HUMAN ECOLOGY FOR GLOBALIZATION

NEW DIMENSIONS *for* ECONOMIC GROWTH

Dr. (Mrs.) SHASHI KUMAR

Foreword by

Dr. MANGALA RAI

SECRETARY
Deptt. of Agricultural Research & Education
and
DIRECTOR GENERAL
Indian Council of Agricultural Research (ICAR)

ATLANTIC
PUBLISHERS & DISTRIBUTORS

Published by
ATLANTIC PUBLISHERS AND DISTRIBUTORS
B-2, Vishal Enclave, Opp. Rajouri Garden, New Delhi-110027
Phones : 25413460, 25429987, 25466842

Sales Office
7/22, Ansari Road, Darya Ganj, New Delhi-110002
Phones : 23273880, 23275880, 23280451
Fax : 91-11-23285873
web : www.atlanticbooks.com
e-mail : info@atlanticbooks.com

ISBN 81-269-0291-4

Printed in India at
Nice Printing Press, Delhi

Secretary,
Department of Agricultural Research & Education
and
Director General,
Indian Council of Agricultural Research,
Dr. Rajendra Prasad Road, Krishi Bhawan,
New Delhi-110 001

FOREWORD

Interactions between human beings and the environment have to be deeply analysed and cautiously planned for sustaining and fostering the present and future of mankind. Providing a quick technological solution to human ecological needs has been in vogue but this practice needs a review. Technological innovations bring with them an array of new problems which need further research, both biological and social. The eco-farming system approach lies in the minimisation of such problems by way of development of technological packages which are realistic, relevant and sustainable.

Global responsibility rests with both the developed and developing countries in order to strike a growth pattern which is harmonised with environmental, social and cultural needs of the mankind. Developing countries in particular have to protect the interest of small farmers and entrepreneurs. Growth has no limit. It, however, has to have a direction and not speed alone. The empowering policy environment has to be created and the governance has to play its role as a facilitator, coordinator and integrator to fulfil the mandate of sustainable global growth.

It is heartening to note that Dr. (Mrs.) Shashi Kumar is addressing the above-stated concerns through her book *New Dimensions for Economic Growth.* I trust and believe that the book will be useful to all concerned towards bringing about a confluence of human ecology and global growth.

(MANGALA RAI)

Preface

The relationship between earth and human beings is the centre of great debate in modern times. Humanity today acts as if it is separate from the natural world. The global crisis in the recorded history played a prominent role in the origin and progress of human race. Man's relationship with his environment now occupies a major place among the problems agitating mankind from the microcosm of separate individual to the population of the planet.

Human ecology is the study of the action below human beings and their environment. It is a means to improve people's lives and environment with the focus on actions of human beings with their environment, emphasizing study of reciprocal effects that take place physically, socially, economically and aesthetically. Its basic approach is the conservation of natural resources.

The peasant household is seen as ancestral decision making unit in rural development potentials and application of innovations. It will be important to ensure that policies in the area of transfer of technology are integrated into broader policy framework beyond economic policy to include science and technology, industrial development, education finance and planning etc., for economic growth.

The book would be of use to readers from all sectors in order to create awareness widely through dissemination of information and use which have the ecodevelopment concern in agrifarming systems and research and development approaches.

SHASHI KUMAR

Contents

1

Globalization of Agriculture

Rural development is the topmost priority of the age and hence a matter of global concern. There is an increasing recognition that women are involved in the World Agriculture. Therefore, until recently it has been difficult to gain a clear picture of where, when and under what circumstances women participate in farm, off-farm and non-farm work. Most farming systems display mixed patterns of women's agricultural responsibilities combining the production cycle.

While examining man-man relationship (needs and participation) and one aspect of man-nature relationship (the environment) the eco-development system has been emphasised on income generation for women. Thus by providing employment opportunities to women, a chain of development activities were initiated, the fruits of which can be observed over a period of time. Beside this, self-employment opportunities were developed for the women and marketing awareness was also created.

The basic mechanisms by which the technologies were transferred to the beneficiaries were : (1) developing need based project, (2) implementing the projects through trained personnel, and (3) constant monitoring at each stage and immediate rectification of any problem arising during implementation. This mechanism was adopted, as what is needed primarily is the development of systems for transference of technologies in their broadest sense. This includes the know-how technique in a manner which promotes the recipient's own ability to become her or himself, a technologist. Those who do not have access to technological knowledge or experience are never likely to become developers of their own technological solutions as those who do.

Any technological innovation brings with it a host of new problems, which necessitate further research, both biological and social. The farmer needs the appropriate technology and the recommended-inputs for increasing production. The farm trials laid out in the farmers field and the field visits made jointly by the research and extension sub-systems bring the extension research and client sub-systems close together. The transfer of income generating technology related activities has profound implication in such fields as energy, environment, science and technology.

The success of the eco farming system approach lies in the development of technological packages, which are realistic and relevant for the target group. It should recognise both the socio-economic background of peasant farmers and external circumstances imposing certain production and consumption condition of moral societies. New production methods, which are consistent with peasant farmers' resources and internal external circumstances, should be developed.

Farmer's involvement is a fundamental step to a successful transfer of information and technology for sustainable land use. Sustainable land system in India refer to the successful management of resources to satisfy the increasing human needs in relation to agricultural livestock and energy, without degrading the environment or natural resources base or without compromising the needs of future generation. However, there is no methodology to develop and promote sustainable land use system. Besides this there is also no considerable experience available for the development and promotion of many of the technologies as social with sustainable system.

Social and economic development must go hand in hand. An incorrigible society cannot secure a viable economy. In the context of the rural development it can be said that the philosophy of "extensive" must yield place to "intensiveness and consolidation". The country is poor economically and exploited for its development.

Keeping this in view integrated system having many components were developed in the mushroom farming as well as triple benefit, fuel yield and various floriculture activities and the concept of participation has been experimented with. The element of participation is difficult to discuss, because we have not had the relevant levels of experience with it. The findings/observations of the projects provide broad guidelines for government and NGOs for planning and implementation of projects at State and National levels. The findings can be utilised effectively by other research organisations to further enhance the work areas. The students also benefit, as the case studies provide a base for work towards achievement of higher education (M.Sc./Ph.D). On the international level the projects can serve as a model for planning, similar work in other developing countries.

Indian agriculture must also capture some more opportunities. The biological revolution has provided the precedented opportunity of transforming any gene from any organism and is already having an impact on agricultural development in several developed, and a few developing countries.

Contribution of technology generation, assessment, refinement and transfer to sector growth: If it is to respond successfully to these challenges, agriculture will have to become more knowledge intensive investments in research will be needed to generate new knowledge. Greater attention will have to be paid to information based technologies. Strengthened means of dissemination will be needed to transfer will have to focus more strongly than before the keys to farming success and sectoral growth. And while ready-made intensification technology may be importable for a few commercials and particularly export producers, most of the needed to generate the new knowledge. Greater attention will have to be paid to information-based technologies strengthened means of dissemination will be needed to transmit this information to farmers. Since vast majority will still have to hectares or use of garble land, or correspondingly small livestock to enterprises, there they will continue to strict limits on the amounts of cost recovery which they can support; much of the adopted technology will therefore remain in the category of public goods. Finally it has been necessary to address growing environmental concerns, especially natural resource conservation. These for better conservation of land and water base of irrigated agriculture and reduction of agro chemical pollution and adverse health effects protection of fragile ecosystems in mountain coastal arid areas and the contaminant of deforestation by traditional shift cultivation to capture some novel opportunities.

To make information transfer more cost effective, greater use will need to be made of modern information technology in communication between researchers, extensionists and their farmer clients. The techniques of frontier sciences of intense biotechnology will have to be further developed nationally.

There is growing realisation that technology generation, dissemination and adoption cannot be taken up in isolation, and a simultaneously unified process of combining all these functions must be turned to fit into high diverse micro situation of farming. Accordingly new paradigms of people participation for increasing productivity, releasing gainful employment, poverty alleviation, environmental securities and strengthening capabilities of local people have been enshrined in various policy initiatives of Government of India. Participatory approaches are bottom up; people centred and demand-driven development of the past. Analysing location specific problems through participatory rural appraisal and working out appropriate remedies by harmonising indigenous technical knowledge with exogenously developed innovations under diverse micro situation are the major considerations of the current research and development programme.

Historically we have been serious minded about environment against western concept of conflict with nature. We have many large scale river valley projects which are carefully worked out by engineers. Even today there are people who believe that there is more money in destroying environment than in conserving it. Tomorrow is not their concern.

Time has come when sustainability in development has to enter in our planning process as one of the basis and permanent objectives. However, sustainable development needs to be properly paraphrased. These would also constitute important slips towards sustainable development in self.

Population stabilisation — to know carrying capacity in conjunction with the availability of food, water, land, energy etc. In practical terms: Integrated land use planning, to set of figures agreed upon by the concerned departments *e.g.*, agriculture, forestry, grasslands, urban and industrial development and transport. Time bound micro level land use survey, starting with village for long term requirement. Land use in relation to soil quality and use. Connected with land use planning-watershed management a problem of almost urgency to solve unplanned irrigation degraded type of wasteland. Himalayas are the most threatened watersheds of the world and need immediate attention. Wherever science based reclamation work has been attempted, remarkable results have been achieved and sediment loads, which are otherwise very high both in our rivers and reservoirs, have come down and productive, protective and economic benefits have accrued.

We need to evolve environmentally sound and economically viable water conservation and management from developmental activities to long term ecological security and sustainable development :

- Integrated land use planning.
- Healthy crop land and grass level.
- Wood land and revegetation of marginal lands.
- Conservation of biological diversity.
- Control of pollution in water and of air.
- Development of non-polluting renewable energy system
- Recycling of waste and residues.
- Ecologically compatible human settlements including slum improvement.

Environmental Education and Awareness at all Levels

The solution to our problem lies in closing the gap between actual and potential yields and thus goes vertical rather than horizontal in agriculture. The latter is not possible, as there is no infusion of genetics, especially genetic engineering and cognate sciences; it is indeed gratifying that ICAR, on its own has taken to biotechnology. This work is aimed at raising productivity permit areas time and in due course of time, it may be possible to release considerable land from present agriculture holdings (47%). Furthermore due to high output agricultural technology our crop land has been diversely affected. Even so, far the foreseeable future the country will have to depend on this model, which cannot be suddenly changed in favour of environmentally sustainable but low input and relatively low output model. During an analysis of the carrying capacity of several countries it has amerced that India, Pakistan and Thailand can become surplus countries only when inputs are guarded at immediate or higher levelled we can feed 2 to 5 time more people. Considerable work needs to be done on organic farming and no till or minimum till agriculture before these can be adopted on a natural scale. Although these methods do confer the advantage of sustainability the immediate problem is to keep on feeding our millions with nutritionally balanced food.

The loss of topsoil quantity-wise is maximum in India being 18.5% of the total soil loss at the global level. This is indeed very serious considering the fact that India has only 24% of the land area of the world. Strategies to reduce the top soil to be developed on an urgent basis.

The problem of grasslands and overgrazing has not received the deserved attention. It has been responsible for eco-degradation due to the fact that we have world's largest number of livestock, particularly in ecologically area, like the hills, leads to very serious and form area big menace and pose a serious threat to a long range ecological security. A concerted effect needs to be made with rangers from livestock survey and improvement methods of feeding grassland improvement, controlled irrigation, fodder banks to settlement of nomadic tribes etc.

The effective forest cover today is perilous low being hardly 14% when it should have been 33% in the plains and 60% in the hills. The causes of distraction through many and varied are reasonably well-known. Coupled with this is the widening gap between demand and supply of wood for diverse uses like firewood (87.5%) timber, and industrial raw material including paper, board, wooden crates, newsprints etc.

The strategy to meet the shortage has to be chalked out against two major objectives of forestry; affording long term ecological security, and supply of goods and services to the people and industry through a well thoughout plant of production. To achieve these objectives, namely conservation production and social forestry need to be practical conservation forestry will cover natural vegetation in watersheds, fragile ecological areas and conservation areas, like Biosphere Reserves, National parks etc. where no commercial exploitation can be allowed. These need to be protected from fuel starving villagers and fodder starving cattle. Production or commercial or industrial forestry aims at meeting the raw material demands of all forest based industries environmental imperatives and production need to be combined. By and large, these should be bankable projects, while in general the non-agricultural land needs to be used for this purpose, it would be in the fitness of things to use good agriculture land once the same is released from agricultural sector after agricultural productivity is enhanced. There is need for a very heavy inputs of S&T in this area. We have not has a culture of science-based forestry much less industry forestry, because we have stock we no longer do so in the case of food and animal husbandry. Time has come to domesticate three crops as we have done in the case of food, cattle etc. There is need to assign this work to ICAR and Agriculture Universities who should treat it as tree agriculture. Infact the whole area of forestry is for S&T inputs and will do so when such time the leadership in this area does not go to technical hands.

The forestry is Social and Community or Agro forestry. These have essentially similar or integrating objectives and have succeeded on non-government land. Basically this is multi purposes forestry for food timber and fodder to meet village needs that would relieve pressure on conservation forests.

The programme is meant for rural poor and is therefore, location specific. In a sense it is an ancient land use where land is used for agriculture forestry and animal husbandry either sequentially or simultaneously. Such as agri-silvi-pastoral model goes well with the predominantly rural setting of the country wither 567,000 villages dispersed over the whole country. Once people develop a stake, there is social fencing created for the protection of such forests. This model also goes to very well with the essentially biomass based society and economy of the country as a whole. There is a number of success stories at micro level in the country. The challenges lies in extending them to micro level by removing bottlenecks and constraints.

There is a need for considerable inputs in forestry, with regards to science and technology, education and training and demonstration and extension. It has to meet foregoing objectives some of the important slips towards this for further success on how well agriculture, forestry and animal husbandry, the three land based vocations can be integrated at village level so as to afford protection to our conservation areas, and ensure production and socio-economic benefits to wood based industry and rural areas at large.

The developing world is facing critical firewood shortage as serious as petroleum crises. The growth of human population is far out pacing the growth of new trees — not surprising when the average users burns as much as tones of firewood a year. The results are soaring prices for wood, a growing drain on incomes and physical energy expanded to satisfy basic fuel needs, the wasteful burning of animal manure to cook food rather than produce it, and ecologically disastrous and potentially inevasible spread of treeless landscapes.

If the pace of tree planting around the world is not greatly accelerated the world bank says "By the turn of century at least further 250 million people will be without wood fuel for their minimum cooking and heating needs and will be forced to burn dried animal dung and agricultural crop residue, thereby further decreasing food crop yields. The potentially valuable firewood crops that deserve increased recognition on species suitable for growing firewood for individual firewood for individual family needs. However species suited to plantation cultivation for fueling and industrial factories, electric generators and crop dries are also considered. Most of the plants are little known in traditional forest production. Some are woody shrubs rather than forest trees, but even those many branched, crocked some time shortlived species may meet many requirements for small scale village use, to such characteristics as : Nitrogen fixing ability, rapid growth, ability of coppice, ability to produce, wood of high calorific value that burns without spark or toxic smoke and ability to go successful to a wide range of environments, including different attitudes soil types, rainfall regions, amount of sunlight.

Keeping in mind those sites now causing the greatest concern: where fuelwood has virtually disappeared. It concentrates on new plantings. These are, however, large areas where tree resources still exists that, with careful husbandry, could be maintained as fuel resources. Moreover, there is scope for harvesting firewood as a by-product for industrial logging and of conventional plantation forestry. The potential for producing fuel from these conditions is also important to consider.

An alternative and complementary approach to the firewood crises is the substitution of well designed stoves or boilers for the generally in efficient devices now widely used.

Unconventional scientific research with promise for firewood include studies of fast growing tropical grasses as fuel crops and some exceptionally promising firewood species related technologies are Leucaena, promising forage and tree crops of tropics, tropical legumes, resources for future producer gas — a little known fuel for motor transport, sowing forest — by broad casting seeds in any trials of fuel wood plantations local species should always be given first priority.

A case study of village Chauawali (Uttar Pradesh) based on studies in relation to fuel yield, sponsored by Department of Non Conventional Energy Sources. The need based crops like cajuns cajan which has multiple uses and fits well in the corporate style of the far households is an example to link between need and socio cultural setting is a complex system still the farming system aimed at harmonizing social and economic objectives with ecologically sound management. Based on the principles of self-reliance, satisfaction of basic needs has proved quite appropriate new symbiosis of man on earth. To make it more adaptive constant education and training is needed to realise that a mismatch between a food crop and land cost us 6 to 12 months but a similar mistake in forestry will cost us one generation. If it has to succeed there will have to be participation of people; building up of an information base and above all treating forestry as S and T activity.

Conservation of biological diversity: the biological wealth of the country is very rich with nearly 45,000 plants, and 65,000 animal species. However, our efforts are conservation has been directed to the conservation more correctly preservation of big cats, as also some large animals, crocodile, birds etc. and we have ignored all together plants, forests trees in particular, as also micro organisms and mangroves and marine biological wealth. There is major lacuna in our efforts. Even in the case of big cats, the stress has been on the art of wild life rather than the science of wild life. All conservation efforts have to be directed to keep the species away from decline. To ensure conservation in space and time, we need to have strategy based on principles of genetic and evolutionary biology. We are far from it. To base the conservation efforts on an ecosystem basis and not only species basis we must take expeditious action and establish the Biosphere reserves. These are areas of vital importance to the country. A gene rich country such as ours, will be left behind if when we have the expertise and experience second to none in the world in this area.

In fact university system has never been encouraged enter the research and development to take science based conservation of natural sites as also the biological diversity in plants, especially forest trees, animals and micro organisms on land in water, and marine environments.

Methodology

To be concerned with man in the social world it is necessary to explore the reality which underlines and characterises 'man', the 'social', and 'world'. Philosophy is inescapable for the social scientist who seeks clarity and rigour in work, who takes the term 'methodology' seriously. It is not merely a question of interest in the logic of scientific enquiry, a matter of paying attention to the status of propositions, models and laws. For paying attention to the phenomena of the social world, symbolism and meaning of social action; men acting in the context of an inter-subjective reality, shared and sustained by temporal beings aware of themselves no less than each other.

A crucial aspect of methodology relates to the relationship between the observer and the observed. A host of philosophical problems concerning the nature of the subject, subjectivity, construction of the subject, and in consequence textual construction of subject, but also of consciously trying to enter into the world of meanings of the subjects under study. The phenomenological critique of sociology has stressed the fact that data gathering is a social process and needs to be understood as such.

With regards to various approaches to methodology that are open today, for anyone looking back over the preceding survey, the most striking fact remains the dominance of the positivist tradition in methodological writing and its influence in the form of the desire for adoption of the 'methods of science'. This has meant, in practice, the devising of a particular mode of enquiry stressing the importance of concepts, hypotheses linked to defined variables, empirical testing and formal analysis. In conjunction with this process social statistics have been used to aid both in the construction of the empirical test and in the analysis and interpretation of the results. The other themes that emerge from the alternative tradition which has been based in social anthropology, village and community studies.

While exploring the themes attempt has been made to identify their problems and implications. These are issues related not simply to techniques of research, but also to the questions of meaning in an inter-subjective world, justification of applying statistical logic and experimental method to a post-positivist universe, nations of objectivity, science reality and realism, methodological implications of construction of subject and test and so on. The general tenor of methodological texts has been to provide a stereotyped account of 'scientific' method, research design, hypotheses, observation, interview in an uncritical fashion, following the model of scientist and without in anyway incorporating the current views of these subjects.

The problem that arises in this kind of work concerns the nature of conceptual categories to be employed and this kind of research method has the inherent danger of allowing the social scientist to negate his vital function of making sense if the data, of consciously constructing the problem rather than expecting it to emerge at some later stage.

Our aim is to go beyond mere descriptions of various methods, to examine the theory, logic and philosophy of the methods and to explore their implications. The questions of methodology proper are linked both with the theoretical issues related to philosophy and to applied issues associated with various mathematical and quantitative techniques. At an abstract level, questions of method and questions of theory overlap and are often identical. They are related to various theoretical positions like positivism, phenomenology, structuralism, post-structuralism and so on. The first task, therefore, is to look at some of the main elements in methodology and how they have been put into operation in the research process.

In the typical methodology text, the 'traditional method' is contrasted with the 'scientific method', and described as something prohibiting proper research. For instance, this is how the features of the traditional methods have been described : (i) methodological ad-hocism, (ii) eminence of subjective perception, (iii) ethical preoccupation rooted in the refusal to distinguish methodologically between facts and values, between 'is' and 'ought', (iv) the dominance of quality against quantity, and (v) the greater use of intuition and imagination, which are regarded as essentially disruptive of modern scientific methodology, are the constituents of the traditional method. The conventional methodology is based on the notion of 'scientific objectivity', which is related to bias in social science. The problem of scientific objectivity is still worsened because of the bias of the social scientists governed by conscious or unconscious political and social attitudes and values.

Fieldwork Methodology

Fieldwork approach in principle rejects the positivist assumption that descriptive concepts are simply a first stage towards the test of explanatory hypotheses. The concern for interpretation of culture and meaning and interest in practices through which social relations become visible from the basis of fieldwork methods. In contrast with the sharp distinction between concepts and explanatory hypotheses within the positivist approach, in the interactions and interpretative fieldwork method 'understanding' the actions and interactions of respondents by virtue of grasping and comprehending the culturally appropriate concept through which the people conduct their social life, is the way in which the explanation is achieved. In the fieldwork method the focus is on naturally occurring situation, the encounters that people have in normal course of events. In this way, it is hoped to produce descriptions and explanations appropriate to the ways in which people actually behave.

There is no dearth of books on research methodology, and almost all aim teaching the novice statistical methods, survey research and its history, drawing up different kinds of questionnaires, interviewing, opinion polls, content analysis and market surveys. Scientific method in the social sciences, in which the need is stressed for the clear formulation of hypotheses to be tested in the inquiry, appropriate research design, the elimination of bias in the collection and interpretation data etc. Throughout, the assumption appears that the social sciences are of the same character as the natural sciences. The new developments in social anthropology, in their view, have blurred the distinction between anthropology and sociology, particularly so in India. Though in methodological terms a conceptual distinction can be made between ethnographic fieldwork and participant observation in which the former involves a recognition of the interdependence of theoretical and methodological issues and the latter relates more to description in terms of participation which often trivialise the issue involved to one meter technique. Like the discussions of how to obtain access and/or to remain concealed and so on — in Indian fieldwork literature no such distinction is made.

The account of fieldwork cover a very wide range of field situations and subjects. The varied locale and subjects cover slums, factories, trade union, industrial cooperatives, college students, school, hospital, minorities, nomads, small towns, and of course, villages. The accounts also point out some important aspects of fieldwork, which are not generally discussed in the available textbooks. However, the fieldwork account argue that hypotheses cannot be formulated in a vacuum, without knowledge of the field. Moreover, the fieldworkers cannot anticipate the developments in the field, which will inevitably guide the course of their investigation. Hypotheses formed without regard to these considerations may turn out to be trivial if not banal. Almost no contribution to this volume has been guided by hypotheses, and some confess that their theorising was only post facts. What most fieldworkers do is to go to the field with a founding in the theory of the discipline, especially in the sub-area of their interest, and with as much knowledge of the region as can be derived from secondary material. The field situation offers them opportunities to reformulate existing concepts and invest them with new meaning.

Survey Methodology

One of the commonly used methods in empirical social science research in India is the survey method. The theme concern how survey research must be designed and conducted as an institution of first accounting of the great variability within them, and second becoming more relevant to the social cultural environment within which measurement occurs. Subordinated to these key issues, the need for using complementary research methods to support and enrich surveys; the need for pre-study exploration prior to conducting the full study; the significance of human errors; the act non-randomly to bias and thereby weaken the survey methodology; the need to study non-random sources and types of biases and describe these methodological findings so that study can be replicated and socio-economic feasibility of implementing results be known.

Inductive Methodology

Provide the basis for research methods can be described as deductive nomological and inductive-statistical system attempts to provide a basis for unification of the sciences and also embodies certain specific features of positivism.

Systems of Social Indicators

With the increasing demand for the present-day literature dealing with social policy for the development of systems of social indicators various methodologies have been geared for developing appropriate measures.

Mathematics, Computers and Formal Analysis

A body of theory in sociology and anthropology that does not call for mathematical treatment, for any theory that conceives of society or culture as a system is committed to the notion of interrelationship of parts, and all conceptions of the cultural consensus and conformity on the one hand and degree of complexity on the other can involve nations of formal analysis, of measure and scaler arrangement as their abstract representations.

2

Globalization for Sustainable Communities

NEW DIMENSIONS OF HUMAN DEVELOPMENT

In the Social Concept and Approaches

In this age of high crime and physical insecurity detective and security agencies offer jobs to those who possess an analytical bent of mind with physical strength to match. The work of a private detective is mainly to investigate and related to fact finding about the organisation/product/individual under surveillance. A detective can be hired to provide information pertaining to :

Domestic problem : problems of divorce, child custody, unnatural deaths or to get information on other family before arranging a marriage.

Family Dispute — Dispute over Wills and Property

A detective work is basically fact finding which involves probing. Some companies could hire detectives to get information about other organisations, infringements or trade marks and copy rights pirating goods or to verify the assets of someone who has applied for loan, pre- and post-employment verification are often conducted by various companies with the help of private detectives. Sometimes private detectives may train and deploy security and bodyguards for different organisations.

Appropriate Home Science for Human Development

Home Science, in reality is deeply and closely related to life being so close, it may often look common place and ordinary in general parlance of human affairs. A model home science curriculum would therefore, care to cover all such factors, fields and interests, which effects a person's fields and interests. This effects a person's development, his life in family and in the community under the world of work. Various aspects of home science on basic scientific understanding of environment and the use of scientific methods in solving daily life problems. Thus various aspects of home science for the improvement of living conditions on the basis of scientific understanding need to be interwoven and integrated in the curriculum at school level. This would need careful shifting of the home science content and practical work expected of children at different stages and streams of education. Home science in its modern context is not nearly restricted to home making or improvement in the prospects of girl marriage. It is on the contrary an immensely broad based discipline full of rich academic, vocational and professional elements, which need to be exploited to the fullest extent in future educational needs. To operationalise the required changes in order to keep in step with the education needs, notes and identity of Asian women. Reconceptualising the "Home Science" may take us to reforming the concept to that of Women Development, Human Ecology or Human Development. It is now possible to reformulate the three years Home Science curriculum with reference to large body of concepts. The fragmented curriculum which was intended to be as multifaceted as the role of women, can now be contextualise with the adhesive of the naturally holistic female self, which has thus far been in sufficiently recognised. The curricula,'theory and practices of B.Sc. degree courses can now be reconceptualised to include necessary internship programmes in relationship with and under the guidance of professionals in the field so as to lead more students with hands of experience to choose to specialise at master's and doctoral level.

As important as the need to reconceptualise the B.Sc. curriculum is the even more urgent need to work in school curriculum so as to socialise boys at an early age to develop their home making and nurturing ability and create these by a real equality of sexes in later life.

The University Grants Commission is a statutory organisation tested by an act of parliament in 1956. This is a national body for the coordination, determination and maintenance of the standards of university education. The UGC serves as vital link between the union/state governments and the institutions of higher learning. In addition to its role of giving grants to universities and colleges, the university grants commission also advice central and state governments on the measures necessary for the improvement of university education.

Higher education provides people with an opportunity to reflect on the critical social economic, cultural, moral and spiritual issues facing humanity. It contributes to national development through dissemination of specialised knowledge and skills.

The Ninth Five-year Plan (1997-2002) launched in the 50th year of India's independence is based on a careful stock-taking of the strengths of the country's past development strategy as well as its weaknesses and seek to provide appropriate direction and balance to socio-economic development of the country. The developmental efforts especially in the social and economic spheres, for its full economic potential for poorest and the weakest will be able to shape their destiny in an unfettered manner. This will require not only the higher rates of growth of output and employment but also a special emphasis on all-round human development, with a stress on social sectors and thrust on eradication of poverty.

The principal task of the Ninth plan, therefore, will be to usher in a new era of growth with social justice and active participation of people at grass-root level.

Recognition of human ecology for the advancement/ evolution of Home Science/Home Economic.

To seek recognition for Human Ecology by UGC for all colleges of Home Science of India for changing in name for the cause of service and education to community.

Educational, Philanthropic

Steps involved in the partnership for the proceedings to Human Ecology : The goal of the school is to provide interdisciplinary study focused on individuals and families and their interaction and their surroundings both material and social.

Furthermore it is concerned with the identification creation, selection, and use of resources by individuals and families in order to provide the means of achieving optimum human development.

Specific Functions

- Formulating and reviewing school policies and procedures concerning academic staff members.
- Development of all school policies and procedures concerning staff members.
- Developing opportunities for participation of academic staff in departments and unit governance.
- Developing opportunities for recognition of academic staff members' contributions to excellence of the school.
- Advise faculty, staff and administration regarding major structural programme, staffing budget, and other decisions.

Significant Importance for the School

- To promote development of research and creative innovations in the school, carryout administrative policy and procedures and make assignment of administrative responsibility.
- To promote and maintain administrative working relationships with cooperative extension outreaches and research efforts.
- To relate education and feedback on school programmes, for curriculum change, programme changes, add options, credits and load.
- Review change of school policies and procedures, graduate students recruiting, undergraduate recruiting, technology review initiative space allocation.
- Review changes required in the department of human ecology in the college of natural sciences for bachelor science in human development and family sciences to meet the academic and professional goal, including human development and family sciences; textile and apparel; food sciences, food system management, human development family sciences or nutrition and training for future design professionals to global industry and consumers to transform the apparel and textile curriculum.

- For bringing research and knowledge for our community for exchange potential of children and youth and families to design environments for quality of life, improving nutrition and health; the community school, family and child clinic; food safety and toxicology initiatives; optimizing economic change.

For international initiatives : for global perspectives for approaches and application in international programmes of faculty and students to participate :

- International exchanges.
- Study abroad.
- Visiting scholars.
- Faculty scholarships and research.
- Earning national attention for the colleges of home science, linked centre for children, youth and families and Delhi University — to bring benefits of shared knowledge in demography and ecology. Partnership for health, especially nursing and osteopathic medicine, for hill community in particular to stay healthy.
- Partnership of active learning and problem-solving in their own community.
- To apply what students heal in the classroom, in realistic need based situation for better health and nutrition.
- The community school project in collaboration between the department of family and child ecology to design the school for supporting the best possible learning environment for each child, for development in design using instructional approaches, compatible with current knowledge about how children develop and learn from traditional school model.
- Partnership for industry and education especially for the apparel and textile curriculum. To create unique facilities for education that meets the needs of emerging industries and professions.

Higher Education. Analysing data and hypothesis testing, essential skills for environmental scientists in applying these skills to environment problems. While referring to software progress, recognising their importance for environmental management for key features and contents, community based environmental protection in action which environmental problem poses the most risk to human health, ecosystem health and quality of life and to develop consensus on action plan to reduce those risks. To improve communities, for the local project, for bringing the major stakeholders and together for problem solving, how does a local community, economy and environment function, what makes it healthy; how do we assess its condition.

The first focus is on the undergraduate course the first degree. In this context, the problems in the undergraduate courses in Home Science are as follows :

1. The course skims the surface of many areas without going into sufficient of any. This may be required for those who become high school and secondary school teachers, after B.Ed. but the feedback from the B.Sc. students is that they study too many subjects.
2. There is a demand, on the part of the students for job oriented and an education with economic returns.
3. While being inter-disciplinary in its orientation, Home science has also tended to become highly compartmentalised.

There is a pressing need for integration and interlinking. Since knowledge is rowing at an exponential rate and no teacher can keep up with all the new developments in our fields, the inclusion of experts from other fields in team teaching should be encouraged. The knowledge would have been integrated into the main stream of Home Science course. The content of social sciences courses taught in Home Science departments need to be reformulated and re-structured. Possibly a theme based approach (poverty, cultural variations and Asian comparison etc.).

Although Home Science is identified in the public mind as being a women's field the courses lack a proper orientation to gender. Gender sensitivity should be made an integral aspect of everything that is taught :

- Population education (including demographic changes generontology and gender) should be part of core courses taught at all home science students and in fact to all undergraduate students of other disciplines.

- Communication, extension and media-method and materials should cut across all specialisations in Home Science areas, and be included on core courses.
- A course on management of institutions (Creche, Balwadi, Old age Home etc.) should be in the undergraduate course.
- If the curriculum is overloaded each of the 4/5 specialisations must decide which course they would be willing to surrender. In that context, it was felt that the basic courses in physical and natural sciences need to be a requirement for human development.
- The sub area specified for the courses :
  1. The early childhood development education.
  2. Theory and principles of child development.
  3. Adolescent development and guidance.
  4. Family dynamics.
  5. Family and child welfare.

Most of the courses should be connected with suitable practical. Orientation course for teachers of Home science in women studies to sensitise them to gender issues must be organised with the expert panels in the UGC and the ICAR should meet together of as far as possible to decide the post-graduate courses in Home Science to have clear identity and job orientation and curriculum change should be discussed.

More diploma courses in Home Science need to be developed, Higher education institutions should gear their programmes offered at different levels (UG & PG) to societal needs, teaching research and extension which form the three components of academic programmes should be so planned that each reinforces the other from the perspective of developing countries. Rapid industrialisation, and technological advancement have created balances in social system aggravating many problems such as poverty, unemployment, migration, equalities in income contribution, resource crunch energy crises and environmental degradation in the quality of life. Because of socio-cultural patterns prevailing in developing countries their human productive power is not optionally utilised, specially with reference to women as productive power and children as potential productive power.

Academic programmes have to be viewed and redesigned appropriately to meet the needs of both students and society which should complement each other in all the four areas of Home Science.

To reorient the community resource management with its community outreaches programme and a concern for management of shared resources into the development of the needs of family and community for social equity and people's participation in truly interactive processes. Combined with outstanding teaching and a strong foundation in the applied and social sciences to work in the community and how to address larger issues concerning the quality of life of people through a well developed and comprehensive course contents. With the institutional commitment to providing quality, carrier oriented professional programmes in teaching research and social marketing for the postgraduate students of CRME for the development of an integral field of study in scientific manner through ecosystem model for multidisciplinary field of study with the committed faculty students the department to achieve greater heights in future. This will help the postgraduates of the departments in important positions with various organisations like government and international agencies. NGO's Food Industries, Hospitals and teaching institutions of India and abroad. Enriched by laboratory experience and community outreach activities programmes with committed faculty and students supported by easy access to the departmental library, computers and other necessary facilities, expansion of different courses to meet the emerging needs and challenges can provide the necessary expertise to the students for self-entrepreneurship and for the reflection to :

- Family and community studies relating to family structure, role expectations, evaluation of various communication aids used for extension work *viz.*, posters, charts, flash cards, flannel graphs, film slides etc.
- Development of communication based on the existing practices and knowledge using the traditional forms, dance, drama, puppetry folks loses.
- Consumer education, income expenditure, and saving practices role of public distribution system, and purchase of consumer durable decision-making patterns.

- Studies on the effect of fertilisers/growth regulators on the nutritive value and yield of vegetables and effect of different methods of storage on nutritive value and shelf life of vegetables.
- Cost control systems in food service institutions and dietary patterns of pre scholars, pregnant and lactating mothers.
- Studies on housing and ergonomics; spatial behaviour, livable studies, slums and resettlements, kitchen and storage design etc., studies on time use pattern, organisational communication, intervention studies in communication and management.

Preparing such extensive courses on every subject could prove to is too time consuming for the Home Science professionals and facilities. Therefore, Home Economists are required to simply record the basic information about every case on digital media or tapes. The dictations are then sent to progressions, who are trained to go through interpret and structure the dictations into full-fledged reports comprising target group assessment, therapy, diagnosis procedures etc. This process of converting dictations into report is called Human Ecology transcription and the professionals who specialise in this IT-enables services, are called transcriptionists. Naturally job requires excellent listing skills accurate typing ability, good written English and extensive knowledge of terminology. This in turn makes it important to first join a reputed training institution.

The students with Science background can do better in Human Ecology. Leading Human Ecology Institutions have evolved easy to learn step by step training methodologies, that can make Human Ecology easy enough for the beginners. Society and science provides knowledge to create human ecology. Its interaction between human and the environment is in the making of technical concepts more realistic and meaningful. The vast and important of the society can be achieved only if concerned efforts are made at the levels of removing the age old syndrome of ten equal treatment towards girl child first at home and later outside. The experts and academicians from far and wide should interact and exchange knowledge and ideas on major issues, of professional orientation to curriculum, enhancing professionals for making graduates self-reliant. The professional courses would provide wide spectrum of experience to graduating students hence sufficient weightage have to be given to make students' professions and befitted in development departments. The discipline of home science is one such innovation which educates/trains individuals to face with vigour and confidence the challenges of the society, for self and family, scientifically, technical, in most befitting ways. This discipline has its existence since last fifty years. Now it is peak time to synchronise our work plan with priorities for the contribution of home science to the society, such as industry, firms, institutions and service related to the employment provided by home science. The effects of new curriculum will affect the employment profile and economic elevation of the community for better utilisation of human resource.

Home Science, in reality is deeply and closely related to life being so close, it may often look common place and ordinary in general parlance of human affairs. A model home science curriculum would therefore, care to cover all such factors, fields and interests which effects a person's development, his life in family and in the community under the world of work. The various aspects of home science on basic scientific understanding of environment and the use of scientific methods in solving daily life problems. This various aspects of home science for the improvement of living conditions on the basis of scientific understanding need to be interwoven and integrated in the curriculum at school level. This would need careful sifting of the home science content and practical work expected of children at different stages and streams of education. Home science in its modern context is not nearly restricted to home making or improvement in the prospects of girl marriage. It is on the contrary an immensely broad based discipline full of rich academic, vocational and professional elements, which need to be exploited to the fullest extent in future educational needs. To operationalise the required changes in order to keep in step with the education needs, notes and identity of Asian women. Reconceptualising the "Home Science" may take us to reforming the concept to that of "women development" Human Ecology or Human Development. It is now possible to reformulate the three years Home Science curriculum with reference to large body of concepts. The fragmented curriculum which was intended to be as multifaceted as the role of women, can now be contextualise with the adhesive of the naturally holistic female self, which has thus far been in sufficiently recognised. The curricula, theory and practices of B.Sc. degree courses can now be reconceptualised to include necessary internship programmes in relationship with and under the guidance of professionals in the field so as to lead more students with hands of experience to choose to specialise at master's and doctoral level.

As important as the need to reconceptualise the B.Sc. curriculum is the even more urgent need to work in school curriculum so as to socialise boys at an early age, to develop their home making and nurturing ability and create these by a real equality of sexes in later life.

The University Grants Commission is a statutory organisation tested by an act of parliament in 1956. This is a national body for the coordination, determination and maintenance of the standards of university education. The UGC serves as vital link between the Union/state governments and the institutions of higher learning. In addition to its role of giving grants to universities and colleges, the university grants commission also advice central and state government on the measures necessary for the improvement of university education. Higher education provides people with an opportunity to reflect on the critical social economic, cultural, moral and spiritual issues facing humanity. It contributes to national development through dissemination of specialised knowledge and skills.

The Ninth Five-year Plan (1997-2002) launched in the 50th year of India's independence is based on a careful stock-taking of the strengths of the country's past development strategy as well as its weaknesses and seek to provide appropriate direction and balance to socio-economic development of the country. The developmental efforts especially in the social and economic spheres, for its full economic potential for poorest and the weakest will be able to shape their destiny in an unfettered manner. This will require not only the higher rates of growth of output and employment but also a special emphasis on all-round human development, with a stress on :

Foods and Nutrition

For combination under nutrition and population growth, using the expanding frontiers of biotechnology and genetic engineering in the agriculture and animal husbandry sector. The various aspects of emerging those trends education in Home Science in general and specialisation in foods and nutrition in particular to reorient as Home Scientists are being recognised for the development of appropriate package of post harvest technology for the villages. These have to be simple, cost effective suited to local conditions, never processing and preservation techniques at the household as well as small sector level in addition to never trends in the areas of food processing and preservation techniques such as microwave heating. Newer packaging technologies for both bulk and retail use of variety of Indian foods for development.

To meet the emerging needs and challenges in the area of food and nutrition. This has been achieved through not only course work but with emphasis given to research, community work, seminars, internship training in hospitals, food industries and related organisations, gained by the students, the postgraduates of the departments to work with various organisations like government. International agencies, NGO's Food industries, Hospitals, teaching institutions in India and abroad. For working as researchers, community based programme officers, nutrition consultant, and expertise to the students for self-entrepreneurship. With the committed faculty and students, the department expects to achieve greater height in future.

Child Development

The child in India has been the major focus. The important task to identify the optional inputs in family and community setting to receive exposure to major theories of human development and to the empirical evidence available from research on children. The influences from the society and culture on the child's development with special emphasis drawing from social sciences especially psychology, sociology and anthropology. The practice courses to train students for working with the children in familial and extra familial settings as well as management of children programmes and institutes. Formal and non-formal education of the child with special needs is an important priority. For this purpose several programmes have to be established at the college level like nursery school, child study centres, enabling centre. Hand on experience at the nursery school provides facilities for the study of young children. For the courses on children with special needs young children with disability for integration with in the nursery school in addition to the enabling centre which provides services for older children. The faculty of the department can supervise these programmes.

Textile and Clothing

The programme can be planned with the following objectives :

- To inculcate a close awareness of current trends, new developments and technological change in the textiles and clothing field.
- To foster appreciation of the tradition and heritage of textiles of the past and draw inspiration for the present.
- To provide depth, scope and professional competency through formal and non-formal education programmes for continued professional growth.
- To equip individuals with the knowledge and skills necessary for creative, managerial and technical careers as wells as entrepreneurship in the field of textiles and apparel industry.
- To contribute towards the economy of the country through research and development.
- Field visits an important component of each course, which includes numerous visit to places of interest and knowledge within the city and at least one outstanding tour during the academic period. Far hand on experience to arrange in house intercept at garment manufacturing units during the vacation period.
- The thrust areas for research in textiles field, with emphasis on the handloom and handicrafts sector operating specially at cottage level.
- State of art studies on traditional textile at in different

parts of country. Apart from documentation of technical information.

- Preparation of database of designs in Indian fabric, technical studies related to processing, specially dyeing and printing to have concentration on the silk industry in India, which is still largely a cottage industry through an important industry in the Indian economy. Natural dyes and economically eco-friendly processed dyes. Textiles and clothing is developing fast and for keeping pace with the latest, the highly trained group of professionals faculty members can develop short term courses seminar, workshop for the development textile and clothing sector.

Bachelor of Education (Home Science)

Skill training in teaching; mastery of classroom management, technique competence to handle children with special needs, facilities to establish warm interpersonal relationships within the class, development of communication skills and competence leading to reflective thinking skill training in various Home Science and Science related work experience.

For close interaction between students and teachers and participatory nature of the programme enables the students to gain confidence and self-reliance, permitting students to manage their own affairs in a democratic ethos and giving them an opportunity to share their thoughts and experiences. The programme cultivates leadership qualities and develops positive virtues like co-operation, sincerity and dedication. In keeping pace with the speed at which knowledge is generated and applied, the emphasis is on learning how to learn. Training in the use of library, audio and video programmes and computer literacy, form an important component of instructional materials for educational communication especially for :

- Educational technology.
- Legal structure for empowerment.
- Extension education with community approach.
- Programme planning, monitoring, evaluation.
- Networking with government and non government agencies.

- Comparative studies — in order to share development in home science institutions in Asia, comparative studies need to be taken up.

Studies of home science programmes in developing Asia Utility of home science training in the context of knowledge, expectations of the employers and need for retaining :

- Comparative studies would assets in establishing advanced centres in Home Science to be recommended by concerned panels for specific vocations of the education and extension department, which is location specific.
- Specific training for vocations at various level; high to low for *e.g.* dean, professor, teacher, school teachers and lab teachers.
- Create acceptance of education and extension graduates for new areas of job.
- Train students for jobs through extension courses, which have come up through immigration of women for jobs in Asian countries within and outside Asia.
- Extension should be a component within other areas of B.Sc. with 30% weightage.
- Home science graduates in agricultural colleges/ universities should implement full-fledged courses rather than agricultural science.

Home Economics a Science

Home economics has been understood hither to as a group of the studies before mentioned, which were common in interest from the point of practical usefulness to our family life. So some explain that Home economics is an applied science of these sciences such as natural and social sciences and human studies. Each science has been varied both in qualities and aims and home economics has been understood, they say as a sum total of the studies of all sorts or conditions, so any systematisation of Home economics as a science has been considered impossible.

How to consider Home Economics as Systematic Study

Man's practical life is carried on in a unity of various facts of living. Could we deny the scientific nature of Home Economics simply because actual facts of human life are excluded from the category of sciences, like natural sciences which is apparently based on a fundamental science? Men have personality and are able to elect and organise those contradictory elements which are different both in their objective and quality, and which extend to clothing, food, housing, nursing, family finance, the relationship among neighbour, speaking and activity and further, they are able to systematise more various facts in life into a life unity without any contradiction.

The Theory of Scientific System

A scientific principle of a system and that to the world living science is often used. What is it originally living science has been suggested and is often used. The world life is a cultural idea which involves economic ideas, so there should be distinction between the natural idea of existence and the science for living, which deal with the farmer to consider the developmental principle from existence to living. We have to perceive materials like clothing, food, housing and those belong as a developmental process from material, as regards natural and social science respectively. Although material as regards to the relation between them is being established as a common conclusion from the field of biochemistry, biology and medical science.

Besides the problems of life there have been a great deal of data from both science and philosophy. But the study on the nature of life belongs to biology and not Home Economics so we are concerned more with the problem of living as the actual condition of life. So we may comprehend the gist of our study as a basic entity of living.

Living is a problem to all living things, which is indicated by having life and of living. It is a basis type, one being accompanied with underdeveloped consciousness and thought like the higher men. They should be differentiated due to the difference of their respective way of living. Here is an establishment of a science of living for the continuance of healthy living. Our livelihood deals with manhood of living. It concerns with a constitution of our economical aspect. So it belongs to social science. The naming of a science for living applied to physics and chemistry is a camouflaged use just as we say a living for moulds vegetable and animal — which has no academic basis and accordingly the name "man" is originally an animal, so one half of man's livings animal and another, spiritual, there lies significance of living as a human animal behaviour such as impulse, instinct and custom, from any act which represents conscious and thoughtful movements.

Behaviour and conduct is a practical expression of living. What is called the original behaviour of life referees to an animal movement, which extends from voluntary movement; a movement practised in default of the activity for human brain control, and belongs to the category of behaviour. The behaviorism of pedagogy is justified from the point of behaviour being a basis of activity.

In principle we deal with moral at home and religion (human relation). It is an important problem but we shall observe the peculiar character and limitation of the field of study as a principle to yield the problem to its individual special standpoint rather than to Home Economics.

In our practical life are observed the existence of various different elements each in opposition among themselves. But they are not solved in isolation, bit as a whole entity if life or a life unity as they are related to each other. That is why we are kept from having contradiction, opposition and breakdowns in our daily life and why the formation of our life in a dynamic way has been possible.

ACTION MECHANISM FOR RESEARCH AND DEVLEOPMENT

Globalization, a dominant force in the 20th century's last decade, is shaping a new era of interaction among nations, economies and people. It is increasing the contacts between people across national boundaries — in economy, in technology, in culture and in governance. But it is also fragmenting production processes, labour markets, political entities and societies. So, while globalization has positive, innovative, dynamic aspects — it also has negative, disruptive, marginalising aspects.

Stronger policies for human development more investment of equip people for the globally competitive economy, and to participate in the global network society — are needed to promote human development. But they are also needed to make globalization work. Ultimately, people and nations will reject global integration and global interdependence if they do not gain from it and if it increases their vulnerability. Pressures will mount to retreat to isolationism in economic policy, culture and political priorities.

To pursue human development, globalisation has to mean :

Ethics — less, not more violation of human rights and disregard of human values.

Development — less, not more poverty of countries and people.

Equity — less, not more poverty of countries and people.

Human security — less, not more vulnerability of countries and people.

Sustainability — less, not more depletion and degradation of the environment.

Accurate effort needs to be implemented. The following measures have been undertaken for the success of policy and programmes :

- Appropriate policy implementation from grass-root level.
- Training facilities.
- Repairing workshops.
- Rewards for successful implementation of the policy.

3

Ecology and Community Approach

Ecology is a developing science, and still more is the awareness of the value of the recent environmental crises that has stimulated the politicians, administrators and public in the understanding of natural ecological perspectives concerned with the system that supports man. Its emphasis is on the study of behavioural aspects implied with the interrelationship of biotic and abiotic components.

System Approach to Farm Women (Rural Development)

- The economic efficiency of production system.
- Sustainability of production system.
- Intra household distributional and nutritional effects. of innovations and change in income.

The Integrated Systems Deals with

- Income generation.
- Sustainable development.
- Integrated land use planning.
- Health of animals and human beings and soil fertility.
- Ecologically compatible system.
- Environmental education and awareness.
- Development of Non-polluting Renewable Energy System.
- Organic farming.

Farm Household Systems

- The household as the decision-making unit.
- The farm, its crops and livestock activity.
- The off-farm component.

Development is viewed as an integrated process focusing on small farms and comprising technical and socio-economic aspects.

Institutionalisation and Fund Support

- To provide basic needs like supplying the improved techniques to the demand on time.
- For the success of policy and programmes.
- Appropriate policy implementation from grass-root level.
- Training facilities.
- Repairing workshops.
- Reward for successful implementation of policy.
- Functional literacy and adult education.
- Prioritisation of rights to resources, employment, just wage and basic needs.
- Adopt a multidisciplinary to perceiving development and problems and solutions.
- Capacity building of NGO's to strengthen the capacity of poor people's organisations and withdrawal of direct work.
- Enhance sectoral strengthening efforts and enhancing accountability and learning of NGOs.
- Developing multiple organisations and forms.
- Trying out experiments for away from the outreach of the community.

Vision and Mission

New thrust for

- Diversity pluralism and equal opportunity.
- Strengthening relations with equal environment work.
- Cooperatively with public and private institutions, industry, state and community organisations and other units in the university.
- Close linkages of faculty and students and real world.
- Interrelations between the various components of human ecosystem with planning and principles.

Future Planning for

- Expansion of research and outreach with people, resource and facilities.
- Postgraduates degree/diploma programmes for pre-service and in-service graduates.
- Other training programmes — short term and doorstep (tailored programmes as per need).
- To conduct research towards programmes in home economics and human ecology to be viable and dynamic in creating and implementing knowledge through teaching research, service and outreach. A catalyst for "Systematic thinking" our vision and efforts to provide the boundless opportunities of global technological challenges as we meet the needs of individuals and families in a transitory society.
- The purpose of Home Economics to be concerned for well-being of individuals and families. .
- Focus — common philosophical base for several disciplines and destructive subjects that made up the total field, for the application of science to everyday life in home, family and community.
- As a change in the family, including greater attention to the development. This development reflected scientific, technological, socio-economic and political changes as well as changes in the family step towards the continuing vitality of home economics as a unified field — A variety of specialisation to flourish.
- Concern increased over the effects of human actions on the environment, including widespread pollution which endangered human health.

The Ecosystem

Richards (1892) — had announced to the world let *Oekology* be the science of (our) normal lives...the worthiest of all the applied sciences which teaches the principles on which to find...healthy and happy lives.

A.G. Tansley (1935) — system resulting from the interaction of all the living and non-living factors of the environment. In the term, ecosystem, eco refers the environment, whereas system implies an interacting interdependent complex.

Odum (1971) — any unit that includes all of the organisms in a given area interacting with the physical environment. The ecosystem, consists of interacting abiotic components and biotic components. The biotic and abiotic components are linked through energy flows and nutrient cycling.

- An ecosystem may also be regarded as energy processing unit, which is restrained or limited by the amount of nutrient and water available to it.
- Primarily responsible for the activities of home and family, women were the major focus of home ecology. Michigan State University (MSU) applied to the family and home economics to Human Ecology in 1970.

Characteristics of Ecosystem

Each ecosystem has several fundamental characteristics that derive from interaction of its components has emphasised the following characteristics :

- It is a major structural and functional unit of ecology.
- Its structure is related to its species diversity; the more complex ecosystem have high species diversity and *vice versa*.
- Its function is related to energy flow and material cycling through and within the system.
- The relative amount of energy needed to maintain an ecosystem depends on its structure, the more complex the structure the lesser the energy it needs to maintain itself.
- It matures by passing from less complex to more complex states.
- Both the environment and the energy fixation in any given ecosystem are limited and cannot be exceeded without causing serious undesirable effects.
- Alterations in the environment impose selective pressures upon the population to which it must adjust. Organisms, which are unable to adjust to the changed environment, must vanish.

Goal

Adoption of ecological model for all units and programmes.

Family and Child Ecology

Child development prepares students for leadership roles in teaching, administration and other applied fields related to children and families. Child development is studied in relation to systems of the family, the child development centre, and the community, as well as to the larger society and economy. The programme is concerned with critical, continuing problems and issues related to the optimum development of children and their families.

Community services. Community services emphasises an ecological approach to problem-solving in all areas of concern for families, focusing on the inter-relationships of families and households and their environments. Graduates understand and take on effective leadership roles in community institutions which provide human services to support families. Research and intercept experiences frequently involve community agencies as field laboratories for students.

Family studies. Family studies focuses on the role of the family in human development, meeting social economic needs of persons throughout the life cycle, and examining the family as a significant ecosystem. Graduates are prepared for professional positions, which apply an understanding of family system to education or action programmes.

Home Economics Education and Outreach

Home economics education and outreach provides preparation for teaching, programme planning, and administrative roles in the school, as well as community programmes which focus on resource management, consumer education and family and child services. This programme is designed to meet occupational and educational goals of increased knowledge in home economics related consent, and improved methodological skill for administrative or supervisory roles.

The Ph.D. programme in family and child ecology is unique in its study of the relationships of human beings within the family and their interaction with the environment that affect the family, areas of specialisation are offered in child development, family science, home economics education and outreach, and marriage and family therapy. Original research with a family ecology orientation is an important programme requirement.

Food Science and Human Ecology

Human Nutrition. Both masters and doctoral students in human nutrition select a focus area in Biochemical Nutrition or community nutrition. Biochemical nutrition includes research interests in biochemical nutrition and nutrient bioavailability food intake regulation and obesity, function and metabolism of vitamins, and nutrition and chronic disease. Community Nutrition includes research interests in diet and exercise treatments in obesity, nutrient assessment and surveillance, maternal and child health, nutrition education, computer application in dietary assessment, nutrition and aging, and evaluation of nutrition programmes, Faculty in each of these focus areas have national/international reputations.

Human Environment and Design

Apparel and Textile. Apparel and textile focuses on the ecological integration of knowledge worth respect to the design of, and human interaction with, apparel and textile product from historical and contemporary perspectives. Specialisation is offered in Apparel Design, Historic Costume and Textiles Studies and Human Behaviour and Ecological Relations.

Interior Design and Facilities Management

The interior design and facilities management programme explores design and function in conjunction with technology, user satisfaction and perception. This is a post professional programme, which provides graduate students with advanced knowledge and understanding design and management, human shelter, and interior design preservation and conservation.

Merchandising Management

Merchandising Management focuses on instruction and research in retail systems. Faculty members conduct international research and emphasise international issues in their courses. Specialisation include international retailing consumer behaviour and human Resource Management.

Human Environment : Design and Management

Human environment design and management students develop individual programmes of study in one of six emphasis areas : Theory development, human environment relation's behaviour, and interface with the environment, marketing and management, Design analysis, History and culture, or global economics. Specialisation is possible in Apparel and Textile, Interior Design and Facilities Management and Merchandising Management.

Doctoral Programme

Family ecology programmes. Integration of human development, family dynamics and family resource management, such as housing, nutrition, clothing and textile, family economics, or home economics, education, related to family ecology.

Outreach and Service

As a separate component in the context of curriculum and instructional programme as an integrated part to offer off campus courses in several locations to increasing needs of early childhood educators and other childcare professionals, and para professionals.

Cooperative Extension Service Programme

The home economics component or family living education to meet the need for closer working relationships and greater communication and integration among resident reaching, research and extension faculty.

Home Economics specialists in family economics, to see the usefulness of ecological ideas to family environment concerns and problems. To incorporate practical applications of an ecological approach to their subject matter.

The ecological framework changes thinking; it becomes part of what many extension staff did and how they did towards improving the lives of families and individuals. It will be an important part of becoming Human Ecology. The curriculum is part of Home Economics and between home economics and background sciences on which it has always learned. Formerly in framing the students were helped to build between them, and individual students build them more or less successfully by themselves. The new curriculum builds firm bridges.

Change and Continuity in Undergraduate and Graduate Programmes

Many social, economics, political-scientific environmental and technological changes have occurred. The computer revolution and world-wide electronic communication, other use of advanced technology and internationalisation of economy have affected the lives of everyone within the university a variety of evolution and strategic planning endeavours have taken place related to undergraduates and general education, graduate study and outreach emphasis on diversity by ethnicity, gender, race and other factors have influenced the student body, faculty, staff as well as academic programmes.

Internationalism has become an increasingly important dimension of all programmes. In the face of challenges the colleges have continued to discover and apply knowledge in variety of modes and setting and adopt and create programmes to educate young people and adults to deal with changes and complexity. Change and continuity in core, undergraduate majors and graduate programmes are highlighted. A teacher can never truly teach unless he is till learning himself. A lamp can never light another lamp unless it continues to burns its own flame.

What is Human Ecology?

- It is simple parable that reveals profound truths.
- It is an amusing and enlightening art as well as science.
- Makes the story of characters who live in fields, look after the fields which make them happy.
- Human ecology is a metaphor you want to have in life — whether it is a job, loving relationship, money or a possession, health or spiritual peace of mind.
- Human ecology helps you to look for, what you want, the organisation you work for, the family or community you live in.
- It will show how to :
  (a) Anticipate for changes.
  (b) Adopt changes quickly.

(c) Enjoy changes and

(d) Be ready to change quickly again and again.

Thinking Globally the Concept of Human Ecology

- It examines the distribution and growth of the population as well as movement of the people from one place to another. Why do some places of the earth contain large number of people or attract newcomers.
- It analyses the distribution of different cultural trait and beliefs and the problems including political systems.
- Human Ecology in Action — it relates principles and concepts, to applied practical issues. It reviews important concepts covered in detail.
- To bring health, wealth and happiness to your life.
- Human Ecology build the power of subconscious mind.
- Case study revisited — additional information related to the case study may be used to reinforce some of the main point.
- Thinking ecologically-based on the concept themes developed in the investigation. The investigator student can apply geographic concepts to explore issues more intensively.

4

Consultative Group Meeting on Human Ecology

"Society and science provide knowledge to create human ecology. Its interactions between human and their environment is in making the technical concepts more realistic and meaningful."

For the values of holistic perspectives in addressing the human environmental issues

"To make human social ecology conducive, human ecology through education and outreach will wake up science and technology for ecological needs of any multi focal ecosystem of the community."

Establishment of Asian Centre for Human Ecology for Equality for Women and Child in New Delhi, India

Proposed site for Implementation of Programmes : As per the decision of the Chairperson in consultation with Delhi State Government :

- Adoption of national policy for the empowerment of women with measurable goals to be achieved by 2010.
- To bring about powers of physical, emotional, dynamic, intellectual, ethical, aesthetic and spiritual potentialities.
- Diversity, pluralism and equal opportunity.
- Strengthening relations with the equal environment work cooperatively with public, private institutions, legislative bodies industry, state and community organisations and other units in the university system.

Outcome of Consultative Group Meeting on Human Ecology held on 13th March, 2002 at New Delhi, sponsored by Department of Women and Child Development, Government of India.

For creation of vibrant new partnership — to reach the most disadvantaged and underserved and the most vulnerable — the young child, the emerging strategy focuses on innovation, fostering decentralised flexible responses to the care of young children, girls and women and reaching through integrated family and community based interventions for survival, growth and development of socially backward villages and urban slums. With the special preference to those areas which are predominantly inhabited by vulnerable and weaker sections of the society *i.e.* Scheduled Castes, Scheduled Tribes and low income families found in economically backward areas, drought prone areas and areas in which development of social services requires strengthening. It also believes that these goals are an integral parts of all efforts to achieve sustained and sustainable social and economic development that meets needs, ensures well-being and protects the natural resources on which all life depends.

The philosophy of human ecology provides the context for developing and serving the individuals and their families from a human environment perspective towards building and sustaining a productive quality of life. The scientific expertise, infrastructure facilities and research needs to be strengthened by bonding the relationship between research and educational institutions and industry in a symbiotic mode of conversion of research findings into products, processes and technologies for human resource development.

Recognising the empowerment of woman and development of children for human resource development to enhance the principles of both gender, equity and gender equality, the scientific expertise, research between educational institutions industry and community will help them to meet the challenges imposed by new economic and social order. It will also guide us to demonstrate the programme effectiveness with the strength based focus in partnership for sustainable solutions of healthy communities and to contribute to understanding the solution to a sustainable path to ecological stability, bearing in mind that equity and justice ought to prevail within and between human generation.

Education raising of public awareness and training are linked to virtually all areas and even more closely on meeting the basic needs, capacity building and data and information, science and role of major groups. To bring human ecology in action for the significance of education for sustainable development at all levels through educational programmes with interdisciplinary and integrated approach for :

- State of knowledge and basic concept of functional literacy.
- To deliver human service and programmes.

Man's relationship with his environment now occupies a major place among the problems agitating mankind. Therefore, it is necessary to demonstrate the scientific programmes a way towards meeting the sustainable and safe future to mankind. To achieve this institutionalisation should be taken as a meeting point for partnership and networking in educational programmes.

To respond to human needs, the main thrust will be directed towards youth employment, income generation and mass awareness about development. The activities which are socially benefited and economically viable like farm, off-farm and non-farm shall be taken up for the benefit of the community by doorstep and on-station technology transfer through short term training programmes to ensure continuous benefits to the rural poor so that resources and environment may be preserved for future generation.

Consultative Group Meeting on Human Ecology

Time has come when sustainability in development has to enter in our planning process. Twelve areas have been identified where priority action is needed as one of the basic and permanent objectives. The policy has to be enunciated not in isolation but in concert with a number of Ministries/Departments of the country.

Priority Areas

- Integrated Land use Planning.
- Healthy Cropland and Grassland.

- Conservation of Biological Diversity.
- Control of Pollution in Water and Air.
- Development of Non-Polluting Renewable Energy systems.
- Recycling of Wastes and Residues.
- Ecological compatible Human Settlements and Slum Improvement.
- Environment Education and Awareness.
- Updating Environmental Law.
- New Dimensions to National Security.

To develop measures to upgrade higher education and research programmes for wider access by linking higher education with community service and Home Science programmes to make them relevant to all sections of society, partnership for sustainable development at different levels.

Thrust Areas

- Human Ecology for Globalisation.
- Partnership and networking.
- Restructuring the curriculum for linking higher education with community service to respond to the local needs for advancement/evolution of Home Economics to Human Ecology.
- To gain insight from contacts between knowledge resources and socio-cultural realities in the entire curricular system and for higher education, international cooperation/partnership for action, sharing their successful experience, technologies, materials, financial resources and learning for pilot studies.
- Research and training for human resource development in on-farm, off-farm and non-farm sectors and its institutional for :
  - Case Studies on Conservation of Ecosystems.
  - Studies on Women, Agriculture and Rural Extension with special reference to Biodiversity.
- Setting priorities in research to help community in

areas of agribusiness, biodiversity and Environment, non conventional energy systems and Human resource development.

- Promote post doctoral research and granting awards for strengthening its focus on rural life.

Major Themes

1. Linking higher education with community service.
2. Changes required in the area of Home Economics and Home Science programmes to make them relevant to all sections of the society.
3. Setting priorities in research to help community in the areas of Agribusiness, Bio-diversity & Environment, Biotechnology, Non Conventional Energy System and Human Resource Development.
4. Action Mechanism for Research and Development.
5. Partnership for sustainable development at all levels (local, nation, regional and global).

Drivers

Rural Development, Human Resource Development, Promotion of educational and economic interest for all sections of society, Multinational collaborations for building, scientific and academic community by linking with partners, networking to increase and contribute to International research.

CONSULTATIVE GROUP MEETING ON HUMAN ECOLOGY FOR GLOBALISATION*

Opening Remarks by the Chairman/Chairperson

Shri Srivastava while welcoming the members to the meeting expressed that the important job on Human Ecology is a subject of global importance and all of us should contribute with all our might to this effort.

Stressing the need of Human Ecology which is essentially the interaction between human beings and their environment. The crux of human ecology is the development of human resource and its environment through an appropriate interaction

* 13th March, 2002 at International Youth Hostel, 5, Nyaya Marg, Chanakya Puri, New Delhi-110021.

between the two. In view of rapid technological advancement, information explosion, diverse condition and growing capabilities, it has become imperative to develop HRD skills, which may comprise of holistic and system perspective moving from individual to the entire global ecosystem. Human ecology attempts to break the barrier between rational scientific thoughts and the traditional beliefs and technologies. It is, therefore, important to link up the scientific education with the community service by setting up priorities in research to help the communities to develop in the areas of agribusiness, Bio-diversity and Environment, Bio-technology, Non-Conventional Energy System and Human Resource Development.

He further said that agriculture is one sector, which has a direct bearing on environment, ecology and natural resources. Agriculture is the mainstay of livelihood in India. It accounts for about one-fourth of the Gross Domestic Product and is the source of livelihood for nearly two-third of the population. The sector provides food and nutritional security to million of Indian population. The agriculture sector in India has been successful in keeping pace with the rising food demand of a growing population, which has crossed the one billion mark. Food grain production has more than quadrupled since the early 1950s from 51 million tons to over 210 million tons in 2000; while population nearly tripled from 350 million to one billion during the same period. Since agriculture has the direct impact on the environment, it is essential to take up agricultural development in totality, environment and ecological imbalance, depleting natural resources and widening of regional and socio-economic inequity and have to maintain the bio-diversity. Efforts are being made through number of programmes/projects and necessary policy intervention to conserve the two important resources for agriculture *viz.* soil and water.

- We need to have a holistic approach in increasing agriculture production for which efforts are being made to generate and disseminate technologies which are focused more strongly than before on the themes of optimisation by produces of their available resources, sustainability, ecological or social circumstances and creation of a policy environment that promotes profitable, productive and sustainable farming.

- In relation to the role of women, he stressed that since Human Ecology deals with the development of Human resources and capacities, it is essential that women who form 50% of our Indian population and have played a key role in the conservation of life support system should be mainstreamed in the development process we need to Engender the Development Process. Women have protected health of the soil through organic recycling and promoted crop security through maintenance of varietal diversity and genetic resistance. Women as an agriculturist tends to look at problems in their totality — from sowing of the crop is ultimate utilisation wither as food, feed, fodder, fertiliser or raw material of industry, the total intellectual and physical participation of the farm women and women farmers in the process of the agriculture development is absolutely essential.
- While speaking about the role of home science he said that Home Science is one subject, which is very closely related to the daily life of human beings. So, Home Science courses should be so developed to cover all such aspects, which affect a person's development, his life, in the family, community and in work.

The curriculum of Home Science should affect improvement in living conditions on the basis of scientific understanding of the environment and use of scientific methods in solving daily life problems. The discipline of Home Science should synchronise the work plan with priority. It should aim to educate and train individuals to face with confidence the challenges of society for self and family, scientifically and technically in the best possible way. It should aim at developing the capacity of girls and women mainly involved in farm and home making activities and should be multi-dimensional and interdisciplinary since it involves various aspects such as technology, growth and investment opportunities for women, building up the capacity of women, their roles and responsibilities.

Dr. K.L. Chadha, President, mentioned about the two Conferences on Human Ecology that in various aspects to deal with the problems of the involvement of the university community in the programmes of Adult Continuing Education of UGC and to deal with interdisciplinary curriculum. Considering the response of individual in the environment for the processes occurring with the ecosystem in order to unlock the human resource and to the mainstream of national life. He also gave the background of the past projects carried out by Dr. Shashi Kumar. In this connection he asked the organising secretary to show the slides to the members for their information and to facilitate them in their work for expediting action on the various facets that need to be looked into the establishment of the faculty for Human Ecology for conducting studies on Globalisation.

Dr. Shashi Kumar showed various slides based on the projects developed by her on thinking globally the concept of human ecology address by Dr. R.S. Paroda, in the inaugural speech of the Second Congress on Human Ecology. She also showed the resource material developed for thinking globally entitled "New Dimensions for Development and Growth" — Vol. 1-3.

Dr. P.L. Gautam while focusing with the in-depth thought on human ecology observed that to expedite the action on various aspects of research and development programmes to help community. He also emphasised to take up the project which was submitted by her to World Bank entitled "International Centre for Human Ecology" to take up with Ministry of Agriculture for its establishment at South Delhi Campus, University of Delhi.

Dr. Tej. Verma emphasised that the discipline of home science is one such innovation which educates and trains individuals to face with vigour and confidence the challenges of society for self and family, scientifically and technically in the most befitting ways to meet their physical, emotional, social, cultural, economic and spiritual needs. This education is recognised all the world over by different names *i.e.* Home Economics/Human Sciences/Human Ecology/Consumer Sciences in USA, Philippines, Switzerland, Belgium, Holland, Canada, Domestic Economy in U.K., Home Science in India and New Zealand.

- In this century we ought to be sensitive to the evolutionary changes that the taking place irrespective of the work of this discipline. We have to be risk taking and innovative in view of the dynamic changes of global liberalisation and marketing strategies.

- The current climate of re-organisation of Higher Education in Home Science as really broken into two parallel efforts — one within the State Agricultural Universities and within the General Home Science arena. Whether these two efforts will eventually merge and reach consensus in higher speculative, although the need to educate the general public about the changes in home science may form the necessity for solidarity across Home Science. Home Science is already much more than it was in its founding days of the 1930s, and it is growing and changing regularly.

Dr. P.L Gautam felt that there is an urgent need for more effective sectoral development programmes to improve food security and nutritional adequacy among the poor. The green revolution had generally by-passed vast rained tracts, especially arid zones, hill and mountain ecosystems and coastal regions, this exacerbating agro-ecoregional and social disparities. He felt the requirements for location-specificity, social acceptability and environmental sustainability for contribution of technology generation, assessment, refinement and transfer to sectoral growth in order to reduce the absolute number of people living in poverty and to reduce regional imbalances.

Dr. Tej Verma emphasised the mission of home science for the empowerment of the community to support families and established interlinkages with other departments/state institutions/corporate sector/non-governmental organisations to provide through innovative and technologically sophisticated delivery systems appropriate to the family lifestyles.

- In order to achieve greater impact on issues involving families and emphasise focused on coordinated programmes of research, which have direct relevance to the mission of advancing the well-being of families.
- In extension, we have to achieve recognition as the model for development and implementation of educational programmes that respond to community needs for information in ever-changing content

areas. It will be provided through innovative and technologically sophisticated delivery systems appropriate to family lifestyles.

- A four-year programme with career orientation — mix issues culminated in the decision in 1995, at least among the SAUs, to create a four-year B.Sc. programmes with the career orientation built-in. The traditional three-year programme was condensed and courses were reorganised to make room for an increased emphasis on practical career and job skills throughout the three years.

This can be implemented to broaden the UGC base to fill gaps in critical areas of research related to regional problems for developing staff skills through extension, education and outreach programmes.

- It was resolved to establish International centre for Human Ecology at South Campus, University of Delhi and Centre for Social Justice and Empowerment at Institute of Home Economics to work in partnership with SAUs to take up the concept of Human Ecology to enhance the principles of both gender, equity and gender equality to demonstrate the programme effectiveness with the strength based focus for healthy communities.
- To respond to human needs the farm, off-farm and non-farm activities to be taken up for the benefit of community by the doorstep and on-station technology transfer short term training programmes to ensure continuous benefit to the poor.
- The international centre for human ecology to be established by DARE to Delhi University, South Campus in concert with Ministries and Departments of the country.
- It is proposed for UGC to establish the Centre for Human Ecology for the discipline of home science for the evolutionary changes that are taking place irrespective of the work of this discipline to educate general public about the changes of home science.
- To realise the concept of human ecology to four years

programme with carrier orientation for the holistic and integrated perspectives for action in respect to :

(a) How Human Resource would be better utilised?

(b) Compare Home Science education at par with other countries.

(c) Effect of new curricula for the economic elevation of the country.

(d) The Home Science Education be recognised as Human Ecology in India.

For the new dimensions to national security to upgrade higher education and research programmes to deal with the development of Human resource and capacity in the conservation of life support system scientifically and technically in best possible ways. It should aim at developing the capacity of girls and women mainly involved in farm and home making activities and should be multidimensional and interdisciplinary to involve various aspects such as technology, growth and investment opportunities for women, to their roles and responsibilities.

To undertake ecosystem research for the principle of diversity with local communities whose survival and sustenance is linked to biodiversity utilisation. The educational philosophy of the university to get translated into its faith in the unity of knowledge as a Centre of higher education and training in agricultural sciences at national and international level.

RECOMMENDATIONS

- DARE should support the project for ongoing initiatives to meet the long term goal of human resource development with reference to in-service and perspective graduates to impart relevant education and training to young men and women for managing income generating and development activities on behalf of rural, urban and slum communities.
- DARE should also support the International Centre for Biodiversity and Environment at Interdisciplinary Applied Sciences, Delhi University, South Campus to establish the Department of Human Ecology for :
    - (i) Developing links to build bridges between researchers and extension worker.

(ii) Expand linkages at all levels macro, meso, micro level, household food security issues for agriculture production in home economics extension programmes in rural areas to strengthen its focus on rural life in reaching the un-reached.

(iii) The project forwarded by Delhi and Concept papers submitted to various national and international agencies should be re-examined.

(iv) To harmonise the course for the major themes and drivers to combine and to conduct research towards improving the sustainable productivity and to support rural development to ensure continuous benefits to the rural poor.

Linkages Human Ecology for Social Justice for Empowerment of Women and Child Development

- ESTABLISHMENT OF UGC CENTRE FOR HUMAN ECOLOGY.
- PROJECT — HUMAN ECOLOGY FOR HUMAN RESOURCE MANAGEMENT AND DEVELOPMENT AT INDIRA GANDHI OPEN UNIVERSITY.
  - Sectoral programmes of development.
  - Agriculture and allied activities and cooperation.
  - Service delivery and Programme Support.
  - Empowerment and development through institution building and training programmes for tribal development.
  - Promoting linkages for urban sustainable training programmes.
  - To provide support to the academic activities of the University for Bachelor Degree Programme for courses in science, home science, computer science etc.
  - Planning and development of academic programmes at the certificate, degree, diploma, undergraduate, postgraduate and Ph.D. levels.
  - Training to individuals sponsored by national and international agencies.

- To provide opportunity for higher science education to working persons, people living in rural areas, remote areas and belonging to disadvantaged section of society.
- Programmes in rural development and poverty alleviation.
- Environment and forest.
- Village and small industries and food processing industries.
- Health and family welfare.
- Housing, water supply and sanitation.
- Social welfare.
- Science and technology.

5

HUMAN ECOLOGY FOR GLOBALIZATION

GLOBALIZATION AND HUMAN DEVELOPMENT

Human development over the life span is a process of becoming something different while remaining in some respect the same. Development involves individuals in orderly and sequential change as they move from one period to another in the course of their lives.

Life is never a material, a substance to be molded. If you want to know, life is the principle of self-renewal, it is constantly renewing and remaking and hanging and transfiguring itself. Scientists refer to the elements of change and constancy over the life span as development involves these process that are biologically programmed within the organism, and those process in which the organisms is changed or transformed through interaction with the environment.

Social and behavioural scientists who study human development focus upon four major issues first they undertake to describe the changes that are typically occur across the human life span. When for instance does the child generally begin to speak what is the nature of speech? Does the speech alter with time?

More technology less jobs secures to be further limitation to the fulfilment of the dream. Scientific knowledge does not postulate unconditional truths, but truth hypothesis valid for range of specified conditions. To act on strategies to be adapted to further the social relations and excellence to the capacity of NGOs is through provoking on the science at an opportune time. The importance of child care, early childhood development to improving researchers, planners and practitioners in India, but also to their counterparts in many countries as they face the growing challenge before them.

The need for early childhood programme is growing a pace for many reasons. As infant mortality rate have declined for instance, it becomes increasingly necessary to run out attention to those children who survive and live in circumstances which put them at risk for delayed or deliberated development in crucial early years. Continuing changes in traditional family structures and child rearing patterns have increased the demand for programmes of care and education. These changes are often associated with urbanisation and irrigation. They also occur as cities reach out into rural areas, through mass media and with improvements in transportation. In many parts of the world, increasing labour force participation by women of care and support? To these long term trends and changes, we can add a recent and marked change in the international climate for investing in programme for young children. This is associated with three recent events.

The first event was the adoption of the convention on the rights of the child by the United Nations assembly in late 1989. The convention signed by more than 100 nations urges signatories to ensure to the maximum extent possible child survival and development. The convention also indicates that states must render the specific suggestions for improving the linkages, these include :

1. Encouraging policy oriented research.
2. Sensitising graduate students to the importance of making the linkages, by introducing appropriate concepts in methods, courses, by organising research and by establishing internships to govern bodies or advocacy groups.
3. Seeking a greater understanding a policy and programme processes and then selecting the research topics, with a high impact potentials.
4. Paying greater attention to research that delves into why some programme succeed and others fail.
5. Building evaluation into programme from the start and on a continue basis.

For the most part, the above suggestions depend on a traditional model describing the research, policy and programme relationship in which research results are first created and then communicated from researchers to the potential users. The communication may be face to face or may occur in written or visual form. An intermediary acting on behalf of the researchers, such as policy institution may break the research results, or a professional association engaged lobbying. "Basic" research findings may also be transformed into a technological application, which is passed on to practitioners. In addition policy maker and practitioners are associated with Government, and therefore the main interface is sought with Government personnel.

The traditional way of thinking about research and its practical consequences have served characteristics that should be made explicit. First the researchers and the user are always separate. Second the following from the first, knowledge is always transferred from one person to another. Third, research results are first arrived at, then disseminated (perhaps after being repackaged or turned into technology), when judging the success of transfer of knowledge to action, there is tendency also to associated specific pieces of research or specific outcomes of research with specific policies or action into world of policy and practice.

The traditional way of approaching to relationship between research and its use into practice is not wrong. Such interface can occur and they can and should be fostered. However, this view is limiting and in my opinion, probably does not represent the principal way in which research gets converted to action. What are the alternative conceptions and what do they imply? These are the use of media to research the public in corporating researches into the evaluation of ongoing programmes and encouraging the students to become involved in research with policy orientation. Indeed, the difficulty of making these more direct connections and of building the desired partnership was illustrated by the failure of many invited individuals from the policy and programming side to participate in the symposium. The only interface for researchers who would like to see their research results translated into action is with governments it recognises that research can be used directly by the public and can be empower. But less often recognised, reason for taking public limited to necessarily to a literate public in these cases as an audience is that, in democracies, the public in these cases as an audience is that, in democracies, the public put pressure on their government to change policies as seems to be the case at present. In this case the journalist and proper writer and even the television producer or actor may become the most important allies of the researcher, an indirect interface between research and practice. Directing research results to public is an important option for researchers, but this approach barely breaks away from the traditional way of thinking about the research-practice nexus. It avoids the leniency to associate specific research findings with specific changes in policy and practice by looking beyond those in governments who set policy and plan programme. However, the approach continues to separate researcher from user and is linear in conception. In this non-linear view, the dissemination and use of knowledge begins to occur with the conceptualisation of a research project. It occurs over the course of the research process. It is embodied in people who carry out research and who then use the technology without having the knowledge, without having to transfer what was learned to others.

In this more radical view, we are led to think as much about who formulates and carries out research and about the specific content of the research. We are led to the idea of participatory research; along side the academic purpose, become to change the attitude and behaviour of the research/practitioner.

Involving graduate students in research whereby they will use what they have learned in the course of the research, is the most obvious case fitting the model. But it is far from being the only case. For instance, there are situations in which knowledge acquired in themselves move into policy or programme making positions or because practitioners are incorporated into research with the idea that the research is directed towards informing their own work.

Attempts to incorporate practitioners directly into research becomes important as incorporating researchers into practice. One can imagine, for instance, cases of classroom teachers or early childhood promoters who are involved in continuing education or training in which they take their own classroom as the basis for research. It may reflect a desire to impart the truth discovered in previous research and which deserves to be transmitted. It may effect a desire to avoid reinvestigating the wheel. Even though a case can be made for the efficiency of such reinvention because it increases the chances that the new wheel will actually be used. Given the proper atmospheres and methodologies linking action to reflection such participatory research can overcome the possible problems of bias in observation can be done without sacrificing rigour and can lead to immediate use of research results. Incorporating directly into research is not a realistic, involving teachers in research is to place the students in internships in government offices, where policies are made and programmes are carried out. These study opportunities could be planned around projects directly related to their work and around research that would feed into their work. The reader will certainly be able to think of others feasible combinations that would bring the researchers and user back to face between research policy and programming.

Making community policy to make market based mechanism to address climate change and promote transfer of finance and climate friendly technology to developing countries.

Established with contribution from government and private sectors to operate and to improve environmental pursuing profits. While a vibrant and growing agricultural sector is vital for reducing poverty agriculture alone is insufficient to solve action oriented phase the policy framework and a good rural strategy are critical, sustained commitment to rural development is important. Data availability is a serious problem.

A doubling of food production to feed a extra 2 billion people by 2025 most of them in developing country will require new and improved agricultural technologies in promoting policies, indigenous people, and cultural property has been improving. Promoting increased participation in civil society in natural level policymaking is more responsive and transparent.

Community driver approaches to development — giving local organisations more say — can make resource allocation more responsive to the need of poor and increase of power of poor community to interact with government, the private sector and civil society in planning and implementing their own development programmes with similar efforts envisaged to disseminate information on legal and procurement matter. Training programmes for in-service community to promote best practice and piloting of initiatives in conflict prevention.

Cultural identity is an essential part of empowering communities to take change of their own destinies from tourism to restoration, investments in cultural heritage promote labour intensive economic activities that generate wealth and income.

GLOBALIZATION WITH A HUMAN FACE

The real wealth of a nation is its people. And the purpose of development is to create an enabling environment for people to enjoy long, healthy and creative lives. This simple but powerful truth is too often forgotten in the pursuit of material and financial wealth.

Globalization is now new, but the present era has distinctive features. Shrinking space, shrinking time and disappearing borders are linking people's lives more deeply, more intensely, more immediately than ever before. Globalization offers great opportunities for human advance but only with stronger governance.

This era of globalization is opening many opportunities for million of people around the world. Increased trade, new technologies, foreign investments, expanding media and internet connections are fuelling economic growth and human advance. All this offers enormous potential to eradicate poverty in the 21st century — to continue the unprecedented progress in the 20th century. We have more wealth and technology — and more commitment to a global community than ever before.

Global markets, global technology, global ideas and global solidarity can enrich the lives of people everywhere, greatly expanding their choices. The growing interdependence of people's lives calls for shared values and a shared commitment to the human development of all people. The challenges is to find the rules and institutions for stronger governance — local, national, regional and global markets and completion, but also to provide enough space for human, community and environmental resources to ensure that globalization works.

Globalization a dominant force in the 20th century last decade is shaping a new era of interaction among nations, economic and people. It is increasing the contact between people across national boundaries — in economy, in technology, in culture and in governance. But it is also fragmenting production process, labour markets political entities and societies. So while globalization have positive innovative, dynamic aspects it also has negative disruptive marginalising aspects. Today interaction between nations and people are deeper than ever. Driving integration even faster are the recent innovations in information and communication technology. But global integration is still very partial — for one thing the flow of labour is restricted, with borders closed to the unskilled.

6

Education for Human Resource Development

There is a great demand for expansion of higher education on account of increasing expansion of primary and secondary education and rising social expectation. Consequently emphasis has been on the removal of disparities and to equalise educational opportunities attending specific needs to those who has been on the removal of disparities and to equalise educational opportunities attending to specific needs to those who have been equality so far.

Educational development is participatory process. Education was incorporated in the list to facilitate evolution of all Indian policies in the field of education (Government has assumed a larger responsibility to look after the integrated character of education, to look after international aspects of education, culture and human resource development) in the general to promote excellence in the sectors of education throughout the country. Having regard to the size of population, diversity and economic frailties the challenges are enormous. This realisation has resulted in steadily rising levels of budgetary allocations, and resource transfer for education to the states.

Elementary Education. Universal access, universal relation and universal achievement are broad parameters to achieve the goal of universalisation of elementary education is yet to be achieved. Considering the magnitude and the complexity of the problem, meticulously formulated strategies to have been adopted in the form of operation black board (OB), Non-Formal Education (NFE), Teacher Education (TE), district primary education programme to address the specific problem areas, gender and regional disparities. Special problem areas, gender and regional disparities, special focus has been laid on the access to education for millions of girls and working children, who cannot participate in the school system on account of socio-economic compulsions. These segments largely constitute girls SCs/STs and other deprived sections of the society.

Although special programmes have been taken up to improve upon specific deficiencies in the educational system, no strategies can succeed in achieving UEE without specifically addressing its gender and regional dimensions.

Human Ecology for Women

The status of women in a complex society like ours, is not uniform within the Indian sub-continent, there have been infinite variations of the status of women, different according to the cultural milieu, family structure, caste class, occupation, property rights etc. All these factors are significant determinants of variation in her position in different groups.

The scheduled caste women who constitute a sizable population of India is subjected not merely to gender bias, but also to indignities arising out of age old traditions of untouchability from which, incidentally the entire social group of scheduled castes suffer. The deep-rooted social discriminations have compelled this section of India's population to lead a life of bare subsistence level, both in respect to economic terms and human values. The scheduled caste households are largely rural based. They have tied themselves to land owners — that happens to be from high castes, by a variety of complex relationship to ensure survival. The variety of complex relationship is reflected in a much larger number of scheduled caste farm servants and attached labourers. This very distinction warrants the scheduled caste women agricultural workers to be recognised as a separate social sub-group in the directed empowerment process.

In rural India more than 80% of people are involved directly or indirectly in agricultural and allied activities like animal husbandry, poultry, fishery, sericulture, mushroom, floriculture, and a number of other related pursuits. This sector is the mainstay of Indian economy; and nearly 50% of the country wealth if not more, in this share is generated through women.

Women's contribution is in fact very intensive and intimate in agriculture. It is not universally accepted that women were the first agriculturists; while men went out of hunting, women were envisaged in homestead cultivation as well as food gathering activities. Recent research suggests that it accounted for satisfying 80% of society food requirements. Women were also discovers of first tool of agriculture and it was they how started making baskets and earthen pots for storing foods. Ever since the beginning of civilisation women have played an important role in agriculture in almost every country of the world. In fact one cannot think of agriculture without women. There are as many women farmers in the world as men farmers. However with the passage of time and new technology inventions, the status of women in agriculture has undergone as sea change and they now play a subordinate role. They have lost all property rights and have little say in decision making.

The commissioner for scheduled castes and scheduled tribes submitted 28 reports (under article 338) on the working of the safeguards provided in the constitution for scheduled castes and tribes.

Besides, the planning commission has set up on the eve of the commencement of each five-year plans, working group for the development and welfare of scheduled castes and scheduled tribes, apart from above institutions, several commission, committees have been set up by the Government of India and state governments from time to time, to go into the problems of the SCs and STs and also women and agricultural workers in general.

However, very scanty information is available with regards to the socio-economic status of scheduled caste women agricultural workers in the published material. However, efforts have been made to collect information as applicable on agricultural labourers on one hand and scheduled caste women on the other, and to integrate the collated information into a meaningful whole.

It would not be absolutely irrelevant to mention that the socio-economic factor responsible for the poor wretched living a scheduled caste woman and agricultural workers in general, and then make observations, recommendations, with respect to the scheduled caste women in agriculture within the available data information base.

In brief, the tribal women enjoy a better position than her counterpart in many tribal societies. However, the phenomenal changes occurring in the socio-economic field of the country affect the tribal women and tribal areas much more harshly than others.

In considering application of science and technology in tribal areas, focused consciously at tribal women would demand consideration of certain essential aspects relevant to their life and culture. To understand its ramifications and its impact role to play in the former than men. Her contribution to the economic well-being of a tribal family is crucial.

When dealing with tribal societies, as they are in our country in the application of technological inputs, it might as well be appropriate that traditional attitudes and values give pre-eminence to authority and custom in the modulation of behaviour is recognised. It makes for stability and continuity of tradition. By the same token, it can also resist force of change and adaptation. Rationality or scientific temper based on authority but would accept as valid only those things of which evidences have been collected scrupulously. What is distinctive about the scientific methods is what is built into it, namely, the possibility of disproof. It is an adaptive, integrative, feedback process. Where inputs and new data, and new hypotheses as to what the underlying theories might be. If experiences an expectation differ either the body of scientific knowledge or the input hypotheses as to what the underlying feedback process where inputs are new data and new hypothesis or the data are refined or adjusted until observations and prediction can be brought back into agreement. We are not positing a kind of polarity between science and tradition but change and development can take place only if there is a willingness of examines previously held beliefs. Scientific knowledge does not postulate unconditional truths but thrush hypotheses valid for a range specified conditions.

If these women are to be empowered as well we must start looking for a new vision, an alternative way of development.

It is against all oppressive structure. It is all exploitation inside the family and outside. So the alternative development is a people based development and the answers should come from people.

Home Science

The field of home science research is today at the crossroads. Researchers in Human development and family studies are in the process of becoming aware of the need for building indigenous theories, developing their own tools and experimenting with research designs and methods of investigation most suited for the study of human behaviour in the Indian cultural context. With its long history of involvement and commitment to the cause of children, women and families, it was felt that the department has a moral responsibility to respond to the need to think of ways to strengthen the interface among research public policy and programmes. For conducting studies on women agriculture and rural extension :

1. What facts do researchers in human development and family studies have to offer policy and programme planners?
2. How can information be most effectively reached to these agencies?
3. What modifications are needed in the approach to research in Human Development and Family Studies, to make it more socially relevant and useful?
4. What is the role of human development and family studies research in social development?

This shall support :

- To revitalise their curriculum in human development and family studies.
- To plan relevant and meaningful research for their institutions.
- Lacunae in research that need investigation on a priority basis.

The need for translating the research funding of child development and other allied disciplines into a language and format that can be accepted by policy planners has also been stated. Several themes which reflect common concerns and point to future agenda and course of action for researchers in human development and family studies and allied disciplines.

Finally, a very important that has emerged is that of setting up an interdisciplinary task force in Early Childhood Care and Education. Its function will be to prepare a research agenda, and play a leadership role by evolving a comprehensive framework to guide research efforts of various institutions across the country; monitor the translation of research findings to policy and programme and coordinate the effective dissemination of information between and among programme and policy planners, and other relevant agencies and the general public.

As one who has in a small way been instrumental in shaping the destiny of this institution during its formative years, to give me great satisfaction and a sense of immense pride in having your kind support for the cause of humanity.

World conferences on women have invariably aroused worldwide enthusiasm and awareness amongst all quarters concerned with gender issues. In our own country and have been acted as prime mover to initiate and promote very many innovative policies and programmes to bring about gender equity, equality and justice. The fourth world conference at Beijing in September 1995 was momentous. The Indian publications on women's issues have come a long way from a small shelf of books on the status of women, into a library of a wide range of collection on women's issues, women's rights, laws, cultural and social issues, employment and labour aspects, poverty and economic issues, and to mention a few. A brief review of the study made on reproductive health care of women in Delhi slums, it was found that as far as the prenatal care was concerned less than 33% of women could utilise it, because they were not aware of such service. Thus it was disappointing to find that information was not percolating down to the grass-root level and the claims of awareness generation by official machinery were not wholly true. If such was the situation right under the nose of the government in Delhi slums, one could imagine the condition in rural areas and other remote places. So far as the educational level of women in the areas studied is concerned, a sample survey of about 500 women in reproductive age of 15 to 40 years was made. It was found that only 22% of these women were literate as against Delhi Literacy rate of 67%.

Population and food raise many questions for human race. This reflects the compelling interest, which especially seeks to establish links with other intellectual disciplines such as philosophy history and social sciences.

Modern ecological studies have been increasingly directed towards measuring the productivity of various kinds of ecosystems and to determining the factors that influence it. When plant material is eaten by herbivorous animals roughly only about 10% is transfer into carnivore tissue, we thus arrive at the idea of a chain each stage of which represents a loss of energy of 90-95 per cent and this leads us to well-known pyramid of numbers which is to be found in ecosystem and to the concept of primary and higher order of secondary produces, ecologists now presents their a loss of energy of 90 to 95% and this leads us to well-known pyramid of numbers which is to be found in ecosystem and to the concept of primary and higher order of secondary producers, ecologists now present their information in terms of bio-mass of total weight of living organisms involved.

Rural household and farming systems have become prime focus of development assistance in recent years. Both in applied research and project work a farm family perspective has been adopted to achieve successful agricultural development.

The farm is no longer viewed solely as a production unit. The focus has shifted to the rural household in its relation to its socio-economic and cultural environment.

The rural family is seen as a central decision making unit for the utilisation of existing development potential and the application of innovations. Simultaneously, the rural household accounts for social stability in the society and for securing the material and non-material essential needs of individual members.

The peasant household is seen as the central decision making unit in rural development. This refers not only to utilisation of existing development potentials, the implementation of development measures of the introduction of innovation of various kinds but also social stability in the society and to the satisfaction of material and non-material needs of its individual members.

Legal and political impediments to Gender Quality for women.

Among the developing countries of Asia, India remains an interesting case study for investigation into variety of analytical issues related to emerging gender structure. Women constitute nearly fifty per cent of the total population of our country and yet the participation rate of women in decision making levels very low. Despite the constitutional provisions and other legislative measures, policy guidelines and programmes and projects, the inequality of opportunity unequal access to material resources of greater number of women, especially the working women, still persists in a large measure.

As we approach the 21st century the eyes of the world are turned towards Asia characterised by rapid economic growth, an unmatched diversity of political and economic systems and a kaleidoscope of people, culture and religions, the region offers the most interesting field for understanding the location of 'gender' of women as well as for seeking means for redressing gender inequality.

Asia is the fastest growing regions of the world in terms of GDP while it holds dramatic diversity with respect to economic growth impulses and strategies, it has a building unity in its cultural roots and modes — offering a veritable laboratory to understand the play of different models of growth on the social fabric. Asia is a varied experience form the G-7 Japan at one end; to the east Asian export led growth success; the incredible, awakening out of one political economy model at another resounding success; to the poverty bowl-south Asia at the other end.

Economic growth and greater influence in the global arena have been achieved at a heavy price. Poverty and inequality in Asia is growing. Asia's culturally strong society is being transformed into more typically agitated society characterised by the strong scars of civic restlessness, a deterioration in women's position in increasing violence, especially against women.

India will march ahead if grass-root workers are given the opportunity for decentralised efforts. Village level activists, to handle the responsibility entrusted to them to the cause of rural women and children. Notwithstanding their handicap of little or lack of education, in fact we have found them to be experienced and articulate in the rural context.

We also found that farm women are highly committed to their duties and women's welfare. Even though they operate in a dispersed set up, they work in unison with one another in implementing the state policy on women and children, which is entreated to them. The exposure, training and support structure provided them not only has enthused to work efficiently and effectively but also help them in shedding their traditional inhibitions and this awakening amongst the farm women and girls with whom they come in contact. Thus they are working as catalysts and change against in the village.

An overall assessment suggests that the effort case with which the women could mobilise women for social change was neither offensive nor unwelcome by the village community, barring some case prejudices here and there. New awakening amongst the rural women folk will indirectly be a very supportive awareness to the Panchayati Raj. In fact women can be great aid and ally to the Panchayati Raj movement in different districts and states. Therefore, we feel that the change, that both government and non-governmental organisation expected from the educated members and workers of social welfare the village women may be called partners can exert their innate potential for the good of the people. The social and community problems cannot be triad carbonate. As part and parcel of the community a village woman's ability to ingratiate herself within the villagers to introduce social change, is a significant landmark in the history to community.

Social welfare is as old as humanity itself. Helping the needy and the person in distress has been in existence particularly in all the civilisation communities. From time immemorial, social welfare has recently developed into a scientific programme for poverty, sickness suffering, social degradation have always been known to man in long course of history of mankind, but after the industrial revolution new social problems were erased, which could not be faced by the older human institutions — family, neighbourhood and local community. In fact this was not the situation only in industrial societies particularly in the wet, but such a situation is being created in the developing countries also. Apart from the humanitarian aspect, the development of scientific knowledge provided the tools for investigating the causes of poverty, of human deficiencies and dissatisfaction with the sole object to find out a remedy for various social problems facing the society. Hence social welfare development into a scientific concept based on a scientific knowledge of the problems facing the society, particularly in free society with the object of finding out ways and means of solving these problems.

The concept of service of one's fellow men has been an integral part of Indian traditions. The ruptures shared the responsibilities of meeting the needs of the individuals and groups in difficulties, the rich and the members of the general community shared the individuals and the group's difficulty. Religion institutions also played a very important part in providing social service. We come across men and women and group of persons who devote their lives to the service of helpless. The measures of goodwill and some leisure time with the industrialisation and urbanisation, our social problems are becoming more and more complex. There is also a growing recognition that for handling such complex social problems of social, economic and human relationship, we require certain technical knowledge concerning human behaviour, social institutions etc.

Thus understanding of social relationship, social psychology and social economics has helped to understand the social problems and the ways and means of organising social welfare services on scientific basis with the help of a tested body of knowledge. An orphan child needs more than food and clothing in children's institution. The problems of aged and infirm persons are partly social and partly psychological in nature. Therefore, the institutions of this basic human needs. There is a need for social welfare programmes like balwadis, holiday homes, youth hostels etc. which help in the prevention of occurrence of social problems. The programmes of social assistance have also to play a very important part in building up the human material. Various services like crèche, orphanages, and homes for the blind, workshops of the orthopedically handicapped persons, community welfare contract were set up by the interested citizens for the purpose of providing welfare services to the needy and the destitute.

Whereas, there has been a large measure of goodwill and dedication, there has been dearth of technical knowledge required to run various welfare services. Foreign literature was available on various social welfare services but this was not suited to the requirements of Indian condition. Attempts have been made in certain areas of welfare, work to provide material on different kinds of social welfare service, like minimum standards on child care institutions, worked out by the Indian conference of social work, and the minimum standards for different welfare programmes by the central social welfare board etc. Some useful material is also available from the reports of various committees and proceedings of conference and seminars on social legislation. All this material is not only inadequate but is not available to the social workers in one place.

Attempts have been made in certain areas of work but this was not suited to the requirements of Indian conditions. Dedication of service towards one's fellowmen, love for charity and brotherhood existed even in times religion emphasised the values of charity philanthropy and mutual help. Indian history revert that the responsibility of assessing the individual in need was hired by the community and the rulers. During the period of King Ashoka one reads about the appointment of Gopas who were supposed to keep the records of caste, gotra, occupation, births, deaths, marriage etc. The duties of gopas were akin to modern social workers. The king took more and more responsibility towards providing social services to the public. During the early British period the impact of education and economic the reformers fought for equality of rights for women and abolition of widow re-marriage. The voluntary organisation like Arya Mahila Samaj, Anjuman-e-Jimayat-e-Islam, Ramkrishna Mission, Theosophical society, Servants of India society and a large number of Christian missionaries contributed considerably to the provision of welfare services for the needy and the handicapped.

These traditions of social services were influenced by various social and economic factors. The social institutions like the joint family, the caste system and the village panchayats provided mechanism, which would meet the needs of the sick, the aged, the destitute and the handicapped members of the community. Industrialisation and urbanisation also changed the pattern of life. New social problems cropped up, for the solution of which the existing social institutions found themselves ineffective. Without the development of social science it beacon possible to make a systematic study if the social problems in order to solve these on a comprehensive and scientific basis. We, therefore, started moving is nonbeing laid on the application of scientific methods to the solution of social problems *i.e.* by studying the social and economic factors of the problem and acquiring special skills and techniques, in dealing with them.

Social welfare board. Social welfare services were brought on the political map of India in 1953 with the setting up of the central social welfare as a part of first five year plan. During the recent years there has been increasing realisation that with a view to improving and preserving the human capital which is one of the most important factors of production of any economic development. It is necessary to provide opportunities for growth and development of the child. The social welfare field has so far been a combination of various social welfare activities without aiming at an integrated approach either to the child or to a family or to the community.

Voluntary agencies. Voluntary welfare organisations have been rendering useful service in the past and sharing the burden of welfare services of the state. In many areas they have playing pioneering role in providing relief and assistance to the people in distress. Many of the agencies are a century old now occasionally financial assistance helps the organisations to expand their programmes. But the absence of continued help and outmoded methods of collecting funds impede the planned development of social welfare in the voluntary sector. Coupled with these difficulties in the dearth of voluntary welfare workers are now going away from the beneficiaries and bureaucracy is also entering into voluntary agencies. The voluntary workers with a few exceptions are no longer able to provide human touch for which they were known.

With changing needs due to changes in social and economic system, there is need to reorient the methods of provided services by the voluntary agencies or organise social services on certain minimum standards. This has not been possible so far. The central social welfare board has decided to create machinery for field counselling service to assist and guide the welfare organisations in improving the standard of their services.

Social security measures. Various field of social welfare pertaining to children, women and aged and infirm handicapped and various other community welfare services, etc., there are still many gaps and weak points in social welfare activities in this country. For the development of the human material it is necessary to link social welfare programmes with the programmes of social services, and social security which is still infancy in this country.

Child welfare. In order to preserve and to improve human capital, investment in the child is very important, in any plan of economic development. The child should be looked after as much as look after our dams, factories etc. and that in many welfare programmes priority should be given for meeting the basic needs of child. These needs are healthful food, adequate clothing, comfortable home with love and understanding, educational facilities, healthy services recreational activities etc. In order to satisfy these needs, the child should be looked after as much as we look after our dams etc. and that in any welfare programmes priority should be provided with all basic services necessary for its physical, mental, emotional and intellectual growth. As investment in basic preventive services for the child is a must in order to prevent blindness, deafness, mental illness or other social handicaps. This will minimise expenditure on the services meant for the treatment of these social ills. These services must be coordinated and integrated so that the total needs of children are met and we have a complete child physically, mentally, and intellectually strong. It may not be possible at this stage to provide all these services to the entire child population in age group of 0-16 but it is necessary to make start somewhere. The Government of India worked on this principle and have initiated demonstration projects of integrated child welfare services in similar community so that all the needs of child are met on integrated comprehensive basis, methods adopted and the results achieved are demonstrated to the community so that the programmes could spread in future.

HUMAN ECOLOGY FOR GLOBALIZATION

When the world and inevitably India are in the throes of major social, economic and technological change, the process will affect the market economy of the nation and also the whole system of higher education. The system has to prepare its graduates for participation in the social economic development of the country, and type of cultural environment and ethic it will need to foster. Information technology is further contributing to this change and will have a major impact on structure, management, and mode of delivery of the educational system.

To develop basic theoretical understanding of discipline but that the understanding should relate to its operational implications for application on making theory-practice an integrated whole in the area of the discipline. The traditional courses should also be encouraged to provide regular field placement of the students to have a "hands on" experience. Due to regional imbalances universities and institutes are developing programmes, which focus on access to quality development of the university/institutes, and colleges located in such regions should receive special attention to the university/institute and the college in backward areas. The expectation is that the universities will also develop greater emphasis to project greater relevance to societal need and legitimise its public support through reaching out to the more disadvantaged groups by undertaking field outreach activities.

These activities should be for undertaking social change functions with respect to women's studies. The centre should be essentially interdisciplinary and headed by a professor/reader with teaching and/or research experience in the area of women's studies and other extension/field action experiences. UGC should deliberate on academic matters of common interest for development of higher education. The contribution of higher education to national development of backward areas, UGC decided on 26th March 1996 at the meeting of commission that no university will be allowed to enroll candidates for one sitting for the BA degree courses from the academic year 1996-97 onwards. There were 214 universities and deemed universities including 27 agricultural universities, 2 veterinary universities, 4 medical universities and 2 technological universities with the affiliated colleges constituting the target segment of the higher institutions of higher education, the total teaching staff in the universities and affiliated colleges was 3.21 lakhs as against 3.10 lakhs in the previous year.

We are a country of rich heritage. Our culture accorded a high position to women in society. It is unfortunate that over the years the very security that was built for women became a barrier for their advancement and deprived them of education and confined them to home. We now have the opportunity to show the world how this trend can be reversed and women accorded an equal status with men.

7

Partnership for Sustainable Development

In the present age, when everyone is aware of the importance of sustainable environment, training the mass in environment management is the need of hours. It is necessary to change people's attitude with regard to environment. A new environmental behaviour is necessary in which quantitative demands and qualitative appreciation and coordination must replace confrontation. This will hopefully lead us into new era of human harmony where all care for well-being of life on earth.

Deterioration of environment tends compelling weight to the need to find a balance between human development and exploitation of natural resources. Some people still claim that the environmental alerts are somewhat exaggerated. The world's population must be limited in the struggle for survival. Department of environmental efficient technology, participation of individual, and change in our thinking and behaviour should help guide us to a sustainable path to ecological stability, bearing in mind that equity and justice ought to prevail with in and between human generations.

The concept of human development is much and richer than what can be captured, simple tool is needed. HDI reflects achievements in the most basic human capabilities — leading of long life knowledgeable and enjoying decent standard of living. These three variables have been chosen to represent that dimension :

- Life expectancy, educational attainment and income.
- Show the improvement in methodology and data can affect country's ranking.

- Deprivation in knowledge by illiteracy and deprivation in income between ethnic groups, man and woman, in political and professional life.

New information opens people's lives to culture and all its creativity — and to the flow of ideas and knowledge. Today's flow of culture is unbalance, heavily weighted in one direction from rich country to poor. Weightless good with high knowledge contents rather than material contents. What is needed is support to indigenous and national cultures with the cost of communications and innovative tools easier to use, people around the world have burst into conversation.

Fundamental rethinking of policy and governance is again required the key priorities :

- Putting human concern and human rights at the centre of national policy and action.
- Reform driven by concern for people, not for capital.
- Development priorities for people for poverty reduction, equity, sustainability and human development.

Globalization offers great opportunities for human advances — Global markets, global technology, global ideas and global solidarity can enrich the lives of people everywhere. The challenges are to ensure that the benefits are shared — An agenda market place and translate them in more equable into human advances with a human face. The growing interdependent of people's lives call for values and shared commitment to human development of all people — but only with stronger governance — local, national, regional and global — to preserve the advantages of global markets competition, but also to provide enough space for human community and environmental resources to ensure that globalization works for people — not for profits, globalization with ethics, equity, inclusion, human security, sustainability and development.

Globalization is often described as a natural phenomena. However, globalization is not inevitable. There is not one but many alternatives to globalization based on the rights of people rather than the rights of corporations, based on democracy rather than corporate rule.

Globalization is a political process, which has been forced

on the weak by the powerful through political institutions such as the Structural Adjustment projects of the World Bank and IMF and the free-trade arrangements of the World Trade Organisation.

Globalization is not new. It was earlier simply called colonialism. The first wave was the colonisation of the America, Africa, Asia and Australia by European powers over 500 years. The first free-trade treaty was a treaty between the East India Company and the declining Moghul Empire in India.

Globalization is basically a take over of the rights of citizens by corporations through a dismantling of the structures of the state that protect people. It is, therefore, leading to less freedom for people, but more freedom for capital. The search for absolute freedom by corporations is expressed in the rules of the Multilateral Agreement for Investment being negotiated by the OECD, to then be imposed on the rest of the world.

The growth under globalization is not a growth in goods and services, but a growth in international trade and a growth of the financial economy. For the poorest of the world increased free trade internationally leads to an increase in poverty by the diversion of or destruction of the resources on which they survive and by the dismantling of institutions which protect their rights.

Materially emptied cultures are then pitted against one another, because their common economic base has disappeared. Cultural diversity is then pushed into conflict. Globalization will protect the environment by leading to economic growth and hence creating more resources for environmental resources and a greater appreciation of environmental values. This assumes that only the rich are environmentally aware. The movements of women, peasants, small fish workers, indigenous people and tribals for environmental protection empirically falsify the assumption. Globalization is increasing violence and disintegration in society by increasing economic insecurity and by ethnicising and ghettoising all forms of dissent, protect and articulation of alternatives.

Capital is defined as a source of freedom, but this freedom is based on the denial of freedom to the land, forests, rivers and biodiversity that capital claims as its own and to others whose rights are based on their labour. Because property obtained through privatisation of commons is perceived to be depriving the owner of capital of freedom. Thus peasants and tribals who demand the return of their rights and access to resources are regarded as thieves. It seems that the western powers are still driven by colonizing impulse to discover, conquer own and possess everything, every society, and every culture. The colonies have now been extended to the interior spaces the entice codes of life forms from microbes and plants to animals including humans.

Today's patents have a continuity with the patents issued to Columbus. The conflicts that have been unleashed by the GATT treaty, by patents on life forms, by the patenting of indigenous knowledge and by genetic engineering are grounded in processes that can be summarised and symbolised as the second coming of Columbus. At the heart of the Columbus discovery was the treatment of piracy as a natural right of coloniser and necessary for the development of the third world communities.

Through patents and genetic new colonies are being carved out. The land, the forests, the rivers, the oceans, the atmosphere have all been colonised, eroded, and polluted. Capital now has to look for new colonies to invade and exploit for its further accumulation. These new colonies are, in my view the interior spaces of the bodies of women, plants and animals. Resistance to Biopiracy is a resistance to this ultimate colonisation of life itself — of the future evolution as well as the part and future of non-western traditions of relating nature and knowing nature.

Globalization is not the cross cultural interaction of diverse societies it is the imposition of particular culture on all others. Nor is globalization the search for ecological balance on a planetary scale. It is perdition of one class, one race and often one gender of a simple species on all others. The "global" in the dominant discourse is the political space in which the dominant local seeks global control, and frees itself of local, natural and global control and responsibility and limits arising from the imperatives of ecological sustainability and social justice. The global in this sense does not represent the universal human interest; it represents a particular local and parochial interest and culture, which has been globalised through its reach and control, its irresponsibility and lack of reciprocity.

When the rights of farmers to save, exchange, evolve seed are denied, when the rights of consumers to safe and adequate food is denied, what we have is totalitarianism of a most basic kind since it is a totalitarianism based on the total control over the vital necessity — food.

How do we build alternatives in the context of this totalitarianism of a new kind — a totalitarianism based on the rule of fictions rather than the gun boat, a totalitarianism built on dispensability of the majority rather than their bondage, a totalitarianism in which there is no dictator, no person, no government, but all pervading corporations which are themselves a legal fiction?

Rejuvenating our knowledge and skills to meet our needs with our own resources, and our own capacities is the alternative to the monopoly on life inherent to patents on life. The Third World people and women have from the beginning of the waves of globalization have had to organise ourselves again and again to define our presented so that we too could govern ourselves, fulfil our humanity, defend our community and other species. We know what it is like to excluded. We need to remember how we have organised in the past, how we have built democratic institutions and cultures. Corporate rules have excluded all people as persons.

Diversity is intimately linked to the possibility of self-organisation. It is, therefore, the basis of both Swadeshi and Swaraj of economic and political freedom.

Decentralisation and local democratic control are political corollaries of the cultivation of diversity. Peace is also derived from conditions in which diverse species and communities have the freedom to self-organise and evolve according to their own needs, strictures and priorities.

Living societies, living ecosystems, living organisms are characterised by three principles :

(a) the principle of diversity.

(b) the principal of self-organisation, self-regulation, self-renewal.

(c) the principle of reciprocity between systems, which is also called the law of return.

Our diversity makes mutuality and a critique of give and take possible. Mutuality makes self-organisation possible. There are two conflicting paradigms of biodiversity. Local communities, whose survival and sustenance is linked to biodiversity utilisation and conservation, hold the first paradigm. Commercial interests, whose profits are linked to utilisation of global biodiversity for production of inputs into large scale, homogeneous, uniform centralised and global production systems hold the second.

The educational philosophy of the university gets translated into its somewhat unorthodox academic structure. Grounded in a faith in the unity of knowledge, department structure of the conventional universities, preferring instead to bring allied disciplines within a few broad and inclusive parameters called schools under whose interactive ambit are placed the more specialised units called centres. At the Master's level, where most of the schools begin their academic programme, training is largely oriented towards single discipline. At the research level it is the development of research solutions that the going becomes precarious. A series of regional workshops that have focused on linkages between research and development. Certainly the linkages are not near and certainly the processes that give the utilisation of research are complex phenomena that are not completely understood. The problems associated with the practical application of university based research have been taken place in Latin America, North Africa and the Middle East, Eastern and Southern Africa have had a special focus on the problems associated with practical application be brought into line with the real needs of agricultural communities. Understanding the world beyond the research system countries to be one of the principle objective. Parallel efforts will be undertaken to ensure that these technologies are brought to bear within the context of the user themselves and resources will be directed towards increasing the effectiveness of research.

As such research utilisation programme has been designed with three main pillars. The first will be the sub-programme on applied R & D systems. The thirst of this initiative will be to understand better R & D from a system perspective. Failures in the transfer of technology may not be solely attributable to the transfer itself. It is possible that there is a failure in research design, or that there is a system failure. Activities relating to commercialisation of research, within a particular client/market orientation will form the core of this sub-programme. The second sub-programme will focus on institutionalisation capabilities for research application. Here the principle objective will be to built and strengthen the capabilities of research and research supporting institutions to engage in activities related to development for creation of communication of infrastructure network.

The growth of India's agriculture during the past nearly 100 years is closely linked with the researchers done and technologies generated. As a centre of higher education and training in agricultural sciences at national and international level :

- To conduct basic and strategic researches with a view of understanding the processes, in all their complexity and to undertake need based research and sustained agricultural productivity in harmony with the environment.
- To serve as a centre for academic excellence in the area of postgraduate education and human resource development in agricultural sciences.
- To provide national leadership in agricultural research, extension and technology assessment and transfer by developing new concepts and approaches and serving as a national referral point for quality and standards.
- To develop information systems, add value to information share and serve the information nationally and serve as a data base.

Linkages and Collaborations

For the national leadership in all major agricultural research areas, IARI has close linkages with almost all annual crops and horti crops research institutes, centres, project directorates, coordinated project, as well as few selected institutes of ICAR;

similar linkages exist for natural resource and socio-economic research institutes; collaboration exists with almost all state agricultural universities (SAUs).

Institutional Setting

To supporting and promoting research the task of activising diverse partners in a network of necessity is certainly a challenge for students of organisational design. Indian agricultural research efforts has three institutional basis : SAU system, ICAR and the private industry. The last is yet to carve a niche for itself.

The SAU system consists of 26 universities, at least one in each state. Some states have more than one *e.g.*, Maharashtra and Uttar Pradesh. SAU's have admission capacity of over 1400 undergraduates and nearly 5000 postgraduates while the SAU concept owes much to the US Land Grant college model. The university education commission perhaps described the need rather well catering for the establishment of rural colleges and universities where no field of human concern should be foreign to them.

The SAU system has about 19,000 scientists engaged in education, research and extension activities. The agricultural university concept was based on the need for a project in which research teaching and extension would be fully integrated and geared towards solving the felt need of the farmers. ICAR and SAU work together supporting each other's activities. The relationships are complex and for our purpose it may be worth nothing that SAU are state Government institution while ICAR is central in character.

Agriculture research in India is a mega effort. A vast network of teaching, research and extension groups with such competence employed in solving farmers' problems, the productivity in Indian agriculture should have been better than what it is. A large volume of research solutions to farmers' problems is made available to the community but a few are accepted. The fault may be inadequacy of solution, the transfer mechanism, the limitations of the understanding of the adopters; all or some of them to check the systems of faults and leakage :

- Are we conformable in managing such a mega system.
- Does the size itself post its unique problems of reduction to put it bluntly; can the civil service system foster a

culture of innovation where age and seniority are not at advantage.

Management of research seems to be as important as the research activity itself in Indian agriculture. These problems are of motivation of achieving excellence and coping with externalities.

TOWARDS SUSTAINABLE COMMUNITIES

Action Mechanism for Conservation of Global Biodiversity Education

India recognises the new global scenario poses unprecedented challenges for the higher education system. The university grants commission has appropriately stated that whole range of skill will be demanded from the graduates of humanities, social sciences, natural sciences and commerce as well as from the various professional disciplines such as agriculture, law, management or engineering.

India can no longer continue the model of general education as it has been persisting in for large bulk of student population. Rather, it requires a major investments to make human resource productive by compiling the older general disciplines of humanities, social sciences and commerce to their applications in the new economy having adequate field based experience to enhance knowledge with skill and develop appropriate attitudes.

International Cooperation

To adopt the new information society technologies such as distance education and internet to forestall the further widening the gap seen in the context of partnership by sharing their successful experience and technologies, material and financial resources and learning to appreciate each other's cultural heritage marked by integrated powers bound to expand new researches to arrive at new equations and new combination. However, it is essential to consider the specific national environment of user and to adopt training material to local situation to ensure their suitability in different context. The HRD movement through new HRD departments to look after or appointed HRD managers to take initiative to strengthen their personal departments to look after the HRD functions to take off the HRD movement, for the organic relationship.

Stepping into the 21st century, India can legitimately take pride in the remarkable progress it has made in every area of human endeavour over the last five decades. Synergy between science, technology, organisation and public policy has helped to bring about a sea change in agriculture, food and environment. Foodgrains production has increased four-fold, to support a rapidly increasing population. Per capita income has doubled. There is also an impressive increase in the life expectancy and decline in the infant mortality. Thanks to the cutting edge science and technology. India has moved from the chronic shortages to an era of self-sufficiency in food grains.

The cabinet on 20th March 2001 finally approved the national policy or the empowerment of women. A new scheme on integration of women empowerment project was approved. A distance education programme for women self-help groups was also launched during the year for the holistic development of the child, the department has been implemented the integrated child development services schemes (ICDS) which provides a package of services comprising supplementary nutrition immunisation, health check up and referral services now covers 4384 blocks and is the world's largest and most unique outreach programme for early childhood care.

The department of women and child development continued to recognise the contribution and potential of rich and vibrant civil society organisation, especially the women's groups, all over the country and forged a strong partnership with them for the implementation of many of its innovative schemes and programmes. These organisations also contribute in a big way for the empowerment of women and development of children. Under the schemes of Day Care Centre for Children 12,470 creches provided day care services to children of migrant, casual, agricultural labourers and construction workers. The Central Social Welfare Board and Indian Council of Child Welfare are implementing the scheme. Under the National Creche Fund, the Department has set up 2455 additional creches.

Early childhood education scheme was started in 1982 to reduce the drop out rates and to improve the rate of retention of children in primary schools. The scheme is being run by voluntary organisations in nine educationally backward States of Andhra Pradesh, Assam, Bihar, Jammu & Kashmir, Madhya Pradesh, Orissa, Rajasthan, Tripura and West Bengal. At present there are 2616 ECE centres in the country integrated with the ICDS network.

Government of India had declared the year 2001 as the year of Women's Empowerment. The Department has finalised a calendar of activities for celebration during every month of the year on themes like, Human Rights for Women, Economic Empowerment of Women, Women and Technology, Women and Governance, Women and Education, Women and Health, Women and Media, Entrepreneurship and Women.

Since the inception of the scheme of Working Women's Hostel, 841 hostels have been sanctioned to provide accommodation to 52,140 working women and day care facilities to 8,012 children in 309 hostels. During the year 20 new hostels were sanctioned. The Cabinet Committee of Economic Affairs has approved the restructuring of Indira Mahila Yojana (IMY) into an Integrated Women's Empowerment Programme (IWEP), and expand it from the existing 238 blocks to 650 blocks by the end of the Ninth plan. The main strategy of the scheme is to create an organisational base for women and to come up together, to analyse and fulfil their needs.

Mass education initiatives through print media for generating awareness and publicity through postal media was also undertaken to inform, educate, and motivate people for bringing about attitudinal changes to receive social education and motivate people for bringing about attitudinal changes to scheme social development goals through electronic and print media are being effectively used to inform, educate and motivate people for bringing about attitudinal of children, women's empowerment, early child development, nutrition, equal status, for women and social civil child marriage, dowry, gender equality, sexual abuses of girl child, exploitation for women and children has been the focus of all media activities. Grant-in-aid to voluntary organisations in the field of women and child to coordinate by the central office to coordinate various activities for women, social awareness, sanitation and hygiene and nutrition education with special emphasis on pre school children, dissemination of knowledge of family welfare for innovative programmes in the field of women and child development during the year 2001 is given. The National Film Development Corporation media unit of the department can provide multimedia facilities for which the electronic and print media are being effectively used for different issues concerning women and girl child. Press campaign can also be launched for generating awareness about child labour, nutrition, and infanticide and domestic violence.

Training, Employment and Education

ICAR has also intensified its efforts for transfer of improved technologies by establishing Agriculture Technology Information Centre — a single window delivery system. The functioning of 53 Zonal Research Stations have been amended to act as Krishi Vigyan Kender in addition to existing 261 kendra, along with the strengthening of institution village linkage programme (IVLP). Under the priority area of crop improvement/management for various regions and production system has been supported by the generation of the appropriate agro techniques, to provide evolved. The research support to provide training and skill development to women for enhancing their productivity, new upgraded skills to poor and assetless women in additional sector — agriculture, sericulture, fisheries, dairying, poultry etc., for enhancing their producing and income generation.

This programme launched in 1987, seek to provide update skills and new knowledge to poor and assetless women in the traditional sectors, such as, agriculture, animal husbandry, khadi and village industries, sericulture, social forestry and wasteland development of enhancing their productivity and income generation. This would enhance and broaden their employment opportunities, including self-employment and development of entrepreneurial skills. Women beneficiaries are organised into viable and cohesive groups or co-operatives. A comprehensive package of services, such as, extension, inputs, market linkages, etc. are provided besides linkage with credit for transfer of assets.

Women's economic programme, which was launched in 1982-83 with assistance from the Norwegian Agency for

Development cooperation. Under this programme, financial assistance is given to women's development corporation, Public Sector Corporation and Voluntary organisations, to train poor women mostly in non-traditional trades and to ensure their employment in these areas. Financial assistance is given to the grantee organisations of hiring of training-cum-production sheds, training costs, machinery and equipment, stipend to the trainees and remuneration for the trainees, the upper ceiling for assistance under this scheme is normally confined to Rs. 8000 per beneficiary.

Distance Education for Women and empowerment and various schemes of the Government of India have shown that strong women's group could contribute substantially to the development and convergence of services and activities. The experience of these schemes has shown that the sustainability of the majority of these groups was a major problem and one of the prime reasons that was lack of proper training strategy. The Department of Women and Child Development, Indira Gandhi National Open University (IGNOU) and Indian Space Research Organisation (ISRO) are jointly undertaking the implementation of the project.

Integrated Child Development Services (ICDS) Scheme

The Integrated Child Development Services (ICDS) Scheme aims to improve the nutritional and health status of pre school children, pregnant women and nursing mothers by providing a package of services including supplementary nutrition, pre school education, health check-up and health education. In addition the scheme envisages effective convergence of inter-sectoral services in the Anganwadi Centres.

Objectives of IDSC

- Improve the nutritional and health status of children below the age of six years.
- Lay the foundation for the proper psychological, physical and social development of the child.
- Reduce the incidence of mortality, morbidity, malnutrition and school drop-outs.
- Achieve effective coordination of policy and

implementation among various departments to promote child development.

- Enhance the capability of the mother to look after the normal health and nutritional needs of the child, through proper health and nutrition education.

The department continued recognise the contribution and the potential of rich and vibrant civil society organisations, specially the women's groups, all over the country and forged a strong partnership with them for the implementation of many of its innovative schemes and programmes. These organisations also contribute in a big way as think tanks, advocates and watchdogs of the development initiatives for the empowerment of women and development of children.

Nutritional Monitoring to be established at state, district, block and community level.

- Community based monitoring mechanism to be established from village level to the level of the state, and responsibility and accountability to be fixed for reduction in malnutrition levels.
- Information on reduction of malnutrition in young children to be reviewed in monthly developmental reviews at district and state levels.
- Database on nutrition situation in the country to be created at the central and state levels and reviewed every quarter by the empowered committee.

Grant-in-aid for Research, Publication and Monitoring

The Department promotes research studies for development of innovative programmes, for testing the feasibility of new proposals, for evaluating the efficacy of existing programmes and services and for analysing emerging problems and services and issues in the field of women and child development. It also supports workshops and seminars which help in formulating research proposals and disseminating research findings of social situational analysis, which are likely to be helpful in planning, programming and review of implementation.

These activities are being carried out through Research Institutes, Universities, Colleges/Schools of Social Work and Social Organisations. Under the scheme, the organisation should have registered under any state in India and normally have experience for three years in the field of women and child development.

Priority is given to research projects of an applied nature keeping in view factors such as the policy priorities of the department, social problems requiring urgent public interventions and evaluation of the programmes implemented by the department.

Constitutional Provisions

Women and children who represent more than two-third per cent of the country's total population, constitute the most important target groups in the context of developmental planning and therefore, their concerns are placed high on the priority list of the country's developmental agenda.

The concern of safeguarding the rights and privileges of women and children found its best expression in the Constitution of India. While Article 14 confers equal rights and opportunities on men and women in political, economic and social spheres, Article 15 prohibits discrimination against any citizen on the grounds of sex and article 15(3) empowers the State to make affirmative discrimination in favour of women. Article 39 enjoins upon the State to provide equal work and article 42 directs the state to make provisions for ensuring just and humane condones of work and maternity relief. Realising that children have neither a voice nor a political constituency, the Constitution of India and laid down certain social safeguards to ensure their welfare, protection and development. Article 45 provides for free and compulsory education for all children upto age of 14 years.

In order to give a practical shape to the constitutional directives a number of laws have been enacted and schemes and programmes have been formulated for the development of women and children. These have definitely brought forth a perceptible improvement in the status of women and children in the country, although there is still a wide gap between the *de jure* provisions and the *de facto* realities.

Women's Component Plan

The ninth plan directed both the Centre and the States to adopt a special strategy of women's component plan through which, not less than 30 per cent of funds/benefits are earmarked in all the women-related sectors. It also suggested a special vigil to be kept on the flow of the earmarked funds/benefits through an effective brings forth a holistic approach towards empowering women. The Department of Women and Child Development which was designed as the Nodal Machinery for the development and empowerment of women is playing a crucial role in the formulation and monitoring of women's component plan. The department has advised all the concerned Ministries for inclusion of an identifiable women components plan in their programmes right from the planning process and implementation and monitoring of their programmes to ensure that the benefits of their programmes to reach the women. The committee has been renamed as Committee for Monitoring Gender Mainstreaming in the Government of India.

Special Component Plan (SSP) for SC and Tribal Sub-Plan (TSP) programmes for women and children implemented by the Departments are primarily directed towards the most disadvantaged groups of population like scheduled castes and scheduled tribes and other economically backward classes living in backward rural and tribal areas and urban slums. The basic consideration in all the schemes is to ensure that the benefits of the schemes flow to the disadvantaged sections of the population the SCs and STs, women and children.

Most of the programmes of the department implemented through voluntary organisations. Efforts are made to encourage more and more voluntary organisation to come with proposals in tribal and backward rural areas by special concessions and relaxation under the grant-in-aid. The department at the instance of cabinet secretariat prepares the Annual Action Plan (AAP) for the scheme and activity of the department, setting out the target fixed at the beginning of the year.

Agricultural Research of India's ninth five-year plan (1997-2002) DARE requested with the endorsement of parliamentary standing committee on agriculture, for allocation of 1 per cent of AGDP for public expenditure on agricultural research, extension education. From previous precedent, plan allocations usually fall some twenty-five per cent short of requests. They nevertheless customarily exceed funding available from domestic sources incorporating an assumed contribution from external financing to cover the projected gap. These have been steady growth in ICAR, SAU & ZRS infrastructure and staff employed. The system now serves almost all of India agro-climatic zones yet despite of this build up there have been a number of funding problems.

Production practices and systems will need to be adopted to respond to new market demands and export opportunities, poverty alleviation or growing labour shortage, depending on the setting. Technical solutions will be increasingly location specific, matched to the huge diversity of India's 20 agro ecological regions, 60 sub-regions and 120 agro-climatic zones. More detailed indigenous knowledge and greater skills in blending modern and traditional technologies to optimise productive efficiency will be more than even before — the keys to farming success and sectoral growth. And while ready-made intensification technology may be importable for a few commercial and particularly export producer, most of the needed technology will still have to be generated and adapted locally to make it compatible with the social and economic circumstances of Indian farmers. Much of the adopted technology will therefore remain into the category of public goods. Finally it will be necessary to address growing environmental concerns, especially natural resources conservation. These include the needs for better conservation of the land and water base of irrigated agriculture, a reduction of agro climatic pollution and adverse health effects, production of fragile ecosystems in mountain, coastal and arid areas and the containment of deforestation by traditional shifting cultivation.

Mechanisms needed simply to improve timely communication would be very different from those required to launch an integrated research and extension programme. Similarly, the mechanisms needed to develop collaboration between two groups that resent losing their autonomy will differ markedly from those needed to link groups that recognise their interdependence but simply do not set enough time to work together and share information. The basic types of linkage mechanisms. These mechanisms apply to link between on-station and on-farm research as well as between research and technology transfer agencies. Many of these mechanisms can also be used to forge link directly with the farmers. The specific to highlight each mechanism's particular utility for building links, its management requirements, and the kind of institutional conditions under which it can be used most effectively through planning and review process. The mechanisms also functions best when managers set them up to advisor, with professional pooling their respective area of expertise, rather than supervisory with one group acting as watch dog over the other for joint problem diagnosis; joint priority setting; and planning exercise joint programming and review meetings.

Indian agriculture must also capture some more opportunities. The biological revolution has provided the precedent opportunity of transforming any gene from any organism and is already having an impact on agricultural development in several developed, and a few developing countries.

Contribution of technology generation, assessment, refinement and transfer to sector growth. If it is to respond successfully to these challenges, agriculture will have to become more knowledge intensive investments in research will be needed to generate new knowledge. Greater attention will have to be paid to information based technologies. Strengthened means of dissemination will be needed to transfer will have to focus more strongly than before the keys to farming success and sectoral growth. And while ready-made intensification technology may be importable for a few commercials and particularly export producers, most of the needed to generate the new knowledge. Greater attention will have to be paid to information-based technologies strengthened means of dissemination will be needed to transmit this information to farmers since vast majority will still have to hectares or use of garble land, or correspondingly small livestock to enterprises, there they will continue to be strict limits on the amounts of cost recovery which they can support; much of the adopted technology will therefore remain in the category of public goods. Finally it has been necessary to address growing environmental concerns, especially natural resource conservation. These for better conservation of land and water base of irrigated agriculture and reduction of agro chemical pollution and adverse health effects protection of fragile ecosystems in mountain coastal arid areas and the contaminant of deforestation by traditional shift cultivation to capture some novel opportunities.

Biodiversity and Environment

Projects may vary from research involving extensive fieldwork or social surveys based on those of a more theoretical nature. The aim is to produce a written thesis which is a sustained argument based on a thorough review of evidence and critical inquiry offering original insights at a theoretical or empirical level for life on earth. The ground breaking reports shall indicate the profound changes that continue to occur in social, institutional and economic systems. The students are required to undertake taught courses in research methods drawn from the M.Sc. research methods in social science during the first year of M.Phil. and Ph.D. studies. Other courses from across the university may be taken if they are relevant to the student research.

A main supervisor shall be appointed when the student arrives at the school/centre and within a few months other people may be appointed as appropriate and in consultation with the student. Supervisors appointed provide advice on all aspects of the form and content of research, and the research process, and ensure that students meet the universities various quality control requirements. Undertaking research and producing a thesis can be a long process and supervisors are also important in helping to keep students motivated.

Entry Requirement

Successful research relies a great deal on motivation, considerable personal commitment is vital. Research students generally have ethic a good honours degree, a master degree or relevant professional experience. The required standard increases substantially from M.Phil. to Ph.D. they must also research interest which match those of potential supervisors. Acceptance is based on formal application form and interview. Applicants are expected to have prepared an outline research proposal at the point of application.

Finding

Significant progress has been made in confronting environmental challenges. Nevertheless, the environment has continued to degrade in nations of all regions. Progress towards a sustainable future has simply been too slow.

A regional and participatory process was used to produce analysis of environmental impact of alternative development scenarios and policy action will be included in the further GEO report as well as more extensive analysis of current policy responses, their impact, and the reasons for their success and failures. The introduction of these elements in the continuous GEO assessment has already started. As a result several countries report marked progress in curbing environment pollution and showing the rate of resource degradation as well as reducing the intensity of resource use.

International Agenda in 1992 in Rio de Janeiro provides the global consensus on the road map towards sustainable development. UNEP continues to be the environmental voice of United Nations responsible development, scientific analysis monitoring and assessment. Increasingly, United Nation Organisations, the World Bank and regional banks are "greening" their programme. New approaches to international policies are being developed, tested and implemented.

Collaborative arrangements. with the network of institutions on JNU campus like Institute of Mass Communication, the Indian Council of Social Science Research Campus will substantially promote networking amongst scientists and cater to each others needs.

8

Global Vision and Local Action

Exploration for establishment of Asian Centre for Human Ecology for Women and Child

To attain the objective of the society and to re-examine its relationship with social economic development includes the relevance of quality education. The gradual process of internationalisation of education; institutional and organisational structures and management; and funding. To enhance knowledge with skills and to develop appropriate attitudes require in major investment to make this large human resource productive by coupling the older general discipline of humanities, social sciences, sciences and commerce to their applications in the new economic and having adequate field based experience. Finally, education should be an instrumentality for developing not only economically prosperous society, but on which one can live comfortably in the context of pluralism and democracy for equity and social justice with respect for gender, caste, clan and creed for linking the functions and roles of higher education for national development.

The project proposal entitled "Studies on popularisation of mushroom through training programmes" F. No. 8(14)95 Hort.II 7-7-1997 — 6-7-2000. This aid was mainly to promote and coordinate education research for the diverse crop — the mushrooms for income generation and bridging the protein gap in rural slum areas and the community as a whole through training programmes for on-station and doorstep technology transfer to establish linkages of mushroom cultivation and coordinate its application. A congress was organised in congregation with IIT, Delhi, IARI and Department of Home

Science, University of Delhi to increase the relevance of Higher education and research through extension education programmes to reach the community to commensurate with the new challenges and opportunities both at national and global level to include human resource development and technology assessment in new paradigm of holistic advancement in agriculture and allied fields to meet the human ecological needs. The project was a great success and led to the development of the field Human Ecology. Under this congress a background paper was also released.

Under the project the book entitled "Farm Women and Community" was developed along with extension bulletin besides the national and international achievements with the concept of home science extension for the cause of linking higher education for community services, the Second Congress on Human Ecology which was organised by Interdisciplinary Applied Sciences, South Campus, University of Delhi, in February 2001 to promote links among researchers and technology transfer agents.

A Consultative Group Meeting for the research management mechanism to be adaptive for extension education and outreach followed this. Based on concept of human ecology delivered by Dr. R.S. Paroda, DG, ICAR in his inaugural speech, an extended report on Biodiversity and Food Security was also developed. Keeping in view the observations on the variety of training programmes conducted and the work already carried out on the project to serve the objective to promote education research and its application in home science and allied sciences for strengthening and dissemination of technologies to the farm women and community towards ensuring food, nutrition, and environmental security of conservation of agro-biodiversity on household food and nutritional security through horticulture. The evaluation report by the technical experts will help in great deal for taking action to derive maximum benefit for our farmers in poverty alleviation and food security. This will also help the appropriate research interventions and extension strategies required to make home science and allied sector more productive through diversification for the dynamic project development as per the country needs for action in management and reform and functional literacy for the poor.

To cope with a greater diversity of agro-ecological settings and producers, a decentralised approach is needed. Such a decentralised approach should focus on individual production systems and integrate contributions of frontier sciences as well as conventional disciplines and indigenous knowledge in augmenting productivity, stability and sustainability. In contrast to the blanket Green Revolution recommendations appropriate to the needs of the past, the new technologies will have to be tailored to specific locations for more efficient use of the technology.

With the objective of the project to support agro-ecosystem research to raise efficiency, responsiveness and relevance of the system which has been built up over the years, partly to the emerging and future challenges facing India's agricultural sector. To promote the multi-disciplinary, location specific and participatory mode of operation the project fund were used to complement existing resources of the US India project and augment the productivity of the present "standing capacity" by enhancing availability of funds for research operations (contingencies), system maintenance and by upgrading scientific skills which had been of the major cause of current weakness in the system and its difficulty in addressing geographical variations in needs of technology. To address these weaknesses for filling the crucial funding gaps to allow these objectives to be reached using existing staff and research infrastructure and filling crucial skill gap are needed to attain the above objectives.

For the priority setting process considered for the potential contribution of improvement in the productivity, stability or sustainability to a range of national objectives including :

- National food security.
- Household food security.
- Environment quality and conservation or equity.
- Sustainability in the use of natural resources.
- Product diversification to enhance rural income.
- Welfare of tribal people, women or other disadvantaged groups and
- Exploiting commercially viable technologies.

The Centre for Human Ecology at South Delhi Campus, University of Delhi will lead to adjustments in the choice of the programmes to be funded in future and/or the scale of funding allocated to each from the national level for the global programmes and the new vision to conduct research towards improving the sustainable productivity and to support rural development sector.

To attain the objective of the society covered in home science and allied sciences and instituting and promoting transfer technology programme. To provide undertake and promote education research and its application in diverse crop like mushrooms and other floriculture crops it was realised that the process, trials and error and the attempt to think in a multidisciplinary way and its genesis is therefore, very difficult from many academic studies. Rather than starting from a clearly defined research purpose and focusing for a number of years on the same few trial fields or villages, this research was inspired by multitude of practical issues.

It was uncertain whether farming system research with its stepwise approach to agricultural technology could provide solutions in such a case. Later on working as per requirements of the village community, I felt that I am setting more towards the fundamentals of farming system research. I was frustrated by the vagueness of the concept of farming system, by the arbitrary way in which variables and parameters were sometimes defined. My problem statement shifted to the definition of general systems framework that was relevant to the particular agricultural activity and allowed understanding the changes that had taken place in respective villages.

There are many limitations of the studies undertaken by the fund support from national and international agencies. The interdisciplinary approach does not always do justice to the complexity of discipline. Secondly, either due to the absence of quantitative data or the limited validity of many of the existing statistical and survey data, no statistical treatment of the data has been attempted.

Therefore, some of the conclusions rely principally on circumstantial evidence. Partly farmers who have witnessed many of the changes in their existing environment provide this evidence. The project entitled "Research methodology for studies on women agriculture and rural extension through education and training programmes with special reference to pre-service graduates of home science" for the Reorganisation of Home Economics to Human Ecology on Policy framework to reform for the cause of education system for future.

I can only hope that this study presents a starting point of further work on farming system and shifting of cultivation. May be it is helpful to those who wish to analyse shifting cultivation or bring changes in the existing farming systems. The effective partnership with advance institutions in India and abroad will always be required for the technology generation. Our agriculture research systems is aware of these issues and is moving ahead in the required direction.

For implementation and time bound completion of the objectives should be planned under three major components:

1. Agro ecosystem research.
2. Innovation in technology dissemination.
3. Organisation and management system.

Keeping in view the *ad-hoc* schemes working in non profit arena a foundation of a government organisation dealing with such problems need to demonstrate programme effectiveness, strength based focus and community impact on the concept of the human ecology towards bio-diversity and food security under :

- Extension education and outreach for empowerment of farm women to know human resource potential available in India.
- To develop not only national HRD plans but also to develop sub-regional plans based on gap analysis to develop new mechanism for training and also to react towards the post WTO trade scenario.

Linkages

The painstaking efforts taken in the development of linkages as a discipline of Home Science to Human Ecology. The most significant achievement under the project is the emergence of the field Human Ecology. Human Ecology is not a new area of the scientific endeavour. It is an area of multidisciplinary science involving a variety of distinct subjects for rural development which the topmost priority of the age and hence a matter of global concern. There is increasing recognition that women are involved into the world agriculture. Therefore, until recently it has been difficult to begin a clear picture of where, when and under what circumstances women participate in farm, non-farm work. Most farming system develop mix pattern of women's agricultural responsibilities combining the production cycle. The technological interventions bring with it a host of new problems, which necessitate further research both biological and social the farmer needs the appropriate technology and the recommended inputs for increasing production.

The transfer of income generating technology related activities has profound implication in such fields as energy, environmental science etc., the success of eco farming system approach lies in the development of technological packages group. Less sophisticated technologies which are developed locally are more appropriate very little or no "research" has been conducted to determine the best farming system that should be applied in specific situation or system for *e.g.* pastoral farming system are mostly replaced by sedentary farming systems in the west.

Farmer's involvement is the fundamental step to a successful transfer of information. The methodologies that evolved from farmers' participatory research can definitely contribute to the developed of sustainable land use system.

The findings/observation of the projects provide broad guidelines for government and NGOs for planning and implementation of projects at State and National levels. The finding can be utilised effectively by other research organisations to further enhance the work areas. The students also benefit, as the case studies provide a base for work towards achievement of higher education (M.Sc./Ph.D.). On the international level the projects can serve as a model for planning, similar work in another developing countries.

1. Synthesis of sub-systems of sustainable agriculture.
2. Synthesis of a sustainable farming system based on location specific need through on-farm research.

3. Development of research methods for evaluating the farming system with regards to its biological environmental and social efficiency.
4. Development of methodology for monitoring the improved system for a long period of time.

Finally, it has been observed that there are many who, by virtue of their passivity, dependency, fear, laziness seek to be shown every inch of the way, and demonstrated to them that each step will be safe. One of our problems is that very few of us have developed any distinctive first hand information in order to function whereas they possess vital knowledge of which I am ignorant. Confronting and solving problems, is a painful process, which most of us attempt to avoid. And very avoidance results in greater pain and inability to grow both mentally and spiritually. The road is less travelled for new psychology, traditions, values and culture.

To the Journey of Human Ecology

In the present time there is a considerable emphasis and interest in Human Ecology all over the world. As such, there is a need for a publication containing all aspects of Human Ecology which could give update information about the already available literature which lie starred in different books and journals in this direction to provide a comprehensive column containing all available information in a compact form to serve as a resource material to the users.

The painstaking efforts taken in the development of linkages as a discipline of Home Science to Human Ecology. In the same context for creating balance in higher education by introducing the unified field of human ecology. It seems all of us are making efforts for the cause of environmental interaction and seeking collaborations to what, how, why, when of the best alternatives for action on the global vision and mission for human ecology needs? The significance of education for sustainable development at all levels keeping in view the following points :

- Networking in informal sectors, the grass-root level, NGO and the global forum for wider access to higher education.

- To foster among students community, a constant motivation to learn and to develop not only academic ability but also practical skills and talents that are being demanded by the modern world.
- Contributions from experts to place, entire sector of higher education in sharp focus.
- For higher investments and measures to upgrade higher education and research programme.
- To use distance education for training skills in virtual classroom, with the advances in communication technologies.

The legacy of innovative programmes of excellence in time past and time present is a gateway to the relevance for the future. It is my fond hope the field of Human Ecology will be to model the value of holistic perspective in addressing human environment issues with the emerging field of all applied sciences, which teaches the principles on which to find health and happy life. It emphasises interrelations between various components of human ecosystems. On the whole the philosophy of human ecology provides a context for developing a serving individuals and families from human environment perspectives. The science is and will continue to be viable and dynamic in creating, imparting knowledge through teaching research, services and outreach so that the "voiçe" may be translated through education and educational programmes in the field of Home Science. And it may adopt the nomenclature of "Human Ecology". For providing new data and enhancing conditions on Human Ecology in the light of evaluation for : suggestions, international population policy, religions, landscapes, ethnicity, race and increase in the multiethnic society, translations cooperation economic measures of development, development theory and the role of women in development and ethnicity and ethnic changes.

9

Education in Human Ecology

Growing activities of human and his increasing demands on the biotic and abiotic components of environment has brought forth a change in his ecological philosophy. He is now directing his attention more on the study of habitat or ecological system as a whole than on their components. The biotic components are just a small past of habitat or ecological systems. In order to study the environment and micro changes brought in various components *i.e.*, water, air and soil, we study the climate and edifice elements. The distribution, adaptations and functional aspects of the organisms and communities are studied in greater details in ecology and relevant information is obtained from biological literature on biogeography systematic cytology, genetics and physiology.

It is, therefore, imperative for an ecologist to be acquainted with various disciplines of physical and biological sciences in order to get integrated picture of the environmental complex in relation to organic world.

Human ecology is the study of interaction between human beings and their environment. It is a means to improve people's life and environment, emphasising indepth study of reciprocal effects that takes place physically, socially economically and esthetically. Its basic approach is the conservation of natural resources both renewable and non-renewable and interlinks the science of biology as an interpretative science and elucidates the existence in the environment. It comes with the system that supports man.

Life on our planet originated much earlier than man came into existence. Mental set up of man has made him a super animal. Man is no longer slaving to the environment but through his technical skills he has to attain, he has to certain extent attained mastery over his environment. He creates favourable environment for his welfare in doing so, many a times, he forgets that his is a small component of nature and by disturbing nature and by disturbing the environmental balance, he is inviting trouble, change of forests, building roads and dams, industrial set ups and urbanisation, server and waste disposal etc., are some of the activities which are rapidly changing environments of our planet.

The paradigms of biodiversity conservation, which is, held by community whose survival and sustenance is linked to local biodiversity utilisation and conservation. For local indigenous communities, conserving biodiversity means to conserving biodiversity means to conserve the integrity of ecosystem and species, the right of those resources and knowledge, and their production systems based on biodiversity. For them biodiversity has intrinsic value as well as high use value.

The utilisation of biodiversity in people's economy is guided by a plurality of knowledge systems. The implementation of these properties, characteristics and use of this biodiversity is held with the local communities in different languages, and in their diverse epistemological frameworks.

Nature's diversity and diversity of knowledge system is however, undergoing a major or process of destabilisation with the expansion of patents and intellectual property rights into the domain of biodiversity via the TRIPs Agreement of the World Trade Organisation. It is totally inadequate for the objectives of protection and conservation of biodiversity on one hand and protection of our indigenous intellectual heritage and social creativity on the other hand. Changes in our policy and law are being made with respect to our biological and intellectual heritage. The plant variety legislation is being introduced by the environment ministry.

No Ministry is addressing the unique problems associated with the objective of conservation of medicinal plant biodiversity and protection of indigenous systems of medicines and their practitioners especially in the context of TRIPs. The framework law for implementation of Biodiversity conservation can therefore, be covered in a legal framework, appropriate to the domain of biodiversity and indigenous knowledge for protecting our biological and intellectual heritage. In the absence of Biodiversity legislation to perpetuate the piracy as intellectual property rights of western laboratories and corporation, will function as one-sided legislation. Protecting our biological and intellectual heritage in the age of biopiracy requires the recognition and rejuvenation of our heritage and the evolution of legal system for the protection of this heritage in the context of emerging IPR regimes needed globally to prevent piracy.

To promote changes in the way the centre and states develop and employ human resources with the aim to make them and their sectors more productive and to modernise its agricultural sector at Nodal Centre for Human Ecology. To achieve these changes, policy and institutional reform would be carried out. The project would foster changes in the investment priorities resulting from policy and institutional reforms will focus on the process of : (a) improving the quality and relevance of higher education for community service through training programmes, and (b) strengthening the capacity of participating states to develop and manage agricultural human resource.

To upgrade human resource management the project at state level would support development and management programmes (HRD & HRM) including training focused on job oriented needs for (i) systematic need assessment, (ii) training and trainers, (iii) evaluation of training-effectiveness, (iv) better instructional facilities, and (v) improve management of state sector employees. This will redress environmental degradation, desirable resources and environment management practices, common property resource management, improve management skills, self-sustaining capacity, employment generation, mass awareness, income generation. The activities which are socially beneficial and economically viable like on-farm, off-farm and non-farm will be undertaken for the benefit of the community by doorstep and on-station technology transfer for functional literacy, through short term training programmes to ensure continues benefit to rural poor so that the resource and environment may be preserved for future generation.

EDUCATION AND TRENDS IN CURRICULA

Vocational/Career Oriented Programmes

Empowering people at different socio-economic and educational levels, which are appropriate to market demand both in rural and urban areas. For students who have undergone general education courses in continuing education could offer specific skills, for those already in job to update skills or acquire qualifications for career advancement.

The school curricula of 1960s had elements of ecology and conservation of nature and its resources right from primary stage to biology courses of middle, secondary or senior secondary classes. The approach of integrating the teaching of science, social science even the mathematics and language with experience of children was extended to upper primary and secondary stage as part of general education. The environmental concept problems and introduction of social and environmental studies provided teachers with a curricular area in which the need and interest of children could be met through a focus on the local environment. Students must be given the opportunity to develop the sense of ownership, and empowerment so that they are fully invested in an environmental sense and motivated to become responsible active citizens.

Yeshpal Committee Report 1993 strongly recommended Gandhian approach to learning. Many other institutions in different parts of the country use different approaches and methodologies with same results. What runs through them all is the thread of spirituality and ecological thinking. All these institutions is still value education through course work as well as practices. It would be in fact appropriate to describe the institutional framework for training and research in sociology, which as emerged after independence. Sociology in India is largely a discipline of borrowed concepts and methods derived from high prestige centres of learning in affluent wet especially in the USA and UK. This has resulted in chasing high prestige models into quick sand of pseudo-intellection. Sociologists have still not related themselves directly to the people and their problems and still revelling in counter productive intellectualism. Our sociology does not address itself to the living concern of today and tomorrow. As a result it is not able to contribute meaningfully towards resolving many dilemmas of development.

The concept of human resource system therefore assumes that human being is great asset in the organisation. They are not merely necessarily evils to be reckoned with but they can contribute a great deal to the achievement of organisational as an asset with the unlimited potential in the concept of Human Resource Systems. The study of people at most is generally referred to as the study of organisational behaviour. It is the systematic study of the actions and attitude that people exhibit within organisation. The field of organisational behaviour (OB) is based on large number of systematically designed research studies. An organisation is a formal structure of planned coordination involving two or more people in order to achieve in common goal.

Contributing Disciplines

Organisational behaviour is applied behaviour science and as a result, is built upon contributions from several behaviours discipline. The predominant are psychology, sociology, social psychology, anthropology and political science. Psychology's contribution has been mainly at individual or micro level of analysis, whereas the latter disciplines have contributed to our understanding of macro concepts — group processes and organisational behaviour. The psychology explains or sometimes changes the behaviour of humans and other animals. The goals of human behaviour studies are concerned with developing people's skills, help to explain, predict and control human behaviour. The human behaviour studies after technologies that facilitate the control of people. In fact whether these technologies should be used in organisation becomes ethical question. The control objectives are frequently seen by managers as the most valuable contribution that human behaviour makes towards effectiveness on the jobs. Today's managers understand that the success of any effort at improving quality and productivity must include their employees. These employees will only be major force in changing out changes and will actively participate in planning other changes.

Improving People's Skill

The relevant theory and concepts that can help one, plan and predicts the behaviour of people. These are variety of ways to motivate people, how to be better communicator and how to create more effective team to be used in the job.

Motivating the Workforce

Reconstituted into job requiring considerable higher technical skills or taking workers in other countries that will do the same work for a fraction of the wages. In this situation employee tends to perform either low skilled jobs or higher skilled jobs that means to maintain a middle class or upper class lifestyle. This situation leads to a major challenge for managers. How to motivate who are making very low wage and have very little opportunity to significantly increase their pay either in current or through promotion.

System Development and Research

Various systems for human resource systems need to be continuously designed, tested and reviewed. Data being collected also need to be analysed to give dues to the developing interventions. Development of human resource system can be conceived a system with interlinkages amongst its various components. The central concern of various components of HRS seems to be job. Job is defined in terms of critical attributes, background characteristics necessary like education and training and experience person has before he takes up the job we get training needs out of the critical attributes which also contribute to the concept of career planning of education and training. If we further expand we get into several new directions. The concept of human resource management is an approach to the management of the people. The behavioural science movement made two useful contributions to HRM.

Organisation development movement. The organisational development (OD) movement advocated the implementation of programmes designed to improve the effectiveness with which organisation functions and responds to change, with particular emphasis on how people carry out their work and interest with one another. The total approach to organisational behaviour exerted a strong influence on many of these who in the late '70's and early '80's began concentrate on corporate culture as a central issue in the management of human resource. Different organisations have different traditions. In some organisations personal function may already include some aspects like general administration such as general administration such special features will certainly influence the design of some aspect of HRS. The traditional factor where HRS was designed was part of the personal function. Where HRS was introduced, administration was also put along with the department was designated human resource administration.

Challenges and Opportunities

The human behaviour studies solutions or at least some meaningful insights towards solutions. The relevant concepts and theories that can help one, plan and predict. Each organisation has its own tradition. These influence the design of human, resource systems. If an organisation is highly centralised the designs will be own kind; if it is decentralised, the design would be quite different.

Transfer of Technology

The process of transfer of technology cannot be examined in isolation. The effectiveness of TOT is greatly influenced by the linkages between and among those responsible for technology generation. The process of TOT could be examined wholly taking the process as major systems and the research extension client and input sub systems and its component. Prioritisation of research needs and action points for functional literacy to deprive through training programmes and doorstep technology transfer.

Empowerment of women for creation of an enabling environment where women can freely exercise their rights both within and outside home as equal partners :

— generation of adequate human resource to meet the goal of promoting awareness, education through training and research programmes in postgraduate courses, post doctoral programme, short term training courses for service and in-service graduate, doorstep technology transfer.

— Development of education, linked to social education from primary school age through adulthood of all groups of people.

— Enterprise resource planning — under university synergy programmes.

To known better the human resource potential available in the region in order to develop not only national HRD plans but also to develop sub regional plans based on gaps analysis in supporting offered and to develop new mechanism for training.

Development of strategy for food production, income generation through genetic, bio-diversity, natural resource management and education to improve the environment of the community on sustainable basis.

- Provide support with action by providing a consistent internal policy, goals and links.
- Provide leadership by taking part in linkage activities and giving them high visibility and priority.
- Encourage the group for commitments towards the farming related activities.
- Use mechanisms such as problem diagnoses, training and priority and set priorities.
- Promotion the farming community, farmer participation as collaborators and evaluators of alternatives technologies.
- To collect and circulate the information on training programmes to identify common training needs in the country.
- To develop such as web sites to further develop its training activities in research organisations and management in the regions.
- Sharing the management experience whatever the management structure, a measure of autonomy is essential in order to maintain flexibility, objectivity and responsiveness to stakeholder; a single nodal centre handling research and education in agriculture together and able to coordinate effectively with other projects seen one model worthy of consideration. To ensure

that research remains a profitable investment as well as to identify viable investment opportunities for research is important. However, public sector funded research institutions need to be aware of their purpose in research for public benefit so that benefit from collaborating with the private sector should not be captured entirely to private sectors.

Adaptation — is also the man's linking imported technology with domestic R&D. Adaptation therefore, is that it is consonant with the strengthening of the capacity of effective acquisition and mastery of foreign technology as well as building up of an effective research and development system — an essential element of attempts to foster technological self-reliance. Effective adaptation requires skilled manpower, which has atleast several years' experience in related production. The condition is not generally met in all but more advanced developing countries. The adaptation of technology however, is undertaken by engineers, technicians with an enterprise by industrial research institutions and by consulting engineers.

Absorption — the effective absorption and diffusion is dependent upon has an interest in applying the technology. The social carrier which has an interest in applying the technology. The social carrier could be a individual farmer who changes his pattern of production as a result of the introduction of improved plough. The carrier can be an institution. It might be an enterprise or agricultural cooperative that can develop and promote the new machinery and agro technologies. Absorption of technology in a narrow sense could be facilitated by policies, accompanied by adequate training facilities both in terms of number of persons trained and in extent of training. Free horizontal mobility has also been ensured to the pool of trained personnels.

Towards Universal Education

In the third world countries rural areas are the places where majority of people live, pursuing age old traditional occupation like agriculture/cultivation. To food the hungry million, the only way left out is to increase or multiply productivity with majority of the population access to education is a matter of utmost significance not only for the upliftment of women but also for general betterment of society. The inclusion of eradication of illiteracy, the universities have accepted in principal the important place of extension world, besides teaching and research with the participation of 83 universities and over 200 colleges, most of the universities and colleges have been involved in varying degree of programmes of eradication of illiteracy, population education and planning forums. Induction of other areas of extension such as rural development, Science for the people, legal literacy, and environmental education have been undertaken. With the majority of population settled in rural countryside the development programme should aim at generating income and employment to one and all. Access to education is a matter of utmost significance not only for the upliftment of women but also for the general betterment of society. Incidentally some of the programmes with accent on women's participation have indirectly helped women to earn while indoors without distributing their normal households chores.

The development trends have picked up from macro level perspective. The filtration frames the wider Indian experiences in rural development wide range of theoretical inter-relations already settled in growth theory. With the formulation of UGC policy frame 1977 a process of involving university system as such to participate extension programmes was initiated with the specific objective of securing equal importance of extension as a third dimension with teaching and research. Though some universities were conducting continuing education programmes and universities involved in substantial way in the National Adult education programme of Government of India. However, the infrastructure is too inadequate even for minimum performance for institutionalising need based extension programmes to involve identified communities in the life long learning process yet not operationalised in most cases.

Institutionalisation of extension needs academic acceptance which is automatically ensured when the activities enter at a stage of studies and research which enlarges our understanding and contributes to the knowledge. Extension activities can enter into research through project work or field based dissertations at undergraduate and postgraduate level.

Asian Centre for Human Ecology Foundation

To conduct, coordinate and promote relevant agricultural research and education in order to contribute to overall agricultural development on a sustainable basis, through effective research leadership, capacity building and UGC policy formulations :

- To recognise the outstanding contributions of institutions.
- To recognise at various stages of scientists professional carrier.
- For postgraduate agricultural research at Ph.D. level.

In order to promote research for tribal areas and applied research, to encourage post doctoral research to promote multidisciplinary and inter institutional team research at national level for excellence in teaching at International Centre of Human Ecology, South Campus :

- To promote the technology assessment, refinement and transfer process and playing the pro-active role in evolving and implementing the new policy initiative. For institutions and scientists to avail themselves of such vast opportunities to contribute significantly in their chosen profession to maintain the sanctity to peep into the professional qualities of all time and placing the thrust to watch how they reached the pinnacles of their chosen carrier in life with awe and inspiration.
- To encourage the young scientist to learn and imbibe those great qualities, processing them in a time bound manner requires the cooperation of so many sections/ individuals at the Asian Centre for Human Ecology from administration, accounts, audit, transport, publicity deserve special mention.
- To establish strong higher educational programmes in specialised areas of national global relevance such as biotechnology and molecular biology environmental sciences, agribusiness management, post harvest technology, information technology, communication development, remote sensing, non conventional energy sources, disease forecasting etiology etc.

- The trained human resource development and to have a comprehensive picture of agricultural systems of India in collaboration with the institutions of higher learning of agricultural sciences 33 state agricultural universities, 5 deemed to be universities including Allahabad Agricultural Institutes, one Central Agricultural University, Imphal, 3 Central Universities (BHU, AMU & Vishwa Bharti) and 50 developed requisite expertise to meet the future challenges, owing to the non-availability of composite data base on institutions, programmes, eligibility conditions etc., national scenario on agricultural education has rather been somewhat pre summative.
- The publication developed would be a useful document for the students, professionals and policy makers and would enable the readers to have a comprehensive picture.

To Conduct the Programme and Institutions of their Choice

- To help such students in making options for a programme and university.
- To compile information on carrier opportunities available in agricultural sciences.
- To update information by the universities in supplying pertinent information to their universities depicting eligibility conditions intake capacity and other academic regulations at SAUs, DU.
- To be our endeavour a new initiative to improve the quality of education in order to reduce in breeding, inculcate spirit of healthy competition and improve cultural life at the campuses, which include admission to seats at UG level, at PG entrance examinations and award of National Talent Scholarships, Junior Research fellowships on the basis of merit.
- To focus on 11 disciplines at undergraduate level such as B.Sc. Agriculture, B.Sc. Horticulture, B.Sc. (Fishery)/ BFSc., B.Sc Forestry, B.Sc. Home Science, B.Sc. Sericulture, B.Tec. (DT)/ B.Sc. (DT), B.Tec (AE), B.Sc. (Food Science and Technology), B.Sc. (B&C) and BVSc. & AH.

Objectives

- To meet a strong base of agricultural education.
- To meet and to make it suitable fulfilment of immediate as well as further requirements of agriculture in the country.
- To be recognised as national issue in phase manner. Delhi State autonomous status to the institution offering agricultural education.
- Location of home science and relevant technological education at the same campus.
- Integration of teaching by offering courses in any of the institution to provide holistic teaching on semester, trimester based internal evaluation.
- Integration of education, research and extension education.

As a centre of higher education and training in agricultural sciences at national and international level :

- To conduct basic and strategic researches with a view of understanding the processes, in all their complexity and to undertake need based research and sustained agricultural productivity in harmony with the environment.
- To serve as a centre for academic excellence in the area of postgraduate education and human resource development in agricultural sciences.
- To provide national leadership in agricultural research, extension and technology assessment and transfer by developing new concepts and approaches and serving as a national referral point for quality and standards.
- To develop information systems, add value to information share and serve the information nationally and serve as a data base.

Duration of the Degree Programme

The duration of all educational programmes in 4 yrs. with 6 months compulsory internship.

Eligibility Qualifications

- Broadly students with science (Physics, Chemistry) at 10+2 with biology and/or mathematics are eligible for admission for programmes in Human Ecology in University of Delhi. The courses imparted outside SAUs system in order to vocationalisation of agricultural education to prepare a vast network of para-professionals in diversified areas of agricultural practices especially in faculties of Agriculture, Home Sciences, Horticulture, Veterinary Sciences, Fishery and Forestry.

To incorporate new courses on information technology environmental sciences, library sciences, biostatics, bio-technology, biodiversity in all degree programmes to further strengthen skill base training in women agriculture training for one semester have been made integral component of degree programmes. The students undergoing WARE get slipped during the training period.

Asian Centre for Human Ecology

Action mechanism for imparting education and training to the students to develop into centre of academic excellence with latest facilities available in the country, for the formulation of action plan for major activities to bear nexus to the objective and project benefit for :

- Expenditure schedule for each activity and if possible duration and sequence of events for the advancement of student community action and rural/urban slum technology in implementing welfare and development programmes, welfare activities including sensitising, organising and mobilising people at village community level.
- To set a common forum for exchange of information, work out modalities for sharing of resources, experience and expertise and evolve strategies and guiding principle for community empowerment through participatory processes leading to social change.
- In order to facilitate the process of networking, NGOs working for children and women for two-way flow of information from voluntary sector to a nodal point in

government sector to develop modalities to strengthen the ongoing programmes for children and women, and identify innovative and replicable community based approaches.

- Strengthening interdepartmental and government NGO linkages for integrated women and child.
- Networking for promotion of child health and nutrition.
- Community mobilisation networking in health and sanitation for project related to welfare and development of children activities of national rural development society.
- Specific objective to organise support services to help urban slum and street children in fulfilment of his/her basic needs such as non formal education, health care, recreation to provide facilities for skill acquisition and vocational training to help and support self-help projects run by children themselves to organise children for collective action in various cooperatives, credit union, child worker, trade union.
- Organise ongoing documentation of the process of the programme, research studies on related issues that would have the direct bearing on policy formulation and programme refinement with the participatory research so that children can be involved in identifying issues and problems data collection and analysis in support to concretising and organising the children.

Approach : Vehicle student community. A term for reaching out to street children who have little or no family support can present a special problem of constraint abuse and exploitation.

- Building of contacts and sensitivity on the part of adults.
- Establishing a trusting relations based on equity and respect for the key objectives.
- Children participation in planning most of their activities.
- In the fulfilment of her/her basic needs such as :
  (a) Non-formal education, health care.
  (b) Recreation.

(c) To help and protect them from the worse access of exploitation.

(d) To provide facilities for skill acquisition and vocational training

(e) To help and support self-help projects run by children themselves.

(f) To organise children for collective action with the feeling that it is their programme and therefore they have to make a success.

(g) To organise the core of programme for reigning interventions and in the process of organising children : to take a rural decision for needed compromise for alternative education for the children who have never been to schools.

(h) Involvement of educators at times suitable for our children to be involved in designing the curriculum and teaching/learning material to understand the realities in which they live and thereby become sensitive and relevant in their interaction with children.

CENTRE FOR HUMAN ECOLOGY AT INSTITUTE OF HOME ECONOMICS

With the new holistic challenges community based convergent services for the development of women and children meeting at the community level.

- Development programme to encourage flexibility in service approach, more relevant to the needs of women and children meeting at the community level.

University of Delhi Course of Reading for

- B.Sc. Nursing
- B.Sc. (Hons) Electronics
- B.Sc. (Hons) Physics
- B.Com. (Hons) Mathematics
- B.Sc. (Hons) Mathematics
- B.Sc. (Hons) Statistics
- B.Sc. (Hons) Zoology
- B.Sc. (Hons) Computer Science

- B.Sc. (G) Group A — Physics, Chemistry and Mathematics
- B.Sc. (G) Group B — Chemistry, Botany and Zoology

Additional Courses

- B.Sc. Agriculture
- B.Sc. Horticulture
- B.Sc. (Fishery)/BFSc
- B.Sc. Forestry
- B.Sc. Sericulture
- B.Tec. (DT)/B.Sc (DT)
- B.Tec. (AE)
- B.Sc. (Food Science and Technology)
- B.Sc. (B&C)
- BVSc. & AH.

B.Sc. (Home Science) in collaboration with 20 Home Science Institutions — 4-year degree course after 10+2 in any sciences stream having Physics, Chemistry as compulsory subject.

In view of changing complexion of agricultural education a need was felt to redefine the position of Home Science education and thereby the entire programme of Home Science has been restructured and made it relevant to the need of skill oriented training for entrepreneur development in diverse aspect for women technological empowerment.

The revised curriculum of undergraduate programme includes :

- The four-year programme would be 2+2 *i.e.*, core courses and Home Science course to be offered during the first 2 years and professional elective courses to next two years. Further Rural/urban slum, Home Science work experience and implant training would be of one semester during which student will get stipend.
- Professional elective in 5 major disciplines of Home Science are as under :
  1. Human development and Family studies (organisation and management of early childhood programme and special education).

2. Clothing and Textile (Apparel designing and Textile designing).
3. Home Science Extension Education (Journalism and mass communication, distance education and information technology).
4. Family Resource Management (Interior Designing and Institutional house-keeping).
5. Food Science and Nutrition (Post harvest technology).

- B.Sc. (Hons) — Botany courses
- B.Sc. (H) Chemistry
- B.Sc. (Gen) Anthropology
- B.Sc. (Hons) Geology
- Bachelor of Dairy Technology is a 4-year degree programme after 10+2 in Physics, Chemistry and Mathematics. The course is offered in 12 institutions including National Dairy Research Institute, Karnal under ICAR-SAU Systems.

B.Sc. Course Syllabus : Revision with the Changing Needs of the Students

The University of Delhi offers courses in information technology, management and other professional streams for introduction of component of vocational courses in BA courses according to the University act enacted by Parliament; the AC shall be the academic body of the university and be responsible for maintaining the standards of institutions, education and examination within the University. The academic agenda to voice the potential for excellence in search for partnership for quality research for carrying out knowledge based research and its application in B.Sc.

For evaluation to tap the strength of DU the applied science departments, leading centres of in the field of genetics, micro biology, and bio physics for the revision towards the courses with the changing needs and to act as academic body of the university.

Pre-Service

1. M.Sc. Human Ecology, Biodiversity, Biotechnology and Environment Management.

Duration : 2 years.

Collaboration with college of Human Ecology, Michigan State University, East Lansing, Michigan.

2. M.Sc. in Women Agriculture and Rural Extension Management.

   Duration : 1 year.

3. Modification of B.Ed. and M.Ed. courses.

   Duration : 1 year.

   Collaboration with NCERT and Department of Education, Government of India.

In-Service

Course on Women Agriculture, Rural Extension and Biodiversity and Biotechnology.

Duration : 3 Months; 1 year Tailor made programmes.

COURSES UNDER FORMULATION AND IMPLEMENTATION (Research Designed and Methodology)

Programme/Activities Proposed

- Continuing education courses for the university group.
- Adult Extension Education for those eligible for university based courses Research.

Role and functions of the Department of Adult Continuing extension, education and field outreach.

Catalyst Role

- Acting as focal agency in the University system.
- Serving as technical resource centre for universities community activities.
- Assessing the need of the community.
- Developing curriculum and multidisciplinary University programmes, involving faculty students from various disciplines.
- Stimulating other departments of the University to undertake similar activities with respect to their discipline for continuing education of graduates, extension education and field outreach.

Teaching, Training and Research for socially disadvantaged group :

- Under the framework of women participation in management, integration of services, at an institution — to provide feedback guide implementation — to improve quality of life in farm, off-farm and non-farm sector for human resource development.
- Development with special reference to tribal women through the strategy which include social empowerment, education and development.

A project proposal entitled "Research and Training in on-farm, off-farm and non-farm sectors for human resources development with special reference to tribal women."

- Teaching programmes/course in adult and continuing education.
- Conducting need based continuing education courses not undertaken by other departments of the university.
- Conducting activities/programmes for upgrading knowledge skills or acquiring new skills short-term diploma certificates programmes.
- Training short-term aimed at various groups is skill income generation, entrepreneurship development family life education, Para legal training for grass-root workers/activities.
- Community outreach activities — responsibility to reach out to society, specific disadvantaged groups, *e.g.* bonded labour, child workers, urban slum and villages.

Programmes

- Vocational/Career oriented programmes.
- Empowering people at different socio-economic and educational levels with marketable vocational skills, which are appropriate.
- Participation in literacy, post literacy, continuing education under the ground level model.
- Evaluation as per university norms.

Collaborating and Networking

- Networking with government departments and other agencies of the country.
- International collaborations — to implement the programmes for higher education and to draw the programmes of collaboration by the participating institute — for linking higher education in the priority areas of environment, population education and science and technology and gender issues.

Documentation particularly of Field Experience to enrich Theory and dissemination of information :

- Preparing material.
- Disseminating information.
- Use of computers and internet-Publications.

Monitoring and Evaluation

- Monitoring and Evaluating the Department's activities as well as ongoing extension in the university.
- Reporting to Nodal Centre/University.

Education and Outreach Technical Programme at Centre for Human Ecology

- Two years postgraduate programmes in human ecology, Bio-diversity, and environment, Bio-technology.
- Pre-service — Human Ecology.
- One year (In-service, pre-service) programme for development in human ecology Bio-diversity and environment, Bio-technology.
- Modification of B.Ed., M.Ed. courses.

In-Service Courses

- Three months general management programmes in women agriculture rural extension and life sciences related certificate courses.
- Courses on women agriculture and rural extension.
- Courses and training programmes on agricultural education and life sciences-teacher's certificate courses.

Top Down Approach

One of the characteristics of the structural transformation of women in agriculture is the prevalence of substantial women labour force especially those belonging to the backward groups. Such as scheduled castes women ability to make agricultural policy is limited. Indian women has religious sanctions reflected in various religious scripture like Manu Smriti, so much so many of their invisible arduous economic activities in agriculture go unnoticed and unaccounted.

In the process of social evolution, rural economy has undergone a vast changes during the last about one hundred years within each region female participation in agriculture happen to be conditioned by a variety of factors. These are agro climatic endowments in particular, cultivated land among the rural household; presence of ethnic and cultural groups such as scheduled castes and scheduled tribes and also the skill and educational background of female population.

Council for Advancement of Peoples Action and Rural Technology (CAPART) support is directed towards employment, income generation, and creation of community assets and fulfilment of basic needs like housing, drinking water and sanitation. Simultaneously its endeavours to generate mass awareness about development issues whole organising the rural poor, particularly women and SCs/STs in activities which are socially beneficial economically rewarding.

Peoples action division focus on small and marginal farmers in the agriculture sector to provide productive employment opportunity through land based activities and handled in this division. Typical projects include land improvement, agro forestry, horticulture, sericulture, animal husbandry, dairying and minor irrigation. Dissemination of innovative technologies of direct relevance to the rural areas through their adoption trials, demonstrations and training are the principal.

- To organise poor rural women into groups for their own development and empowerment.
- To enhance income for the rural poor.
- To create and increase employment opportunities for rural poor living below poverty line by upgrading and

strengthening their productive activities by introducing new activities.

- To provide for supportive services for women to engage in productive work.

It is important that group building of women is an important first step which may take considerable time. The daily productive routine of poor rural women should be the starting point for identifying an appropriate economic activity generally the poor rural women are working women — at home, in the field and else where women's productive role should be understood.

The training of rural women should be designed to enable them to acquire the capabilities. The VO is expected to organise production either on a centralised or decentralised basis depending upon the nature of activity and beneficiary performance.

The thrust has also been for meeting the subsistence requirements of local people to ecology and satisfying the minimum needs of the people providing fuel wood and fodder and strengthening of tribal forests linkages. The social forestry may be undertaken on lands belonging to the categories of the rural poor are Scheduled castes, scheduled tribes, marginal farmers, small farmers, freed bonded labours and all identified individuals below the poverty line.

Council support projects aimed at :

- Conducting field based study, survey adaptive research and development, field trails, demonstrations and dissemination of appropriate technologies amongst rural poor, strengthening the existing institutions and setting up a new institution for the above purposes.
- Popularisation of new technologies up to the commercialisation stage.
- For upgrading the technical and productive skills of village youths, artisans, women and other largest groups through demonstration and training centres set up by voluntary organisations working in the field of rural development through training programmers, seminars, workshops and meetings.

Institutionalisation of Human Resource Development — Establishment of Nodal Centre for Human Ecology

UGC says education should be an instrumentality for developing not only an economically prosperous society, but one which can live comfortably in the context of pluralism and democracy, as also provide or equity. Several crucial areas have emerged in which university system has been asked to re-examine it and its relationship with social and economic development. These include the relevance of quality education, the gradual process of internationalisation of education is not only the student and faculty cross border but even the system of education are doing so. The institutional structure and the management of funding. The university system has to recognise these issues. A relevant curriculum, which equips them to deal with these issues, in terms of appropriate knowledge, skills and attitude.

To bring incentive to the system the Centre for Human Ecology, which was forwarded by Delhi University to UGC, may be reconsidered by the Delhi University in terms of earth and environment for the establishment of department of Home Science as department of Human Ecology under faculty of Interdisciplinary Applied Sciences. The department should grow to reflect on the critical social economic, cultural and spiritual issues facing humanity. It contributes to national development through dissemination of specialised knowledge. The University Grants Commission also advised Centre and State Governments on the measures of the principal task of the ninth plan in the new era of growth with social justice and active participation of people and their response on quality of leadership.

National Linkages

To implement most of its programmes through ICAR Institutes Research Organisation. NGOs with whom it has strong linkages. These linkages will be further nurtured and strengthened by its follows in the project and institutions.

- Avinash Lingam Institute of Home Science and higher education.
- M.S. University of Baroda.
- National Institute of Public Cooperation and Child Development.

- Central Welfare Board.
- National Cooperative Development Cooperation (NCDC) for marketing of agricultural produce, marketing of horticulture produce, cooperative cold storage, cooperative processing, oil seed processing, fruit and vegetable processing Agriculture trade-APEDA for Agro Economic research studies.
- For natural disaster management to take necessary rescue relief, and rehabilitation measures on natural disaster reduction programmes.
- Agricultural extension management for agricultural technology management and innovations for revamping agricultural extension/research project supplied by World Bank.
- For training in subject matter area.
- Training abroad.
- Research and training programme for wiring the curriculum of school and university. For the considerations of policy makers, dealing with National and International concern on management.

To meet the long term goal of human resource development with reference to in-service and perspective graduates in the light of women agriculture and rural extension there is a need to impart relevant education and training to young men and women for managing income generating and development activities on behalf of rural urban and slum producers.

We have to be very precise about the goal of developing links to build bridges between researchers and extension workers should not make us forget that specialisation and division of labour have contributed to growth throughout history. Sometimes a bit of competition between different sectors will lead to improved performance by each of them as long as social and institutional goals are clear. Working with constraints and responsibility is sheer drudgery, but from another point of view it is the most challenging task that a woman can ever undertake.

Priorities for research agenda and action points :

- Priorities for home economics programmes : need to re-examine historical ties to the agricultural production into home economics extension programming in rural areas.
- Restructure curricula at all levels to make sure it responds to local needs for education.
- Strengthening its focus on rural life in reaching, research and extension.
- Expand linkages at all levels macro, meso, micro level, household food security issues.
- Strengthen research on women's role in agriculture, food security and focus issues specifically on alliance with women in development programmes.
- Bringing researchers together in the field.
- Breaking down disciplinary barriers.
- Approach, basic to on-farm research.
- Interdisciplinary team work in the subsequent stages of research process to identify constraints.

For the projects for the development of Infrastructure for women, agriculture and rural extension

- For the relevance of education, equity and access of management of higher education.
- UGC administration for "financial mechanism".
- For the cause of : The training for the future :
  - The asset way-industry acceptance of asset of the student community.
  - Promotion of ecologically sustainable agriculture.
  - Carry out agricultural research relevant to social sciences including statics, economics, extension, Home Science and Nutrition. Sustainable and equitable use of agro-biodiversity.
  - Eco development concerns in Natural agricultural farming system, R&D approaches.

To meet the emerging demands for — productivity, sustainability, and environmental and ecological security. To coordinate research with the community perception education and reforms.

For the Cause of Linkages

National. To implement most of its programmes through the ICAR Institutes, Research organisations, NGOs with whom it has strong linkages. These linkages will be further nurtured and strengthened by its fellows in the projects and Institutions.

International. To promote collaborative activities in the areas of agricultural research for modalities of cooperation. To establish bilateral linkages with :

Foreign universities for : Development and modification of course curricula at postgraduate and undergraduate level.

Overseas training : Education technology for outreach training programmes : collaboration with the universities of USA.

Texas A & M University : To develop the human resources; faculty exchange for institutional capacity building in the areas of evaluation methodology; ecosystems; meat processing technology; skill development for Agribusiness education.

Collaboration with ISNAR for research training in the various disciplines of agriculture and management of research, joint collaborative projects and study visit in respect of scientist and scholar for international linkages for Human Resource Development with special reference to Agriculture and Rural Extension and other institutions for training on pre-service and in-service graduates.

Key Issues

To help people, help themselves through the practical application of knowledge and resources to improve their quality of life and that of future generations.

Objectives

- To strengthen and to achieve the goal of sustainable development.
- To encourage the environment ethics at both formal and non-formal education.
- Use of media in promoting environmental and development awareness.

- To provide a support network at international and national local level.
- To provide data basis on programmes, projects that created a paradigm shift towards more widespread intellectual voices in higher education.
- Technical programmers will include : Ph.D. in Human Ecology, M.Sc. in Human Ecology, Biodiversity, Biotechnology and Environment Management, M.Sc. in Women Agriculture and Rural Extension Management; Modification of B.Ed. and M.Ed. courses.
- Education and development programmes to involve women right from grass-root level.
- To coordinate network of regional and national centres and to provide a forum for gathering and dissemination of information on experiences and findings of those in the field.
- To facilitate the entry of women into employment in the field of science and technology and their progress within such employment.
- To deal effectively with global development issues and opportunities to broaden their perspectives.
- Training and award programmes to support activities to meet both needs ultimately leading to the production of critical mass of experienced trained researchers for global, sustainable equitable development.

10

Empowerment of Women for Knowledge

As the century begins, natural resources are under increasing pressure, threatening public health and development. Water shortage, soil exhaustion, loss of forests, air water pollution, and degradation of coastline afflict many areas. As the world population grows, improving living standards without destroying the environment is a global challenge.

Women have unique and valuable perspective to bear upon the application of science and technology to development. Women researchers can play a key role to pursue the high objectives of the collective endeavour jointly with men to overcome the barriers of discrimination impede the health education and career of women also the critical challenges on the growing gap between the science rich countries of the north and the science poor countries of south in the production and use of scientific and technological knowledge.

To generate facilities to be used by the scientists, industries and students all over the country for the multifarious activities in the country. Financial assistance to, postgraduate, post doctoral, certificate courses, diploma courses in biotechnology and allied fields of Human Ecology National and International associateships for research and training in leading research laboratories in the country and abroad, short term training courses, to train mid carrier scientists.

(A) Training Programmes

To pursue postgraduate training leader to a doctorate degree at centres of excellence in the country and outside own country. The specific aims of the schemes are :

1. To improve access to educational and training opportunity for young talented women graduates.
2. To increase scientific productivity and creativity.
3. To empower a new generation of talented women to assume a leadership role in science and technology and their application in sustainable development.

Nature

- The scheme to provide fellowships to young female students in and institution outside country, or choose to register as Ph.D. student in her own country and pursue part of her research at another institution under sandwich programme.
- Each fellowship will be offered for a period of upto three years and covers travel expenses to the host institution.
- The host institution will be expected to provide the facilities needed for tuition fees, training, supervision and if possible free accommodation.

(B) To Launch Postgraduate Programme

Training fellowships for women scientists in India at centres of excellence in least developed countries.

Purpose

The general purpose of the scheme is to institute fellowship programmes for female students who wish to pursue post-graduate trainings leading to a doctoral degree at the centre of excellence in India and outside their own country. The general purpose of the scheme is to contribute to the emergence of a new generation of women leaders in science and technology, and to promote their effective participation in scientific and technological development of their countries.

The specific aim of the schemes are :

- To improve access to educational and training opportunities in Science and Technology for young and talented women graduates.
- To increase scientific productivity and creativity of women scientists.

- To empower new generation of talented women to assume a leadership role in science and technology and their application.
- To sustainable development.

Nature

- To enable them to pursue postgraduate studies leading to Ph.D. degree at centres of excellence either outside their country within same region or in other regions.
- A candidate can either enroll as a full time research student in an institution outside her country and pursue part of her research at another institution in some other regions under a sandwich programme.
- Each fellowship will be offered for a period of up to three years and covers travel expenses to the host institutions and a most living allowance, the amount of, which will be determined after consultation with the host institution.

The host institution will be expected to provide the facilities needed for tuition fees, training supervision, and if possible free accommodation.

Host Institutions

Applicants should select renowned institutes outside their own country, preferably where they have already applied for postgraduate admission of the precise field of proposed research and the country/region where the applicant would wish to pursue a postgraduate research programme.

Eligibility

The fellowships are open to qualified young women graduates (generally less than 30 years of age) from India and abroad.

The minimum qualifications of applicant is an M.Sc. degree (or equivalent) or an outstanding B.Sc. honours degree in any field of natural sciences.

Selection

- The fellowships are highly competitive and the selection will be based on scientific competence and merit.

- The applications will be reviewed by a panel of eminent scientists appointed by executive board.
- A limited number of fellowships (not exceeding twenty) will be provided to successful candidates for respective academic year.

(C) For Creative Services (Linking Higher Education for Community Service)

- To fill position in information and creative services.
- Tree scientists/horticulturists.
- Regional coordinators.
- Geologists for the National Resource strategy and policy.
- Leader of the ecosystem Rehabilitation programmes.
- To prepare female entrepreneurs to face in the world of global changes.
- Changing world market; altering social structure, accelerating development in information technology.
- Expanding industrialisation.
- Extending social services and education.

Mission for the Tasks

Enhance effective participation of women in industrial development through promoting of women's ventures that efficiently utilise their potentials, skills and capabilities.

Tasks

- Provide technical and managerial assistance to female entrepreneurs through advisory services, guidance and industrial information.
- Training.
- Create effective coordinated programmes with other women.
- Support entities.
- Conduct studies and research.
- Promote self-employment programmes.

International Centre for Research will Function

- To improve human welfare by reducing poverty, increasing cash income.

- Improving food and nutrition security.
- Enhancing ecosystem resilience in the tropics through improved agro-forestry systems.

GLOBAL PROGRAMME

Urbanisation

Basic services and community participation. The rapid pace of urbanisation in the developing countries and the consequent pressure on urban civic amenities matters of serious concern the world over. Experts, scholars and administrators grapple with the problem for all urban poor access to adequate basic civic amenities in burgeoning cities of developing countries. An important element is local community particularly empowerment of urban communities. Increasing urbanisation accompanied by increasing concentration of the urban population is bigger cities has not only posed the problem of pollution, crime concentration of the mushrooming of huge metropolises congested housing but has housing led to severe pressure on the basic civic amenities and consequently a decline in the living standard of the city dwellers. As a result although the situation is not better in rural areas, the urban areas suffer from inadequate provision of safe drinking water and sanitation facilities. The problems belonging to the developing world are expected to become acute. It may even lead to international welfare. Many factors such as resource crunch, lack of proper management, too much dependence on central authorities as well as very little involvement on the part of the community of the specific problems of patterns of urban growth. To learn from the experiences of other countries suggest concrete recommendations to the situation. In addition it aimed at assimilating further thinking with the status of basic services in terms of drinking water and sanitation facilities, problems of decentralised planning, community development.

Global warming, diminishing vain forests, protection of ozone layer and preserving genetic biodiversity are all subjects of discussion today but closer to ground is the problem of water pollution we have recognised that how much water is needed but rather how best the water demand can be managed and how to optimise the use of available water.

Though only seven per cent of world water is used for domestic demands and 70% for irrigation, the efficiency of water used in agriculture in most countries is around 30% only. The inefficiency is no less in urban areas. Leakage and unaccounted for water in many cities and many countries is around 30% only. The efficiency is no less in urban areas. Distribution arrangements and existing tariff systems have hardly any relevance for water conservation and wastage reduction. The contamination of water resource is now widespread in many developing countries brought about by industrialisation as well as untreated sewage. Surface water pollution is also a major problem. Unfortunately, the cost of conventional sewerage system continue to be very high and the level of technology development and application efforts limited, while man has succeeded in putting one of his species on the moon, he has not been able to deal with his own wastage in an efficient cost effective manner. Technologies like an aerobic treatment and those of recovery of resources from sewage continue to be applied on the limited scale only. The Ganga action plan launched in this country in 1985 was the first comprehensive plan of action to address in an integrated manner, conveyance and treatment of sewage, resource recovery through methane gas, fish farming and irrigation, sustaining aquatic diversity and river quality monitoring and management. But the plan is limited only to Ganga.

Management

Management is concerned with the optimum utilisation of various resources for the attainment of organisational goals and objectives. The proper management of human resources plays an important role for attaining such objectives. The behaviour science is a wholly distinct discipline. It deals with the behavioural aspects of human being, which analyse the factors, which influence human behaviour. Every man by virtue of his own experience as a person, the managerial job involves all kinds of people problems, but he might also argue that he knows from his own experience how to deal with most of those problems. Behavioural scientist has worked on human problems in organisations. But the nature of the problems studied has evolved from individually oriented industrial psychology focused on problems of recruitment, selection and testing to organisational psychology and sociology focused on managerial style. How groups and teams work, inter group collaboration and competition, and total systems analyses of organisational and managerial effectiveness.

Management is the creation and control of technological and human environment of an organisation in which human skill and capacities of individuals and groups find full scope for their effective use in order to accomplish the objectives for which an enterprise has been set up. It is involved in the relationships of the individual, group, the organisation and environment.

The role of urban local bodies in providing water supply has verified from country to country. A community plan to demonstrate to upgrade and extend to such areas to meet further needs. Extension social surveys and distinct packages for the demonstration project to fund the entire project on a grant basis. The only effective way to ensure that cultural factors are incorporated into service programmes would appear to be by involving communities in the design of the project. Water consumption and waste disposal impinge on extremely personal attitude towards bodily hygiene, which are largely cultural in nature.

To conduct need based study, survey, adaptive research and development, field trials, demonstration, dissemination of appropriate technologies among rural poor. Strengthening the existing institutions and setting up of new institution to test technologies suitable for specific geographical area making modification where necessary an initiate the process of transfer of viable technology through demonstrations, training and manufacture. The new institution will act as a focal point of referral of technology gaps in the area and generation of matching solutions to answer the technology needs, identified by government and non-government institutions. It will also conduct training programmes at various levels, especially trainer's training programmes through the demonstrative achievements in the adaptive research and development and dissemination of innovative rural technologies for five years.

The scale of urban growth in many developing countries during the past four decades has been without precedent in human history. Although providing storm drains are separate for servers, open channels with earth banks are generally appropriate in that they are in expensive to construct and easier to maintain.

Government can work directly towards specific community objectives, or by offering contracts that serve those purpose. Further more traditional engineering approach often encourages expansion of infrastructure and supply augmentation rather than alternatives such as demand management. Still, investment in improved technologies, such as design of sewers, design and construction of man holes, inverted siphons protection of water supply, waste water facilities for sewage keeping with current usage for more conventional municipal waste water collection and treatment systems. Innovative approaches to collection and treatment particularly for the very small municipal systems practices for safeguarding of the public health or protection of water quality, for desirable procedure or methods with deviations subject to individual consideration. *The waste water treatment* works for safety, design, essential facilities and laboratory. *Settling sludge* and scum removal, protective and service facilities, *Sludge processing,* storage and disposal, Biological treatment systems, *Disinfection* — chlorine disinfection, dechlorination, ozone. *Supplement treatment* — handling waste water treatment plant.

Innovative construction of a municipal garbage composting facilities, with a small-scale energy efficient sewage treatment plants and fish to change sewage into clear water. Any technology that encourages the recycling of resources should be serious considered by communities that attempt to plan sustainability. The expenditure may be taken as solution to many policy problems.

Status of Water Supply and Sanitation

The global consultation on safe water and sanitation which met here in Delhi in 1990. A part of problem in measuring coverage is that the data are limited to simply arithmetics, usually most national reports describe the total population of a whole town as covered if there is some kind of water supply are calculated even more simplistically by dividing the total installation capacity by population. We need to go very far for the truth.

Evolution of Research system. Expanding the research for pilot scale testing of the technologies already developed for commercialisation would be valuable to organisations within outside UGC system. This fund support would also help to broaden UGC base by drawing upon the strength of individual research institutions, which in term can fill gaps in unforeseen but critical areas of research related to regional problems besides contributing to developing staff skills through extension outreach and study tour — entry of institutions outside the ICAR/SAUs systems for enhanced inter-change with national and international centres of scientific innovations.

Several changes have taken place in the organisation and functional set up of Institute of Home Economics and in their research and development programmes. Commensurate in these, there has been no proper emphasis towards development of management skills of faculty members to make national research programmes more efficient and effective. Projects for R and D activities are time bound, and lay high priority to meet challenges such as poverty alleviation, food and nutrition security, natural resources conservation and overall sustainable development of agriculture and human resource; efficient managers are required.

Selection of species. Energy farms are still in the conceptual stage. It require detailed studies in genetic, agronomic and other aspects particularly the selection of appropriate sites and species, spacing and fertiliser usage and resistance to pest and diseases to maximise dry matter production and increase availability of alternative source of energy. Following criteria need to be adopted for selection of species, case of establishment and regeneration after harvesting, freedom from pests and diseases, ability to reduce transpiration losses in arid areas and minimum drain of nutritionist. Unlike aquatic plants, there is need to replace each harvest with a new crop as quickly as possible, the plants that have high sprouting potential following coppice cutting are preferable to those requiring replanting, using or breeding plants with leaves whose shape and orientation makes maximum of sunlight is another promising area (i) to increase biomass production, (ii) ability to conserve water, (iii) minimum drain of nutrient and ability to improve soil quality. The enormous diversity in the range of ecological conditions in India offers problems in afforestation and biomass production. For successful plantation trees must be raised in the nurseries later transplanted in the field. In order to achieve success in this newly developing challenging areas, steps need to intensify on Resource survey and technological planning.

Setting Priorities

Commensurate with new challenges and opportunity both at national and global level. Ministry of Agriculture has oriented its mandate to include Human resource development and technology assessment and refinement as new paradigms for holistic advancement, in agriculture and allied subjects. While ensuring optional use of natural resources in partnership with stakeholders, especially the state agricultural universities (SAUs) farmers, NGOs, private sector, etc. so as to achieve the ultimate goal of evergreen revolution.

The facilitators of green, white and blue revolution, the technologies generated by the scientists has been the cornerstone of our past successes. To achieve the twin national objective of poverty elevation and welfare of disadvantaged and weaker sections of the society, it has become imperative to increase agricultural productivity, profitability and sustainability through judicious and more integrated use of our natural resources. However, our production of our agri horticultural crops has secured a prestigious position with India being the second largest producer of rice, wheat, fruits and vegetables in the world. We have yet to go a long way in improving our productivity to ensure profitability and sustainability of Indian agriculture, through conservation of natural resources.

We are in evolution of plant and animal genetic resources and their conservation had been the main thrust in order to maintain our biodiversity and the genetic base by having improved variety to increase productivity. The mandate of agricultural research; to plan undertake, aid, promote and coordinate development of skills in soil and water conservation.

Coordination and regulation of programme relating to land resources, conservation management and development at state level.

- Formulation and implementation of land use policy.
- Implementation of plan for optimum utilisation of land resources.
- Review and assessment of land resources.
- Restoration of ecological balance and improvement of socio-economic condition of tribals.
- Generation of employment opportunity.
- Promotion of people's participation.

Strategy

- Adoption project approach to the treatment of catchment.
- Increasing sectoral measure of watershed development and maintenance.
- Vegetative thrust for conservation of ecosystems.
- Institutional and operational mechanism for treatment.
- Promotion of skills of farmers and field functionaries through appropriate linkages with the necessary infrastructure recreated in the project for appropriate institutional linkages and direct control and coordination of the programme.
- Organisation of special orientation and training courses/ refresher courses for pre-service and in-service courses for graduates for maintenance of environmental hygiene.

To achieve the objective the project will undertake in an integrated manner with due support of drainage line treatment, measure, like, spill ways, check bunds, inundation of constriction of water harvesting structures, farm, pond percolation tanks etc.

This project is to improve the income level of disadvantaged and marginal farmers by reclaiming the facilities of the soil.

The components of the project are :

- Preliminary survey and planning.
- On-farm development.

- Boring and installation of pump sets/tube well if possible.
- Improvement of drainage system.

Implementation of the programme lays emphasis on adoption of low cost technology with the use of local material for soil and water conservation to increase the productivity with the components of livestock development and household production with the provision of construction of small water harvesting structure by involving NGOs in the area.

Human Resource Development

Education develops manpower for different levels of economy and empowers with poor masses to become self-reliant enough to participate in the process of national development. Special focus has been laid on access to education of millions of girls and working children, who cannot participate in school system on account of socio-economic compulsions. These segments largely constitute girls : SCs, STs and other deprived section of the society girls, working children, and those belonging to SC/ST and deprive sections of the society stand to benefit from this. To have enough flexibility to provide education at their doorsteps. The major challenges is to maintain quality comparable with the formal system. Although special programmes have been taken up to improve upon the specific deficiencies in the educational system. To consider the objectives of improving the quality of population and environmental sustainability.

International Linkages

To develop linkages and collaborative programmes with related national and international institutions and organisations for undertaking programmes, are mainly to increase the quality of life of farming communities. The Texas A & M University, Michigan State University has three major plans : (a) Agro ecosystem research, (b) innovation in technology dissemination, (c) organisation and management for priority setting, monitoring and evaluation of the project with the focus on policy interfacing activities. The policy to emphasise the issues of right to entitlement, gender equity and employment opportunities for rural population :

- Population with special attention to efficient land use planning.
- To promote, the involvement of the stakeholders in developing research agenda to include elements of indigenous knowledge.
- Promotion of social equity and ecological security.
- Innovative institutional arrangements to correct the existing lacunae in management and use of natural resources.
- Stepping up both public and private investments in agricultural research is critical for social and economic infrastructure, development to realise to goal of rural development.
- To constitute the task force of experts to examine the current projection of action mechanism for interfacing the functional relationship and sharing of information and materials with ICAR and private sector.

HUMAN ECOLOGY FOR HUMAN RESOURCE DEVELOPMENT AND MANAGEMENT

List of the Projects and Centres

1. Research Methodology for studies on women agriculture rural extension through education and training programmes with special reference to pre-service graduates of Home Science.
2. Conservation of ecosystem through community resource management with special reference to hill community.
3. Research and Training in farm, off-farm and non-farm sectors for human resource development with special reference to Tribal women.
4. Studies in women agriculture rural extension through education and training programmes with special reference to pre-service graduates.
5. Establishment of Centralised Quality Control System for cereal and pulses based processed food.
6. Development of training programme in non conventional energy system with special reference to solar systems.

7. Transfer of agro biotechnology of mung bean, chick pea, mushroom and floriculture for income generation and bridging the protein gap for small scale marginal and landless women of Delhi and Haryana villages.

CENTRES

Asian Centre for Human Ecology :

- Nodal Centre for Human Ecology.
- Centre for Human Ecology.
- Centre for Social Justice and Empowerment.
- Centre for Biodiversity and Environment.
- Centre for Biotechnology.
- Centre for Food Processing and Food Safety Systems.

11

International Centre for Biodiversity and Environment

Introduction

Projects may vary from research involving extensive fieldwork or social surveys based on those of a more theoretical nature. The aim is to produce a written thesis which is a sustained argument based on a thorough review of evidence and critical inquiry offering original insights at a theoretical or empirical level for life on earth. The ground breaking reports shall indicate the profound changes continue to occur in social, institutional and economic systems. The students are required to undertake taught courses in research methods drawn from the M.Sc. research methods in social science during the first year of M.Phil. and Ph.D. studies. Other courses from across the university may be taken if they are relevant to the student research.

A main supervisor shall be appointed when the student arrives at the school/centre and within a few months other people may be appointed as appropriate and in consultation with the student. Supervisors appointed provide advice on all aspects of the form and content of research, and the research process, and ensure that students meet the universities' various quality control requirements. Undertaking research and producing a thesis can be a long process and supervisors are also important in helping to keep students motivated.

Internationalisation of Education

Significant progress has been made in confronting environmental challenges. Nevertheless, the environment has continued to degrade in nations of all regions. Progress towards a sustainable future has simply been too slow.

A regional and participatory process was used to produce analysis of environmental impact of alternative development scenarios and policy action will be included in the further GEO report as well as more extensive analysis of current policy responses, their impact, and the reasons for their success and failures. The introduction of these elements in the continuous GEO assessment has already started. As a result several countries report marked progress in curbing environment pollution and showing the rate of resource degradation as well as reducing the intensity of resource use.

Internationally Agenda in 1922 in Rio de Janeiro provides the global consensus on the road map towards sustainable development. UNEP continues to be the environmental voice of United Nations responsible development, scientific analysis monitoring and assessment. Increasingly, United Nation Organisations, the World Bank and regional banks are "greening" their programme. New approaches to international policies are being developed, tested and implemented.

Collaborative arrangements. With the network of institutions on JNU campus like Institute of Mass Communication, The Indian Council of Social Science Research Campus will substantially promote networking amongst scientists and cater to each other needs.

Education for Extension

Linkages for economic status and social power :

- Greater economic efficiency of production technologies to the need for location specifically, social acceptability and environment sustainability.
- To generate new knowledge for information based technologies to strengthen means of dissemination needed to transmit this information to farmers.
- Optimisation in the management by producers of their available resources, sustainability, coping with diversity, by adopting technology.
- To make information transfer more cost effective, in communication, between researchers, extensionists and their farmer clients for effective learning.

- Teach to know what makes both teaching and learning effective for the establishment of a variety of rural services.
- To bring desirable changes in the behaviour of concerned persons through educational methods to improve their general standard of living with their own efforts.
- Educational methods aimed at the dissemination of knowledge leading to systematic learning make process of development a continuous process as a discipline of formal education as informal education.
- To change the attitude and practices of the people with whom the work is done in agriculture, and home economics, for home making or bring about continuous improvement in their physical, economic and social well-being through individual and cooperative efforts.
- To have close relationship of the discipline with technical sciences and social sciences for the needs importance and techniques for cooperative extension work for action programmes.

Objectives

— To update and modify the undergraduate course curriculum in collaboration with ICAR Division with Deans of Faculties of agriculture, agricultural engineering, dairy technology, home science, horticulture, fisheries and forestry.

— Implementation of revised curriculum in all SAUs and Universities under UGC for new courses on computer application, Biodiversity, Biotechnology, Principles of Ecology, Agribusiness Management, marketing and environmental sciences for improvement and assurance of quality education.

— Resource Centre for outreach activities :

  - Working with communities for conducting need based studies, survey, adaptive research, development, field trials, demonstrations and dissemination of appropriate technologies amongst the rural poor.

- Networking in innovations, participation, and demonstrations at national and international level.
- Popularisation of new technologies and designed to test technologies, for the specific geographical areas.
- Linkages and interaction with national and state level science and technology institutes in technology adaptation and exchange.
- Creation of assets/infrastructure to utilise locally available human resource to facilitate implementation of action oriented projects for impact assessment, training facilities, workshops, laboratories, tools and equipment in the areas and generation of matching solutions, conducting training programmes.
- Conducting need based studies, survey, adaptive research and development, field trails, dissemination of appropriate technologies amongst rural poor. Popularisation of new need based research upto commercialisation in agricultural sciences/home sciences, basic sciences for academic excellence in the area of postgraduate education.

— Balancing Higher education for community service :

- For better management of human and environment to improve people's life and environment in the view of rapid technological advancement and community belonging to the poorest of the poor families.
- *Earth ecosystem research :* To mobilise community support in understanding, promoting and enabling better child care through education.
- To provide supportive services through education, women's development programmes such as safe drinking water, environmental sanitation, pre school education below 6 years.
- Nutrition and health education by the community, the referral services in expectant and nursing mothers, and women in age group of 15 to 45 years.

- In partnership with DARE for effective linkages at the national and international level and partnership among different ministries/organisations within the country.

HUMAN ECOLOGY FOR BIODIVERSITY AND ENVIRONMENT

International Centre for Partnership and Linkages with DARE

To provide additional support for training of the faculties and infrastructure development of social sciences and policy includes studies for technology assessment, refinement and transfer. The research extension linkages to strengthen and integration of technology assessment and refinement programmes for :

- Front-line demonstrations including farmers.
- Action programme pertaining to institute village linkage programme.
- Research centre for women agriculture rural extension for the development of appropriate farming system research.
- To test promising varieties in tribal and hill region for adaptation of agro-pastoral systems in hill terrain for valley and hilly areas of Uttaranchal.
- Technology dissemination in innovations with revised curriculum for SAUs.
- Development of training programmes with the centres of advanced studies — the pre-service and in-service training in educational technologies in emerging areas for the development of professional competence for broadening the concept of Home Science to Human Ecology.

Effective linkages at the national and international levels and partnership among different ministry organisations within the country is the need of the hour. Agriculture sector has delivered goods to the country for sustainable and economic reform.

The emerging demand are to be met through increased productivity, sustainability, environmental and ecological security profitability and competitiveness in the backdrop of decline in factor productivity, loss of biodiversity natural resource shrinkage degradation, climate change, intensifying completion in the international trade and widening economic disparities. The challenges are formidable yet within our reach. If the opportunities are harnessed in the interest of small and marginal farmers on the resource scarce situation so that large number of small and disadvantaged farmers are benefited and the efforts to achieve doubling of food production and eradication of poverty can be set in motion. To plan coordinate undertake aid promote and coordinate education research and its application in agriculture agro forestry, animal husbandry, fisheries, home science and allied sciences. Instituting and promoting transfer of technology programmes to look into the problems of broader areas of rural development concerning agriculture by developing cooperative programmes. To include human resources development, commensurate with new challenges and opportunities both at national and global level, for the holistic advancement in agriculture and allied subjects while ensuring optimal use of natural resources in partnership with all stakeholders especially the state with all stakeholders especially the state agriculture universities (SAUs), farmers, NGOs and promote sector etc. To achieve national objectives of poverty alleviation and welfare of disadvantaged and weaker section of the society. However, our production of agri horticulture crops has secured a prestigious position with India being second largest producer of rice, wheat, fruit and vegetables in the world.

In order to maintain our biodiversity and broadening the genetic base by having improved varieties to increase production. To sensitising partners about its plans and programmes. The project Human Ecology for biodiversity and environment has three major components : (1) agro-ecosystem research in research programmes, (2) Innovations in technology dissemination under which technology dissemination and (3) priority-setting monitoring and evaluation to develop mechanism for priority setting, monitoring and evaluation of the project.

For partnership and linkages include International linkages through memorandum of understanding with Director South

Campus, University of Delhi to sign MOU with DARE for the establishment of Centre for Biodiversity and Environment.

To undertake long term research agenda to bring research and knowledge to the community, human ecology combines the interests theories and studies of geographer, ecologists, and anthropologists to include in the undergraduate and postgraduate courses. This will require the links of environmental education organisations. It will be in the interest of botanists, plant ecologists, and conservation biologist resource managers for the management of various ecosystems. This can be combined with the departments of Home Science which will offer both masters and doctoral graduate programmes. The programmes which focuses on management of work place environments and historical preservation in conjunction with technology, user satisfaction and perfection of work and residential environments.

The international research and emphasis on international will provide advance knowledge and understanding of specialised fields. These may require the collateral course work where background is inadequate.

The grants and the projects under consideration by international agencies can support for such courses under exchange programme.

MISSION

- For institution strengthening and linkages for research capacity building in collaborative programmes in research and training.
- To promote participation in education to bring into sharp focus the central role of human development, into poverty reduction.
- To promote behaviour studies with practical application of knowledge across the domains of research, outreach and international programmes.
- For empowering and strengthening families and individuals in addressing the challenges of opportunities in their environments.
- To promote scholarships, and initiative that enhance the positive development of individuals, and families,

address the problem that concerns of families in the community and acknowledge the diversity of families and community served by the college.

- To encourage scholarly efforts across the broad mission of the college/institute of Home Science/Human Ecology.

INTERNATIONAL CENTRE FOR HUMAN ECOLOGY FOR BIODIVERSITY AND ENVIRONMENT

Objective — Setting priorities in Agribusiness

Providing educational programmes to respond to human needs by improving nutrition and health, advancing environmental design and technology, promoting human development and securing economic and social well-being for individuals.

Drivers. Rural Development, Human Resource Development, Promotion of educational and economic interest for all sections of society, multinational collaborations for building, scientific and academic community by linking with partners, networking to increase and contribute to International research.

It will combine the interests, theories and studies of : Geographers, Ecologists, Anthropologists, Home Economists/ Consumer Science Specialists, Psychologists, Agriculture Scientists, Economists and Biologist.

Centres

- Asian Centre for Human Ecology.
- International Centre for Bio-diversity and Environment.
- Other National Centres.

Projects

- Conservation of Ecosystem of Central Himalayas with special reference to Gola Catchment area — A case study of conservation of hill community.
- International Centre for Human Ecology for :
  - — building a successful community through education to empower themselves and their families.
  - — knowledge, technological advances.

- To bring knowledge through their programmes to have access to the latest research and recommendations meaningful to the community.

Countries in Alliance. Austria, Netherlands, Germany, France, Italy, Mexico, Russia, China.

CENTRE FOR EXCELLENCE

For the Cause of Linkages

National. To implement most of its programmes through the 1CAR Institutes, Research organisations, NGOs with whom it has strong linkages. These linkages will be further nurtured and strengthened by its fellows in the projects and Institutions.

International. To promote collaborative activities in the areas of agricultural research for modalities of cooperation. To establish bilateral linkages with Foreign universities for development and modification of course curricula at Post-graduate and Undergraduate level.

Overseas training. Education technology for outreach training programmes.

Collaboration with the Universities of USA

Texas A & M University. To develop the human resources; faculty exchange for institutional capacity building in the areas of evaluation methodology; ecosystems; meat processing technology; skill development for agribusiness education.

Collaboration with ISNAR for research training in the various disciplines of agriculture and management of research, joint collaborative projects and study visit in respect of scientist and scholar for international linkage for Human Resource Development with special reference to Agriculture Rural Extension and other institutions for training on pre-service and in-service graduates.

ICAR CENTRE FOR HUMAN ECOLOGY UNIVERSITY OF DELHI

It is my fond hope that this centre shall help individuals and agencies involved in a development work. And activism in realising the dream for better eco-friendly humane and

HUMAN ECOLOGY FOR SOCIAL JUSTICE AND EMPOWERMENT

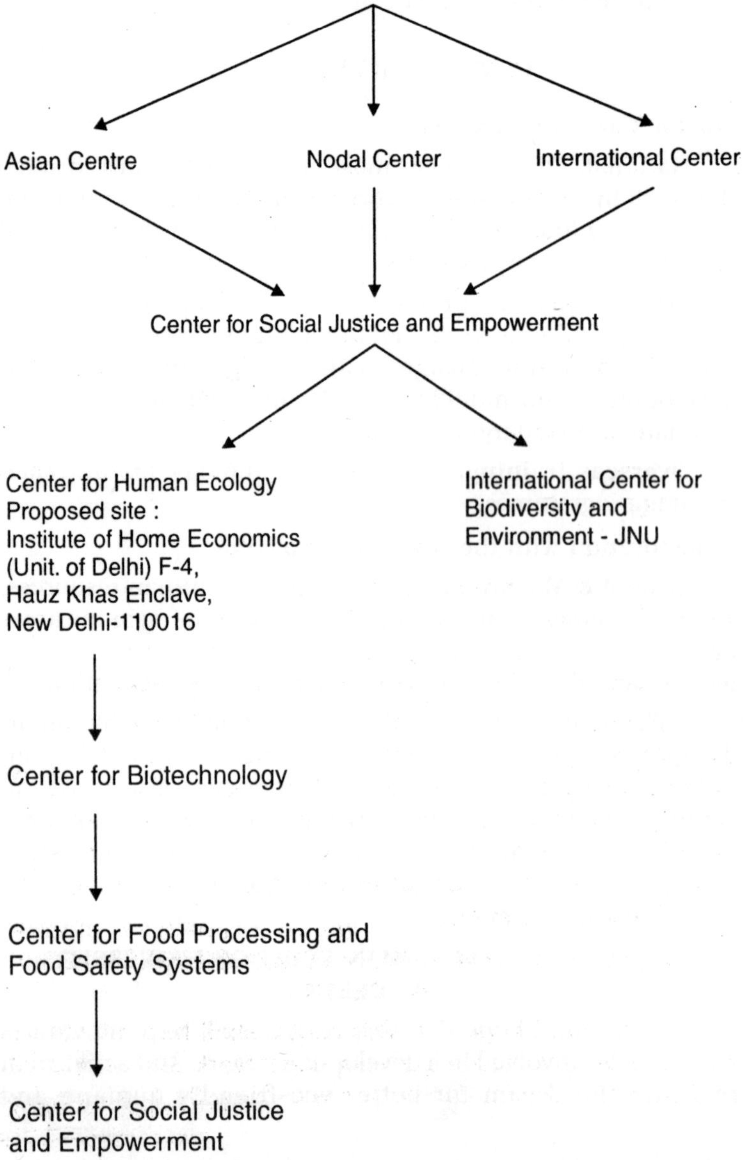

sustainable society by travelling on the road which is less travelled.

Background

The project entitled "Studies on popularisation on mushrooms through training programmes" has organised a "Congress on Human Ecology for Women" to include human resource development and technology assessment and refinement as new paradigm for holistic advancement in agriculture and allied subjects.

The students are alive to the expectation of society and their role in the changing world order. To bring in sharp focus the issues are :

- Strengthening relations with equal environment work cooperatively. To commensurate with new challenges and opportunities both at the national and global with public and private institutions, legislative bodies industry, state and community organisations and other units in the university.
- Close linkages of faculty and students with the real world.
- Interrelations between the various components of human eco-system with the planning and principles.

Strategic Planning

- Improve access to quality education and expert knowledge.
- Achieve more active learning.
- Generate new knowledge and scholarship across mission.
- Promote problem solving to address for society needs.
- Advance diversity within community.
- Make people matter.

Future Planning for Action Points

- Expansion of research and outreach with people, resources and facilities.
- Postgraduate degree/diploma programmes for pre-service, in-service graduates.

- Other training programmes — short-term and doorstep (tailor programmes as per need).
- Research and training programme for wiring the curriculum of school and university.

For the considerations of policy makers, dealing with National and International concern on management

To meet the long term goal of human resource development with reference to in-service and perspective graduates in the light of women agriculture and rural extension there is a need to impart relevant education and training to young men and women for managing income generating and development activities on behalf of rural urban and slum producers.

We have to be very precise about the goal of developing links to build bridges between researchers and extension workers should not make us forget that specialisation and division of labour have contributed to growth throughout history. Sometimes a bit of competition between different sectors will lead to improved performance by each of them as long as social and institutional goals are clear. Working with constraints and responsibility is sheer drudgery, but from another point of view it is the most challenging task that a woman can ever undertake.

PRIORITIES FOR RESEARCH AGENDA AND ACTION POINTS

- Priorities for home economics programmes need to re-examine historical ties to the agricultural production into home economics extension programming in rural areas.

Background

- The First Congress on Human Ecology for Women was held on 4th to 5th February 2000 in New Delhi.
- The Second Congress on Human Ecology was held on 4-6th February, 2001 in New Delhi.

Consultative Group Meeting

In the same context for creating balance in higher education by introducing the unified field of human ecology. It seems all of us are making efforts for the cause of environmental interaction and seeking collaborations to what, how, why, when of the best alternatives for action on the global vision and mission for human ecology needs?

The significance of education for sustainable development at all levels keeping in view the following points :

- Networking in informal sectors, the grass-root level, NGO and the global forum for wider access to higher education.
- To foster among students community, a constant motivation to learn and to develop not only academic ability but also practical skills and talents that are being demanded by the modern world.
- Contributions from experts to place entire sector of higher education in sharp focus.
- For higher investments and measures to upgrade higher education and research programme.
- To use distance education for training skills in virtual classroom, with the advances in communication technologies.

The legacy of innovative programmes of excellence in time past and time present is a gateway to the relevance for the future. It is my fond hope the field of Human Ecology will be to model the value of holistic perspective in addressing human environment issues with the emerging field of all applied sciences, which teaches the principles on which to find health and happy life. It emphasises interrelations between various components of human ecosystems. On the whole the philosophy of human ecology provides a context for developing a serving individuals and families from human environment perspectives. The science is and will continue to be viable and dynamic in creating, imparting knowledge through teaching research, services and outreach so that the "voice" may be translated through education and educational programmes in the field of Home Science. And it may adopt the nomenclature of "Human Ecology" proposed.

The projects forwarded by Delhi University will provide the umbrella for the years to come. For providing new data and enhancing conditions on Human Ecology in the light of evaluation for suggestions, international population policy, religions, landscapes, ethnicity, race and increase in the multi-ethnic society, translations, cooperation economic measures of development, development theory and the role of women in development and ethnicity and ethnic changes.

- Restructure curricula at all levels to make sure it responds to local needs for education.
- Strengthening its focus on rural life in teaching, research and extension.
- Expand linkages at all levels macro, meso, micro level, household food security issues.
- Strengthen research on women's role in agriculture, food security and focus issues specifically on alliance with women in development programmes.
- Bringing researchers together in the field.
- Breaking down disciplinary barriers.
- Approach, basic to on farm research.
- Interdisciplinary team work in the subsequent stages of research process to identify constraints.

For the projects for the development of Infrastructure for women, agriculture and rural extension

- For the relevance of education, equity and access of management of higher education.
- UGC administration for "financial mechanism".
- For the cause of : The training for the future :
  - — The asset way-industry acceptance of asset of the student community.
  - — Promotion of ecologically sustainable agriculture.
  - — Carry out agricultural research relevant to social sciences including statics, economics, extension, Home Science and Nutrition. Sustainable and equitable use of agro-biodiversity.
  - — Eco development concerns in Natural agricultural farming system, R&D approaches.

To meet the emerging demands for productivity, sustainability, and environmental and ecological security. To coordinate research with the community perception education and reforms.

In Partnership — IGNOU

Indira Gandhi National Open University is today virtually a household name. With its headquarter located on 150 acres of verdant land in the south of Delhi and a network of regional and Study Centres spread all over the country, the University has brought higher education to the doorsteps of a vast number of people. IGNOU has over 700,000 students today.

The University now offers 76 programmes. From its inception, IGNOU has been endeavouring to develop its own programme profile, which is a mix of academic as well as continuing and extension education programmes.

- Contribution of professional women in development for more and more openness for women, role of women extension workers in terms of their number, and quality of technology transfer mechanism, to understand with the influences growth of professionals and women in agriculture.
- To identify various issues of graduate women from the study which relate to educate, employment, inability, career expectations, values, problems, and contribution to agriculture and development. To help in policy formation, planning and action.
- To take up the development work in dairy, sericulture and post harvest technologies in required linking and other support services.
- Networking for its academic programmes to enhance learning environment at an affordable cost and that mass media does not telecast the nation-wide telecast of curriculum-based video tapes and live teleconferencing for academic conferencing and counselling.
- Gyan Darshan and Krishi Darshan channels of Doordarshan which in effect is cooperative venture involving host of institutions and organisation in enriching and learning environment in our country with the application of modern technology.

- To transform existing material as a part of field attachment programmes from Open Universities of Bangladesh, Nepal, Sri Lanka to initiate the centre, the project team may include academics, from other schools, interdisciplinary projects, for extension education for the following activities :
  - — Certificate programmes in participatory planning for development functionaries.
  - — Community awareness on disaster preparedness.
  - — Computer literacy for school dropouts.
  - — Certificate course for professional development of adult education and functionaries.
  - — Vocational and skill training programmes.

TRAINING FOR DOORSTEP TECHNOLOGY TRANSFER FOR PRE-SERVICE AND IN-SERVICE GRADUATES

To address specific system constraints, weaknesses and gap in research, extension. The innovation in technology dissemination; agricultural technology management for strategic research and extension; to augment infrastructure support for technology dissemination management at national level. This project has its main focus on women in agriculture especially in Maharashtra, Kerala, Uttaranchal, U.P., Punjab, Haryana, Rajasthan, Himachal Pradesh for village based training programmes for farm women, skill upgradation programmes for link workers, the student community for demonstrations, study tour, for transfer of technologies. To cater to skill upgradation and capacity building of farm women in states namely Andhra Pradesh, Karnataka, Tamil Nadu, Gujarat, Madhya Pradesh and Orissa.

On the farming community it will help in : Seed production and distribution, to ensure increased availability of quality and certified seeds. A seed bank to provide for storing of seeds of important crops, of various agroclimatic region depending upon requirements for promoting quality seed production; to ensure availability of quality seeds; as result of research motivation evolved varieties for the availability of certified seeds to farmers; for seed production and possibility of export in seed sector to neighbouring countries.

Plant Varieties Protection

With the objective of protecting intellectual property rights to be enacted with the plant breeders thereby making the fruits of research in India and abroad, available to the farmers. Thus the breeder or owner of a variety will get protection legally to control its production.

Plant quarantine : To upgrade and modernise the facilities available at new plant quarantine station near international airport at New Delhi. Skill training for functionaries by way of fellowship with latest equipment of international standards like Electro micro scope.

Integrated pest management : extension officers in environment friendly ecological approaches, for managing pest problems with minimum dependence on chemical pesticides, and banning of hazardous pesticides and amendment in steadies act and rules.

Agriculture credit : Institutionalisation the facilities for providing better access to institutional credits to farmers for increasing agricultural production and productivity. Providing better credit for small marginal farmers and other weaker sections to enable thereto adopt modern technologies and improved agricultural practices.

National Cooperatives and Multistate Cooperatives for agricultural marketing to meet the challenges of WTO. Training programmes with the pace for cooperative programmes and to strengthen the democratic management of cooperatives in the legislation for greater degree of autonomy for multistate cooperative societies. Reduction in the control and level of intervention of government for the development of a well knit comprehensive nation-wide efficient and responsive marketing systems at different levels right from rural markets, wholesale markets and terminal markets of national importance. Whereas resources for development of rural periodic markets and improvements of services in the wholesale markets to meet the challenges imposed by WTO agreement in the light of capacity development of agricultural production and marketing systems for adoption of latest technologies of enhancing cold storage technology with the objective to stabilise the marketing of perishable vegetables and fruits in particular; to enable the farmers to get remunerative process for their produces. Comprehensive crop insurance scheme :

- To cover all farmers both loanee and non loanee and optional for non-loanee farmers.
- Coverage of additional commercial/horticultural crops subject to availability of yield data, subsidisation of insurance charges payable by small and marginal farmers.
- Simultaneous introduction of a pilot crop, insurance scheme based on individual farmers as a unit for disbursement of insurance compensation.

Forecasting and Linkage on Computer Network

For coordination and assimilation of various methodologies and technical advancements relating to multidimensional state crops for advocacy, articulation and facilitation to help the state in their efforts for development of agriculture. Besides, a few major programmes of national importance as central initiative. This project will also built on a line, real time capacity to create an enabling environment.

Training in administration : training in the field of computers, personal management, financial management, secretarial procedures and practices, investment planning project formulation and implementation, evaluation, project designing for agriculture development, data processing and use of computers.

The linked project for the cause of soil and water conservation Project : conservation of eco-system of Gola Catchment. The main focus of this project of conservation with special emphasis on soil and water conservation.

Preservation of Soil Loss from the Catchments

- Promotion of multidisciplinary integrated approach to catchments.
- Improvement of land capability and moisture regime in the watersheds.
- Promotion of land use to match land capability. Reduction of run off from the catchments to reduce peak flow into the river system.

- Upgradation of planning and execution of watershed development programme.
- Identification of critical degraded area.
- Increase of productivity of land affected by alkalinity for increasing sustainable agriculture.
- Generation of data on land suitability and capability of regulating land use.
- Preparation of soil resources map and inventory of soil and land resource.

Setting Priorities

To act as a catalyst for resources needed to create financial and administrative infrastructure needed to undertake long-term research agenda to ensure appropriate research priorities :

- International collaborations for building scientific, academic and development communities by linking its national partners and networking with international collaborators to increase and contribute to the international research.

Mission

Empowerment through knowledge.

The proposed centre will be attached to the Nodal Centre.

Technical Programme

- Tapping the strength of NGO system — the private sectors, community group in designing and execution of project work.
- Serving as a financial mechanism for the conservation of biological diversity.
- Mobilising new financial resources for the management of environment like UGC and Ministries and local funding agencies.
- Engaging business small and large and also joint venture that augment but not displace the private and pioneer technologies *i.e.* of keeping in view the development of individual, community and village in focus.
- Setting clear yardsticks for the success of the project as a participatory monitoring and evaluation of the project.

12

DEPARTMENT/CENTRE FOR HUMAN ECOLOGY AT INSTITUTE OF HOME ECONOMICS

PROJECTS :

(a) Establishment of Centre for Human Ecology (Nodal Centre).

(b) Studies on Women Agriculture and Rural Extension through Education and Training Programmes with Special Reference to Pre-Service Graduate.

New thrust and future planning for :

- Expansion of research and outreach with people resource and facilities.
- Postgraduate degree/diploma programmes for pre-service, in service graduates.
- Other training programmes — short term and door-step and tailor made programmes as per need.

ABOUT THE PROJECTS AT CENTRE FOR HUMAN ECOLOGY

The proposal entitled "Studies on Women Agriculture and Rural Extension" through Education and Training Programmes with Special Reference to Pre-Service Graduates forwarded by Delhi University to UGC is to strengthen and sustain university education as an instrument of social transformation and to facilitate the development of capabilities for the overall development of the community.

It is envisaged that under the umbrella of Centre for Human Ecology, Extension Education, including adult education, continuing education through field outreach activities can be undertaken to meet the following objectives :

- To enrich the learning process of faculty and students through exposure to community needs, problems, issues and reaching out to social, economic and cultural groups.
- To extend knowledge and other institutional resources and social cultural realities with a view to reflecting these in the entire curricular system of higher education and to promote meaningful and sustained rapport between national and international universities, its colleges and the community.
- To have the integration between formal and non-formal education and out of school learning process.
- To make education relevant to learners' needs and feedback to the university curriculum.
- Reform, based on the experience, and the experience gained by such interaction or project with the larger community of the people, learner, employers and promoting learning process particularly in preparation of learning material and to have involved students in the major development of programme like adult literacy, bonded labour, gender issue, communal harmony and cultural integration and consumer right issues including skill for self-employment.

The methodological approaches (farming systems research, cropping systems research and farmer back-to-farmers) have been quite useful to develop stronger links between researchers and with poor in resources. The experience gained is useful in active management to :

- Provide support with action by providing a consistent internal policy, goals and links.
- Provide leadership by taking part in linkage activities and giving them high visibility and priority.
- Encourage the group for commitments towards the farming related activities.
- Use mechanisms such as problem diagnoses, training and priority, setting and planning, to set a clear goal and objectives.
- Application of an interdisciplinary perspective to diagnose problems and set priorities.

- Promote the farming community, farmer participation as collaborators and evaluators of alternative technologies.

Foundation Mission

- To improve, access to quality education and expert knowledge.
- To achieve more active learning.
- To generate new knowledge and scholarships across the mission.
- To advance diversity within community.
- To the market demands both in rural and urban areas, for students who have undergone general education courses in continuing education can be offered specific skills.
- For those already in jobs to update skills or acquire qualification for carrier advancement.
- Equivalency programme : Catering to parallel programmes for disseminating knowledge in all walks of life and for different segments of the population through need based and relevant education programmes to fill in the gaps in their intellectual growth, enhance professional and technical competence and promote undertaking of contemporary issues.

With the view of present education system and its human resource development activities programmes for community related to the socio-economic development, Delhi University has forwarded several projects to facilitate linking of higher education with the development process. This confirms the UGC policy of considering extension as the third dimension of higher education of people with diverse needs. This is to facilitate the development of capabilities of the community for the overall development of the community and to help people to improve the quality of their lives. Social development of people needs organic linkages between education and society.

The project proposal entitled "Studies on women agriculture rural extension through education and training programmes with special reference to pre-service graduates" forwarded by

University of Delhi to UGC to establish Centre for Adult Continuing Education, Extension Work and Field Outreach for the optimum involvement of teachers and students where departments, like Home Science, Microbiology, Bio-technology, Physics, Sociology, Psychology, Economics and School of Social Sciences will be the integral part of the academic work. The basic aim of the project is to adopt an integrated approach to help sustainable linkage with all sectors of community, consisting all age groups with the institutional resources to the community and to gain insight from contacts between knowledge resources and socio-cultural realities with the view to reflecting these in the entire curricular system of higher education including outreach and research. It is two-way process between the experts and the people and intellectual intervention in the community living problems which need to be overcome through the educational process.

Aims and Objectives

Impart relevant education and training to young men and women for managing income generating and development activities.

- Offer training courses for policy makers, directors, general managers and those in charge of specific managerial functions in rural enterprises and projects.
- Conduct research on operating problem order to help improve the management of enterprises and projects.
- Undertake basic research into the process of rural urban management to augment the existing body of knowledge on the subject.

After finishing the course the participants will be able to :

- Relate extension education to the development issues.
- Design curricula and programmes that contribute to development.
- Administer curricula and programmes, selecting for different target groups appropriate methodologies and media.

Rationale : Reaching the unreached through education to improve the quality of life.

Programme/Activities Proposed

- Continuing education courses for the university group.
- Adult Extension Education for those eligible for university based courses Research.

Role and functions of the Department of Adult Continuing extension, education and field outreach.

Catalyst Role

- Acting as focal agency in the University system.
- Serving as technical resource centre for universities community activities.
- Assessing the need of the community.
- Developing curriculum and multidisciplinary University programmes, involving faculty students from various disciplines.
- Stimulating other departments of the University to undertake similar activities with respect to their discipline for continuing education of graduates, extension education and field outreach.

Teaching, Training and Research

A project proposal entitled "Research and Training in on-farm, off-farm and non-farm sectors for human resources development with special reference to tribal women" :

- Teaching programmes/course in adult and continuing education.
- Conducting need based continuing education courses not undertaken by other departments of the university.
- Conducting activities/programmes for upgrading knowledge skills or acquiring new skills short-term diploma certificates programmes.
- Training short-term aimed at various groups is skill income generation, entrepreneurship development family life education, Para legal training for grass-root workers/activities.
- Community outreaches activities — responsibility to reach out to society, specific disadvantaged groups, *e.g.* bonded labour, child workers, urban slum and villages.

Programmes

Vocational/Career Oriented Programmes

Empowering people at different socio-economic and educational levels with marketable vocational skills, which are appropriate :

- Participation in literacy, post literacy, continuing education under the ground level model.
- Evaluation as per university norms.

Collaborating and Networking

- Networking with government departments and other agencies of the country.
- International collaborations — to implement the programmes for higher education and to draw the programmes of collaboration by the participating institute — for linking higher education in the priority areas of environment, population education and science — and technology and gender issues.

Documentation particularly of Field Experience to Enrich Theory and dissemination of information :

- Preparing material.
- Disseminating information.
- Use of computers and internet-Publications.

Monitoring and Evaluation

- Monitoring and Evaluating the Department's activities as well as ongoing extension in the university.
- Reporting to Nodal University.

Five Ways to give Push to Human Ecology

- Basic concepts of sciences.
- Attitude of the community (testing through cooperation, collaboration models for behaviour studies).
- Evaluation at every stage for implementation of the projects.
- Experiments with real world situation to bring changes in curriculum.

- Have good public relation at all levels, community, industry, institutions for research, education extension, GO's and NGO's development related organisations.

Strategy

Development of strategy for food production, income generation through generic bio-diversity, natural resource management and education to improve the environment of the community on sustainable basis.

Project planning and project preparation are vital. Efforts to ensure this need, are to be sustained. Following obstacles are faced in course of their improving the standard of living through new plans and policies :

Improper training, insufficiency of technical staff and supervising facilities, lack of need based, non-availability of suitable mechanism to determine the appropriateness of the technology; insufficiency of government machinery to provide basic needs like supplying the improved techniques according to the demand on time, non-involvement of local people and organisation, shortage of funds, need of proper S&T policy measure; non-availability of technical advise, rectifying and replacing the equipment in use, lack of political will. Therefore, accurate effort needs to be implemented. The following measures have been undertaken for the success of policy and programmes :

1. Appropriate policy implementation from grass-root level.
2. Training facilities.
3. Repairing workshops.
4. Rewards for successful implementation of the policy.

Functional Literacy and Adult Education

To act on strategies to be adapted to further the social relations and institutional perspective to poverty alleviation, and enhance capacity of NGOs in poverty alleviation on which organisation is most relevant to :

- Prioritisation of rights to resources, employment, just wage and basic-needs.

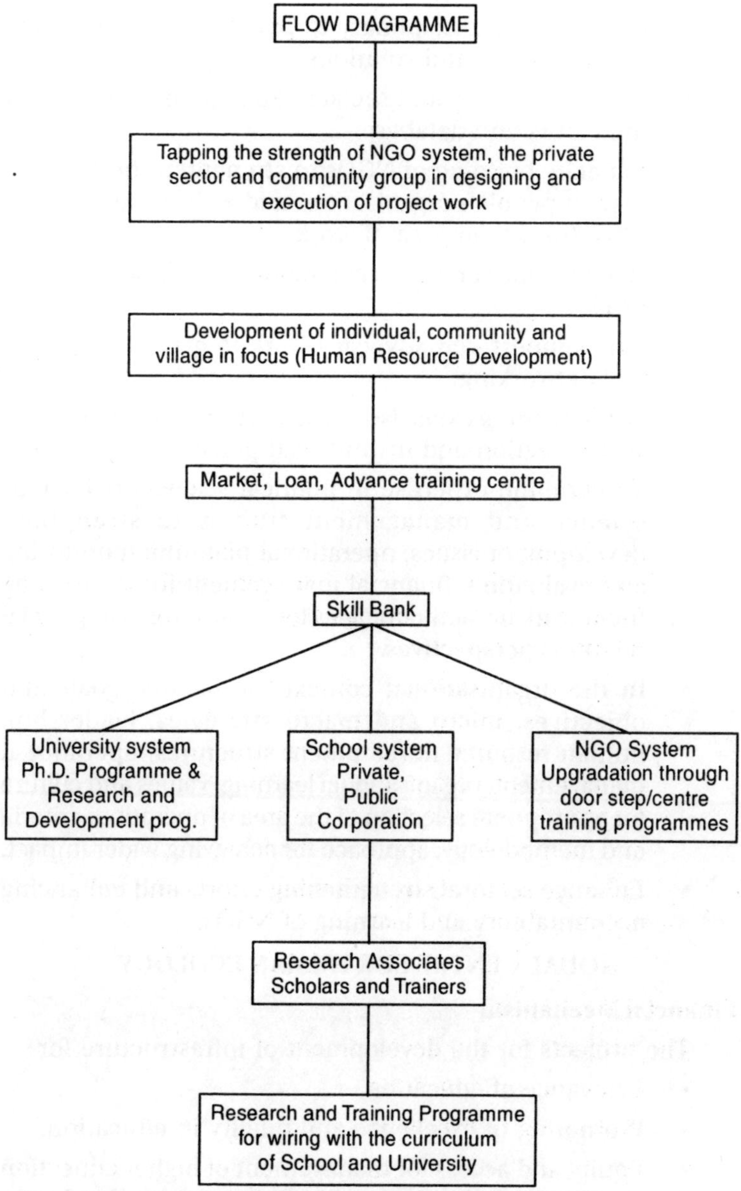

A sequence of steps for matching methods of education and training for putting knowledge to work for conservation of ecosystem through community resource management.

- Adopt a multidisciplinary to perceiving development and problems and solutions.
- Building poverty and social relations sensitive poverty indicators and database.
- Capacity building of NGOs to strengthen the capacity of poor people's organisations and withdrawal of direct work from their area of work.
- Handling the conflicts at community, family, local market level.
- Link support and advocacy work to grass-root action and networking.
- Strengthening expertise in capacity enhancement from social relation and institutional perspective.
- To combine expertise in political science, behaviour science and management studies to strengthen development issues, operational planning monitoring and evaluation, financial management for developing framework or methodologies for institutionalising social relations perspectives.
- In the organisational context the factors, goals and objectives, micro and macro strategies, leadership, human resource development structures, operational management, organisational learning, values and culture for appropriate selection of the area of operation, criteria and methodology, approach for achieving wider impact.
- Enhance sectoral strengthening efforts and enhancing accountability and learning of NGOs.

NODAL CENTRE FOR HUMAN ECOLOGY

Financial Mechanism

The projects for the development of infrastructure for

- Relevance of education.
- Promoting of excellence and quality in education.
- Equity and access for management of higher education and UGC administration for "Financial Mechanism".

Education develops manpower for different levels of economy and empowers the poor masses to become self-

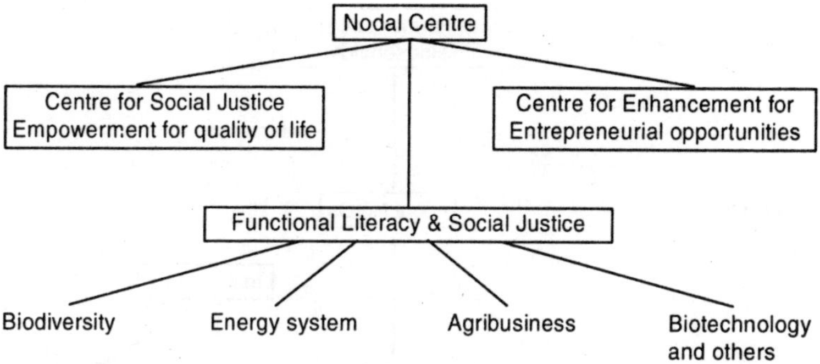

reliant enough to participate in the process of nation development.

The main objectives of the proposed centre will be :

- To identify various target groups of human ecology for women as well as those who are to be trained in imparting and in developing the field of human ecology and consequent.
- To review currently employed teaching methods and assess how far these are suitable, and what appropriate methods and training programmes need to be devised.
- To devise programmes and techniques for sensitising not only the institutions (the teaching faculty and students body) to imbibe human rights culture but also for developing sensitivity and respect for human rights at the community level.
- To identify activity and programmes in addition to running courses, that could be undertaken by the institutions for objectives of human ecology education.

The proposed centre will be located at the Institute of Home Economics, New Delhi.

MULTI-LEVEL APPROACH

Collaborations

1. Village Level :
   (i) Gram Panchayat
   (ii) Van Panchayat
   (iii) Fruit Utilisation Department.

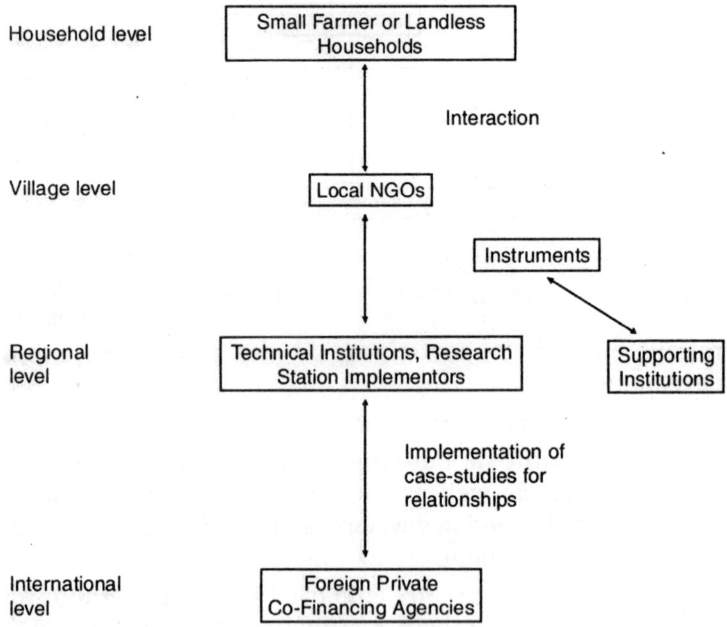

2. National Level :
   (i) G.B. Pant University, Pantnagar
   (ii) Departments of Delhi University, Delhi
   (iii) Kumaon University, Nainital
   (iv) Forest Research Institute, Dehradun
   (v) Indian Council of Agriculture Research Centre, Almora
   (vi) G.B. Pant Institute of Himalayan Environment & Development.
3. International Level :
   (i) Texas A & M University, Texas
   (ii) Texas Agriculture Extension Services, College Station, Texas
   (iii) Michigan State University, Michigan
   (iv) College of Human Ecology, Michigan State University, Michigan.

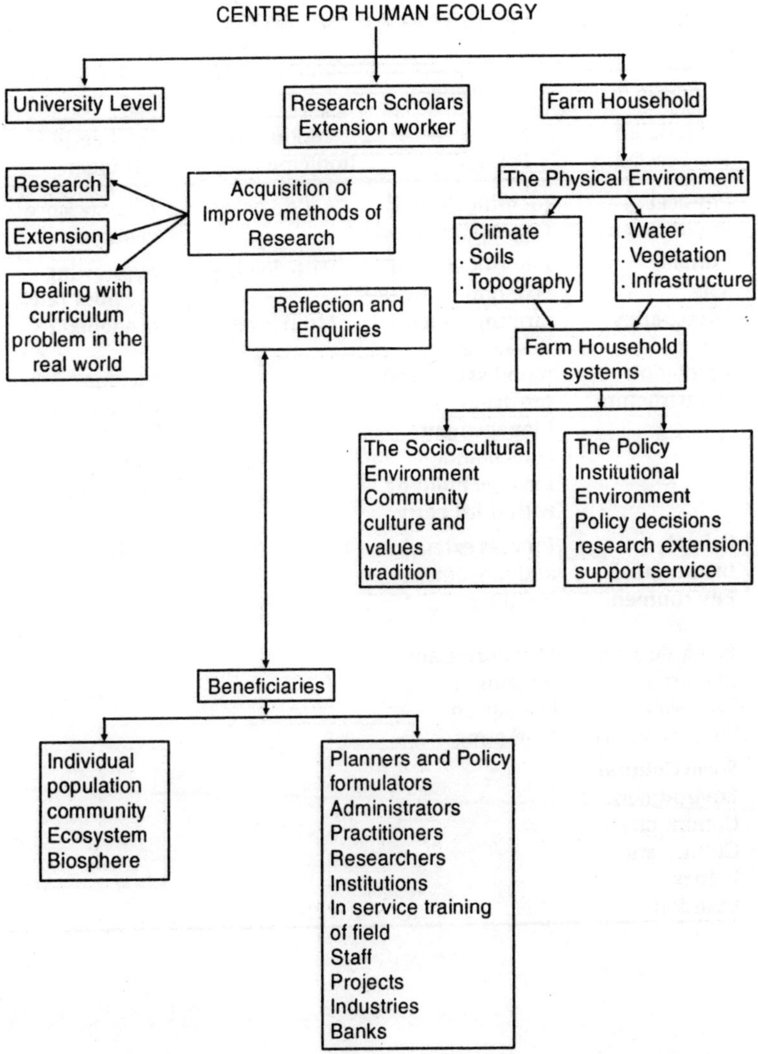

University level approach for reaching the unreached through research, extension and education

Methodology

Research	*Extension*	*Education*	
Module-I Pre-Feasibility	Module-II Feasibility	Module-III Implementation	Module-IV Impact
Physical Environment	Identification of target population	Action based -	An associative economy
Climate Soils Topography Water Vegetation Infrastructure	Identification of economic activities/ farming system Resource mobilisation and provision Management consultancy Linkage building with third party	Participatory Multi level	Supporting the poor rate of adoption Income generation Dietary awareness
Policy/ Institutional Environment	Process extension and movement building		
Policy decision Research, Extension Support services	Monitoring and ongoing self-evaluation Marketing		
Socio Cultural Environment Community Culture and Values tradition			

13

Establishment of Nodal Centre for Human Ecology

Society and science provide knowledge to create human ecology. Its interactions between human and their environment is in making the technical concepts more realistic and meaningful.

ESTABLISHMENT OF NODAL CENTRE FOR HUMAN ECOLOGY

To establish Nodal Centre for Human Ecology, with the view of present education system, the criteria for distribution of funds to the institutes of higher learning and research by a parameter of productivity of the institutes rather than their products and image etc., and to conduct adult continuing education and outreach activities, the department/centre should become an integral part of all departments and constituents of the University through the optimum involvement of teachers and students. The universities need to give a statutory status to the departments with the core faculty eligible for representatives on all the university bodies such as senate, academic council, etc. To establish the Nodal Centre for Human Ecology at JNU for Research, Education, Extension and field outreach for the optimum involvement of teachers and students where Centre will be the integral part of academic work. The basic aim of the forwarded projects is to adopt an integrated approach with no "hidden hunger" for ecological access to our population below poverty line particularly children, women suffering from malnutrition and go to bed hungry every night.

INNOVATION OF THE DISCOVERY OF KNOWLEDGE FOR COMMUNITY BASED APPROACHES

To develop unique scientific culture by linking several disciplines and professionals for ecology of individuals, families in their diverse socio cultural, physical biological environment where diversity of ecosystem is way of life.

To work with the Centres of JNU for organising pre-service and in-service courses, Refreshers training with the centres of excellence like Zakir Husain Centre of Educational Studies, School of Social Sciences, School of Life Sciences, School of Physical Sciences, School of Environmental Sciences and Centre for Biotechnology.

For action to be taken in order to overcome institutional bottlenecks to participatory programmes :

- For the sustained process of endogenous innovation generating activities as indicator of success for continuity of learning in academic structure for the involvement of curriculum work and re-animating the collaborative process of generating knowledge in the classroom and taking independent research by the students.

To develop In-House Research and Development Activities for untrodden path to the journey of Human Ecology requires the support in order to understand the process of development, various institutional technological and environment factors of different regions. For the development of human resources in the area of biotechnology for the exploitation in the field of industry, medicine and agriculture. For teaching physico-chemical aspects of biology, cell biology, bio-chemistry, bio-physics, microbiology, molecular biology, bio-statistics and computer applications.

- Instrumentation CIF (Central Instrumentation Facilities).
- USIC (University Science Instrumentation Centre).
- For Rich Software Library.
- For the Study of Law and Governance.

Basic concepts — Paradigm in shifts in human services that are promoting change for better outcomes for children, families, neighbourhoods and communities processes and tools — ways of operating that can facilitate the new way of doing business.

Best practice-models — Tried and tested human service delivery, basic research and evaluation reports and field experience the best information currently available than decision makers can use in human service programme development.

Education programmes — to over a wide range of diverse topic, programming efforts to address community based issues in many areas including agriculture, natural resources, community and economic development families and children.

Children, youth and family — programme to use the educational resources and methods of following areas to deliver educational programmes within community to enhance the quality of life across the life cycle :

Family strength/home economic.

Food nutrition and health.

Youth development.

Training programmes in horticulture education, location specific training programmes by doorstep technology transfer and on-station technology transfer.

Development Area of expertise team in Family strength/ Home economics — Area of expertise team to help families, succeeded by integrated university and community resources in educational process that applies, knowledge, practice application of research in critical issues.

Field crops — To help crop producers, improve themselves, their business and their environment through an educational process that applies knowledge demonstration and research to critical issues.

Firm — To assist agriculturally related industries business, families and individuals to improve their lives that applies management and economic knowledge to critical issues, needs and opportunities.

Food nutrition and health — To use sound food, nutrition and health principles to help families, improve health through an educational process that applies knowledge practical application, and research to critical issues for food safety.

Forestry to help private landowners, industry, and communities to improve the management and conservation of forest resources through education, outreach programmes and research for traditional forestry, urban forestry. Social and economic issues in resource management, conservation, research and education.

Fruits — To coordinate fruit researchers and extension specialists on station as well as field extension agents working together to solve problems of fruit education, extension efforts for increasing the productivity and profitability of fruits growers.

Leadership — Organisation-wise resources for on campus and off campus that is issue based, action oriented with the viable sense of community.

State and Local government — links to local government related resources.

Tourism — To help the tourism industry, improve themselves, their business, and their environment through an educational process that applies knowledge, demonstration and research to critical issues.

Vegetables — To address the vegetable industry needs; identifies the current state of vegetable industry and help define a vision for it, strengthen the competitive position and profitability of the vegetable industry which can remain a viable asset for vegetable industry.

Water quality — Identifying available resources to answer water related questions and to share about water quality related programmes of outside agencies and organisation.

Natural resources — Generating research and extension to meet economic and environmental need. To generate new research and education programmes to meet a wide range of economic, environmental needs by growers and processors.

The office for research, outreach and international programme with the purpose of facilitating and supporting home science/home economics college faculty scholarships in research, outreach and international programmes. It will be a resource point of access, for faculty in focusing enhancing the generation and application of knowledge across the domains of research outreach and international programmes.

For Establishment of Asian Centre for Human Ecology for Women and Child
(Under Planning Commission, Government of India)

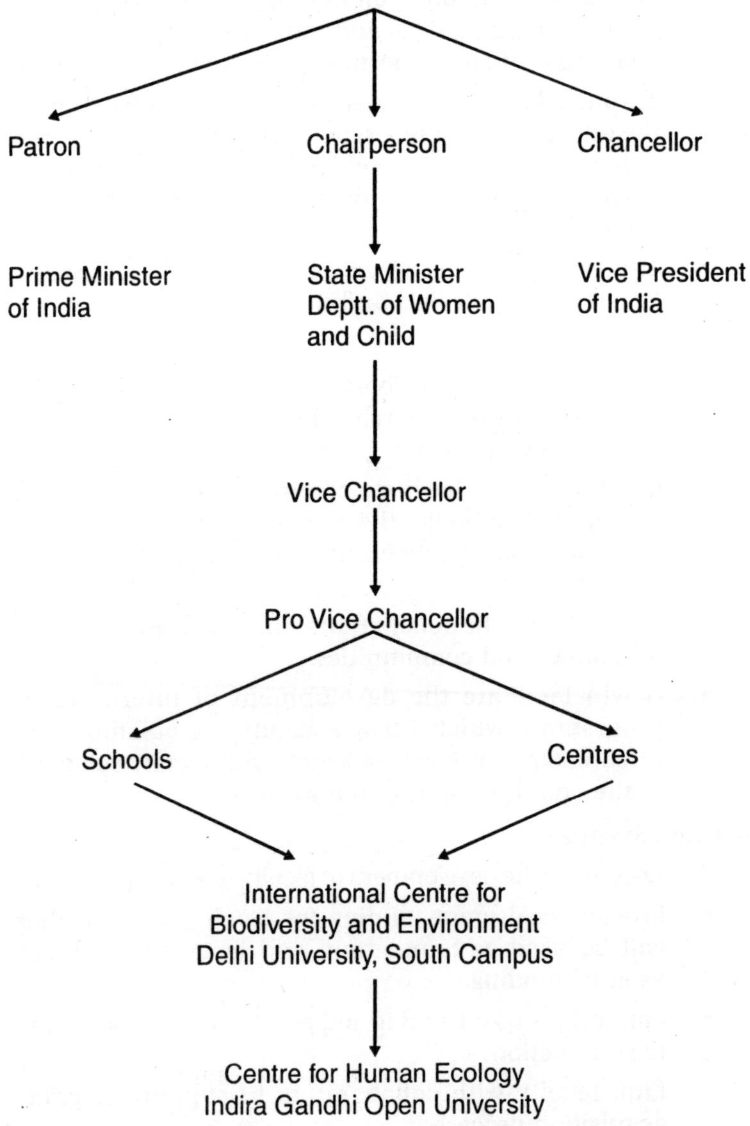

Mission

- The office will be committed to the mission of the colleges of home science of empowering and strengthening families and individuals in address the challenges of and opportunities in their environment.
- Through the support of research, outreach programmes, the office shall promote scholarship and initiatives that enhance the positive development in communities and acknowledge the diversity of families and community served by the colleges.
- The office will encourage scholarly efforts across the broad mission of JNU and its centres.

Goal

- It will support the collaboration of home science faculty in the pursuit of research priorities which cuts across the three departments.
- It will promote, facilitate community outreach which reflects and embodies the influence of college research and scholarship programmes for people, business and industry.
- To initiate public policy efforts which address the needs of families and communities.
- It will facilitate the development of international programme which involve faculty in collaborative research and outreach/research with faculty scholars, in the countries around the world.

Selected Strategies

- Encourage the development of faculty research proposals.
- Provide seed grant funding for faculty research that will be used as foundation, and leverage to obtain external funding.
- Support proposal writing and grants manship seminars in conjunction.
- Link faculty with collaborators to support in grant acquisition process.
- Work closely with university administrations and faculty,

individuals, on specific research interest of the faculty as well as outreach and international programmes.

- Organise and develop faculty research groups in relation to identified research themes.

Themes and Programmes on the Path of Progress by Utilising all Available Resources

- Uplift of schedule castes, tribes and backward classes.
- Minority specific development programme.
- Water resource development.
- Functional literacy programmes.
- Agricultural development.
- Public health programme.
- Health care for all.
- Rural development.
- Land reform.

NODAL CENTRE

Systematic efforts for developing human resource at the grass-roots level in the directions of sustainable development.

Project Title

UGC Nodel Centre for Human Ecology for Projects

"Centre Human Ecology for linking home science curriculum with farm women and community through studies on women agriculture rural extension." (Delhi based)

"Research Management and mechanism for Conservation of Ecosystem of Central Himalaya with Special Reference to Gola Catchment Area (A case study on conservation of ecosystem of hill community)."

Project Summary

To promote changes in the way the centre and states develop and employ human resources with the aim to make them and their sectors more productive and to modernise its agricultural sector at UGC Nodal Centre for Human Ecology.

To achieve these changes, policy and institutional reform would be carried out. The project would foster changes in the investment priorities resulting from policy and institutional

NODAL CENTRE FOR HUMAN ECOLOGY

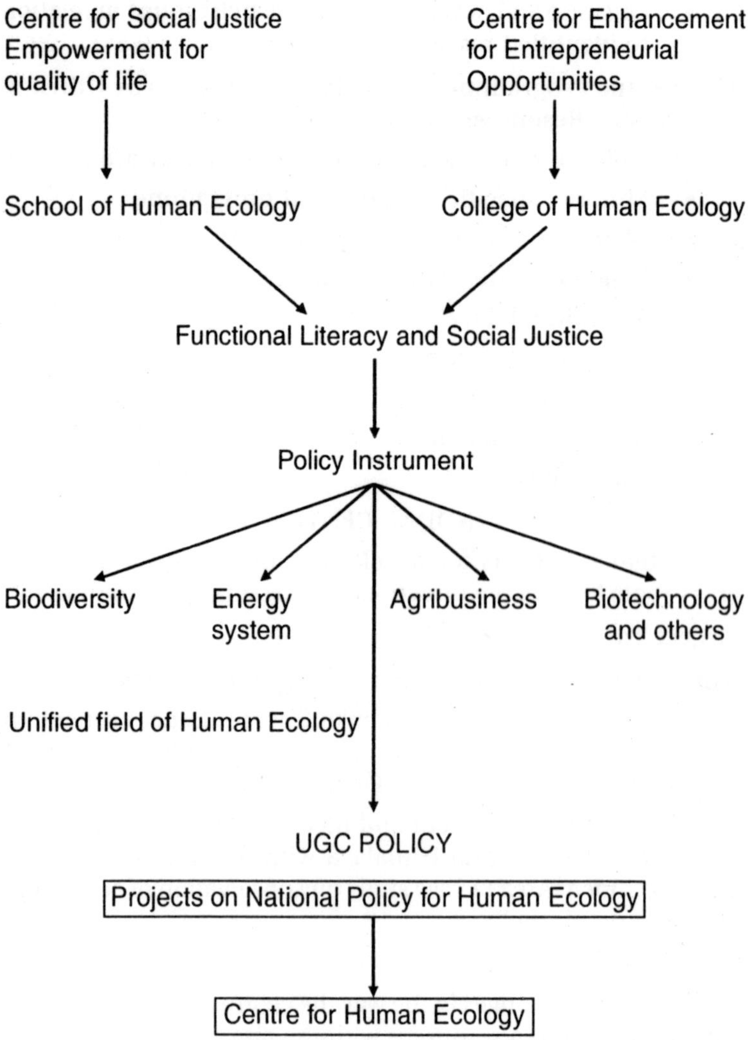

Centre for Food Processing and Food Safety System

Ministry of Food Processing

Centre for Biotechnology—Deptt. of Biotechnology

reforms will focus on the process of : (a) improving the quality and relevance of higher education for community service through training programmes, and (b) strengthening the capacity of participating states to develop and manage agricultural human resource.

To upgrade human resource management the project at state level would support development and management programmes (HRD & HRM) including training focused on job oriented needs for (i) systematic need assessment, (ii) training and trainers, (iii) evaluation of training effectiveness, (iv) better instructional facilities, and (v) improve management of state sector employees.

To secure better livelihood for people by the development for forestry sector to increase afforestation programme to preserve the ecosystem by taking specific action including necessary training and technical assistance. This will redress environmental degradation, desirable resources and environment management practices, common property resource management, improve management skills, self-sustaining capacity, employment generation, mass awareness, income generation. The activities which are socially beneficial and economically viable like on-farm, off-farm and non-farm will be undertaken for the benefit of the community by doorstep and on-station technology transfer for functional literacy, through short term training programmes to ensure continues benefit to rural poor so that the resource and environment may be preserved for future generation. The project will establish and strengthen the institutions to demonstrate desirable resources and environment management practices for integrated community system for sustainability and replication and neighbouring countries and other states of India.

Driver — Production and employment and restoration of ecosystem by the community of the area.

HUMAN ECOLOGY FOR EDUCATION

(Planning, programming, monitoring and evaluation)

Financial Mechanism

For the projects for the development of infrastructure for :

- Relevance of education.
- Promoting of excellence and quality in education.
- Equity and access for management of higher education and UGC administration for "Financial Mechanism".

There are many ways to mobilise citizens and their governments towards sustainable communities, but there are also many barriers and obstacles that hamper our progress in this direction. We cannot realistically expect most people to choose sustainable options if they appear to be more difficult or expensive than unsustainable choices. The question arises, then, how can we change the systems around us.

In recent years there has been increasing interest in the use of "economic instruments" in environmental policy. These tools influence the behaviour of economic agents by providing financial incentives to environmentally improved behaviour, or disincentives to damaging behaviour. As the influence of environmental economics has grown, so the calls to introduce economic instruments in fields such as pollution control and energy consumption have grown louder. Economic instruments should not be seen in isolation when introduced they are inevitably part of a structure and process of community management which in turn reflect wider objectives — environmental, economic, social and ethical — in society.

For communities to move effectively toward sustainability, citizens and their governments should understand the range of policy instruments available to them and the wider context of how community policy is made.

In Asian countries, the standard of living has been improved, with a great many technological innovations and our tremendous economic growth. However, this affluent lifestyle has caused various problems in all aspects of our daily lives; the population explosions in urban areas, the weakening of people's mental health, increasing anxiety about food safety, the depletion of natural resources, environmental issues are some examples of those problems.

Environment has been defined "as the sum total of all conditions and influences that affect the development as life of organisms." It stresses its totality, and every living organism, from the lowest to the highest, including human being, has its own environment. To identify priority areas and the way corrective action could lead to sustainability in development. This has to be done in relation to our particular social, cultural and economic milieu. Historically we have been serious minded about environment and the basic philosophy has been one of harmony with nature as against western concept of conflict with nature.

Time has come when sustainability in development has to enter in our planning process. Twelve areas have been identified where priority action is needed as one of the basic and permanent objectives. The policy has to be enunciated not in isolation but in concert with a number of Ministries/Departments of the country. These are :

Integrated Land Use Planning.

Healthy Cropland and Grassland.

Conservation of Biological Diversity.

Control of Pollution in Water and Air.

Development of Non-Polluting Renewable Energy Systems.

Recycling of Wastes and Residues.

Ecological Compatible Human Settlements and Slum Improvement.

Environment Education and Awareness.

Updating Environmental Law.

New Dimensions to National Security.

To develop measures to upgrade higher education and research programmes for wider access by linking higher education with community service and Home Science programmes to make them relevant to all sections of society, partnership for sustainable development at different levels. For creation of vibrant new partnership — to reach the most disadvantaged and underserved and the most vulnerable — the young child, the emerging strategy focuses on innovation, fostering decentralised flexible responses to the care of young children, girls and women and reaching through integrated family and community based interventions for survival, growth and development of socially backward villages and urban slums. With the special preference to those areas which are predominantly inhabited by vulnerable and weaker sections of the society *i.e.* Scheduled Castes, Scheduled Tribes and low income families found in economically backward areas, drought prone areas and areas in which development of social services requires strengthening. It also believes that these goals are an integral parts of all efforts to achieve sustained and sustainable social and economic development that meets needs, ensures well-being and protects the natural resources on which all life depends.

Interdisciplinary knowledge and skills to deal with the problems through vigorous research, active extension education programme will outreach the community. This will help them to meet the challenges imposed by the new economic and social order and improve their quality of life. The concept and viewpoints developed here will be helpful in framing educational strategies in higher education and research needs in the field of human ecology :

1. Linking higher education with community service.
2. Changes required in the area of Home Economics and Home Science programmes to make them relevant to all sections of the society.
3. Setting priorities in research to help community in the areas of Agribusiness, Bio-diversity and Environment, Biotechnology, Non-Conventional Energy System and Human Resource Development.
4. Action Mechanism for Research and Development.
5. Partnership for sustainable development at all levels (local, nation, regional and global).

The Asia and Pacific region extends from Mongolia in the north to New Zealand in the south and from the Cook Islands in the east to Iran in the west. It embraces the world's largest ocean, the pacific 165 million square kilometres, as well as third largest ocean, the Indian (73 million square kilometres) and a range of important seas (ESCAP, 1992; ESCAP, 1995a). It contains three of the largest and most populous countries of the world (China, India and Indonesia), several mountainous and land locked states (such as Bhutan and Nepal) and 22 small archipelago-states, territories, and protectorates. With only 23 per cent of the world's total land area, the region is home to about 58 per cent of the world's population.

The economics of this region have witnessed high growth rates in the recent past in 1994, the total GDP growth was 8.2% despite this, and poverty persists. Estimates indicate that, of the world's 1.2 billion people who live in absolute poverty. High population growth is exerting pressure on the environment and on natural resources on the environment and on natural resources in the region. Urbanisation and industrialisation have also had deleterious impacts, leading not only to high pollution loads but also social stress.

The pressure of human population expanding cultivation, developmental projects and increasing urbanisation have been posing a serious threat to our natural plant and animal wealth. Environmentalists all over the world have been voicing great concern about the immediate need not only to preserve biological diversity but to protect soil health, water resources and habitats, which are crucial to productive agriculture and the well-being of people.

Human life has been made possible because of the variety of living organisms on earth. Now, innumerable varieties of plants, animals, and other living beings are disappearing from our planet as land alienation, industrial agriculture, use of hazardous chemicals, and other forces push them into extinction. It is that variety, an irreplaceable biological diversity that has always sustained us, particularly at times of natural crisis, that we are seeking to preserve.

India has invested heavily in the past in its public agricultural research, education and extension systems. As a result, there is now a large "standing capacity" in the sense of existing staff and infrastructure in research and extension. Past investments have contributed largely to national success in maintaining food security for a burgeoning population. But while the green revolution technology was the cornerstone of the past successes, demands for agricultural technology are now changing and diversifying. Factor productivity growth in India's Green Revolution areas does not match with that of some East Asian countries and may be declining. Newer approaches like involving frontier sciences such as biotechnology as well as production system, approaches for breaking through yield plateaus are needed for these well endowed areas.

The major environment concerned vary widely across the region. The major issues include :

Land degradation.

Deforestation.

Declining availability of fresh water and deteriorating water quality.

Degradation of marine and coastal resources.

These issues have set a new agenda for the generation assessment and dissemination of agricultural technology. To cope with greater diversity of agro-ecological settings and producers, a decentralised approach is needed. Such a decentralised approach should focus on individual focus systems and integrate contributions of frontier sciences as well as conventional disciplines and indigenous knowledge in augmenting productivity, stability and sustainability. In contrast to the blanket Green Revolution recommendations appropriate to the needs of the past, the new technologies will have to be tailored to specific locations. Producers themselves will need to participate in setting the technical agenda, contributing their own ideas as well as assessing and disseminating results. Because much of the new technology will not be commercially marketable because it deals with broader management of natural resources or is aimed at the rural poor. It will still have to be publicly funded. But pressures on government expenditure means that public funds will have to be more carefully targeted and more efficiently used from now on.

The challenges expected of following a model of economic development based on excessive consumption of energy derived from fossil fuels. At the same time there was threat from global warming, rising level and climate change due to increasing atmospheric pollution caused by the Green House gases emission from economic activities based on fossil fuels.

To conduct research towards improving the sustainable productivity and to support rural development sector, the project on women agriculture and rural extension will adhere to the NGOs through the collaborative research and training. The projects will contribute to the institutional strengthening of voluntary private sector through the development and delivery of packages for playing significant part both as catalyst and prime mover in rural development.

The main thrust will be directed towards youth employment, income generation and generation of mass awareness about development issues. The activities which are socially beneficial and economically viable like on-farm, off-farm and non-farm will be taken up for the benefit of the community by doorstep and on-station technology transfer through short term training programme to ensure continuous benefits to the rural poor so that the resource and environment may be preserved for future generations.

14

THE ASIAN CENTRE FOR HUMAN ECOLOGY

(Resources, Newsletter and Events and Affiliates)

For the first time in history, nearly half of the world's people now live in urban areas characterised by human structures and activities. The way our communities develop will largely determine our success or failure in overcoming environmental challenges and achieving sustainable development. Cities and towns provide enormous, untapped opportunities to solve environmental challenges, they must and can pioneer new approaches to sustainable development and community management.

Earth is the laboratory where biological and physical processes are experimented. An endeavour to improve the quality of life enhances warrants a thorough understanding of various earth system processes. The 21st century is an era of accelerated development in all activities of life conceivable. Any attempt to satiate the developmental urge, neglecting earth, will boomerang and will set in stumbling blocks across our path to progress. The task ahead for planning and development is to comprehend the mother earth in its totality, involving land, water and atmosphere to allow sustainable life possible. The negative aspects of unscientific development with its case carrying effects on society have dawned upon us the urge to understand the intricate dynamics of the earth.

Humanity now faces an unprecedented confluence of changes in the global environment. For nearly three decades, scientific evidence has indicated that human activities are degrading planet earth's fundamental life-support systems : the biosphere, the atmosphere, and the hydrosphere. Preserving and wherever possible, restoring the global environment is now a challenge confronting all peoples in all countries of the world. Since the biosphere, atmosphere and hydrosphere are interrelated in myriad ways, threats to any one of them have ramifications for all, and human existence depends upon the healthy functioning of all.

In this new age, great cultural achievements of the past have to recover and enrich in the context of contemporary advancement so that humanity can successfully meet the evolutionary challenges and bring about a new type of humanity and society marked by integrated, power of physical emotional and dynamic intellectual, ethical, aesthetic and spiritual potentialities. Frontiers of knowledge are therefore, bound to expand unimaginably and new researches will oblige humanities, science, technology and fine art to arrive at new equations and new combinations. It will require contributions from experts for the field of designs and environmental analysis, planning made up of faculty and students with background design, planning and management of settings such as offices, housing and health facilities that satisfy the needs of those who use and are affected by those environments. This will place the entire sector of higher education to sharp focus for community empowerment.

We look upon the child today as a pivot of the family and hope of the future. Families are the hearts of any community and education programme serving the needs of youth and families are at the heart of extension work. The extension "learn by doing" method has a history of success in providing individuals and families with the knowledge for health, financial security and self-sufficiency.

The family and consumer sciences programme to reach to the families in rural, urban, and suburban communities with education for building successful life skills, enhancing nutrition and food safety, promoting healthy lifestyles, increasing self-sufficiency, strengthening the volunteer work force and developing future leaders. Ultimately changing families for the better. A family's success really depends on successfully coping with changes, making good decisions about everyday care, managing credit and debt, or understanding health care options, require knowledge and understanding. Extension educational programmes especially for family and childcare can represent an important field of social work. The need for dealing with the old is not so acute in India. The time is not too far off when the problems of old will become more acute, and is banned to become more serious concern for the government and the civil society. This requires homes for the aged in the urban areas. Generally their children look after the aged. Now the individualism of the west has commode family life and the neglect of the old has not been uncommon.

EDUCATION PROGRAMME

Human Ecology combines the interests theories and studies of geographers, ecologists and anthropologists with the focus on the modification of the earth's ecosystems. Ecology and environment links botanists, plant ecologists, conservation biologists, resource managers, and students at the University or high school levels. The colleges of Home Science are to respond to human needs by improving nutrition and health, advancing environmental design and technology, promoting human development and securing economic and social well-being for individual.

Human ecology considers human affairs as :

- Human factors in their evolutionary and ecology context as part of a way of looking at the world and its animals, plant, natural resources, its geography and its geopolitics for human behaviour studies.
- Engineering and technology, industrial design of industrial hygiene, environment and development, microbial ecology, to improve the practices and educational standard.
- Education for environmental sustainability and social justice, working with communities, business and students to develop consciousness, professional skills, creativity and leadership.

Extension programmes cover a wide range of diverse topics. Programming efforts address community-based issues in many area including agriculture, natural resources, community and economic development, families and children. These are :

Undergraduate and Graduate Programmes

Children, Youth Families

- Children, Youth and Family programmes use the educational resources and methods of the following areas to deliver educational programmes within communities to enhance the quality of life across the life cycle :
  - Family strengths/Home Economics.
  - Food, Nutrition and Health.
  - Youth development.
  - Integrated Pest Management.
  - Integrated pest management is a suitable approach for managing insects, weeds and plant diseases that combines the use of biological control.

Association

In association with *Asian Regional Association for Home Economics, Family Development and Resource Management Extension Programme* — to serve people of all age regardless of socio-economic level, race, colour, sex, religion, disability or national origin in collaboration with the Texas A&M University system, the Texas and Indian Council of Agriculture Research, India.

CENTRE FOR HUMAN ECOLOGY FOR EDUCATION EXTENSION AND FIELD OUTREACH

Providing educational programmes to respond to human needs by improving nutrition and health, advancing environmental design and technology, promoting human development and securing economic and social well-being for individuals.

Drivers

Rural Development, Human Resource Development, promotion of educational and economic interest for all sections of society, multinational collaborations for building, scientific and academic community by linking with partners, networking to increase and contribute to International research.

It will combine the interests, theories and studies of :

1. Geographers

Driver Production and Employment

Training	*Target group*	*Target area*	*Outcome*
Pre Service	Students	Bangladesh	*Good supply of Extension
	Managers	Bhutan	Workers
Degrees	Extension Workers	Burma	*Food Security-appropriate
Ph.D.	Govt. Organisations	China	technology for agro based
M.Sc. (2 yrs.)	Ministries	India	industries
		Japan	*Sustainability in
		Korea	agriculture, dairy,
Diplomas :		Maldives	horticulture, tiny and
Postgraduates		Nepal	cottage industries and
Diploma (1 yr.)		Pakistan	other agrowaste based
		Philippines	income generating
In-Service		Sri Lanka	activities
(3 months)		Thailand	
Short Term (2 weeks)			
Doorstep and			
On-station			

2. Ecologists
3. Anthropologists
4. Home Economists/Consumer Science Specialists
5. Psychologists
6. Agriculture Scientists
7. Economists
8. Biologists

Projects

Feasibility studies on conservation of ecosystem through Community resource management with special reference to hill community.

Programmes

- M.A. Multidisciplinary Programme.
- M.Sc. Research Methods in Social Science.
- M.A. Criminology.
- M.A. Social Policy.
- M.Sc. Psychology and Health.
- M.A./Pg. Dip. Social Work.

- M.A. Social Work 'Top Up'.
- Employment Route M.A./PG Dip. Social Work.
- M.A. Psychoanalysis.
- M.A./M.Sc. Sustainable Environmental Management (Geography and Environment Management) (Water Management).
- M.A. Local Economic Development.
- M.A. Sustainable Rural Development.
- M.Sc. in Arboriculture and Community Forest Management.
- PG Dip./M.A./M.Sc. Inter Professional Healthcare.
- M.Sc./PG Dip. Mental Health Interventions.

Graduate Studies in the Field of Social Sciences

An interdisciplinary approach, particularly with regard to studies of environmental issues, gender, reach ethnicity, is a significant feature. Particular attention is given to the theory and development of advance research methods and acquisition of key skills for the conduct of upto date and innovative research practice.

The postgraduate community which provides its members with support and simulation. Academic staff facilitates the learning in a variety of ways. Academic staff involved in postgraduate work is active in research and producing publication.

The postgraduate programmes are always being update in the line with changing knowledge and demand. For work experience internship modules which can take place of one to two taught options for a taught master degree in school of Social Science. JNU is the first university to have constituted a committee on sexual harassment and gender sensitisation. The committee acts both as a preventive and redresses body. The main functions of this committee are sensitisation and awareness generation, crisis mediation and management and formal redresses and inquiry. The committee has representatives from teachers, students, officers and staff bodies. It also avails the services of external organisations like Sanjeevini as and when needed. The Centre for the study of law and governance is a new concept. But its nature a multidisciplinary Centre — to the management of social order and its concern including globalisation and the legal structure, the problem of work culture and human rights.

M.A. Multidisciplinary Programme

The master programme, which allows students the flexibility of combining modules from two postgraduate programmes.

Programme Structure

Students combine postgraduate programmes solely from within the school of Social Sciences or from other schools within the university to form a major subject with a minor or joint major in social policy could be combined with a minor in Human Resource Management practice. It will give individually tailored advice to help students plan their multidisciplinary programmes both in advance of starting the M.A. and during the study period.

By combining research methods with subject area not only students will gain a strong basis in research training but, understanding or research findings, this is a useful combination whatever carrier path students may take. Students combine postgraduate programme either solely from within the university to form a major subject with a minor. Modules are drawn from these offered in master programme in the school of social sciences and from other schools in the University and students on this M.A. will be studying along this programme. The pattern of teaching, learning and assessment will follow that of the modules chosen for the students specific programme.

M.Sc Research Methods in Social Sciences

The M.Sc. Research methods in Social Science is a multidisciplinary degree programme for those who want to acquire or extend a knowledge of research methods across a broad span of the social sciences. It may lead to the award of M.Sc., PG Diploma or PG Certificate. It also forms a strong basis for research students proceeding to an M.Phil. or Ph.D.

Core Modules

- Methodology and Research Design.
- Qualitative and Quantitative Research.

- Research Context, Process and Ethics.
- Advanced research software and applications.

M.A. Criminology

The M.A. Criminology is designed for those who want to expand their knowledge of the criminal justice system, crime and social policy. It provides a thorough sociological approach to understanding these aspects of society. The programme is integrated into the European Common Study Programme in Criminology, which is taught at Middlesex and Universities at Rotterdam also. Two-week common study sessions are held every year at one of these institutions, on an annually rotating basis. Attendance on these is optional but participation is encouraged. Students who wish to spend a term abroad at one of the six institutions may apply for ERASMUS funding.

Programme Content. Issues of criminology theory, white collar crime, research and evaluation in criminology, issues of criminal justice, crime and victimisation, prisons in context, racism, criminal justice and social exclusion, preparing for criminological research and dissertation.

M.A. Social Policy

The M.A. Social Policy is a well-established programme. It is of particular relevance to students currently employed in the public and voluntary sectors that work in, or may wish to work in, middle management. It is also a good training programme for students who have a background knowledge and experience of social policies who wish to seek employment in the public or voluntary sectors or others who have a first degree in social sciences who wish to pursue to advanced study in social policy.

Programme Content

Core Modules : The Politics of Social Policy.
Public Sector Management.
Care of Mixed Economy.

Skills Modules : Study Skills.
Dissertation Skills.

Internship Modules

Work Experience internships are available in place of options. The Central concern of the programme is to reflect the many sided character of debates on the 'Welfare State' as we approach to the 21st century. These debates related to the respective roles of state, market, voluntary and informal provision of welfare, and the changing institutional context — at international, European, national and local levels, within which welfare needs are met. The focus on contemporary issues is combined with setting the changes in a broad historical context.

M.Sc. Psychology and Health

The M.Sc. Psychology and Health equips students with a knowledge of theoretical issues in health psychology, increases their awareness of the complex multidisciplinary issues which this study entails, and enables them to carry out research in this area. It provides an account of the psychological, social and policy processes which relate to the promotion and maintenance of health and the prevention of its health. The programme is innovative in placing emphasis on the psychological interface between the individual and society as a key issue in the determination of health.

Programme Structure

All students take two health psychology core modules, and research methods modules. In addition, students choose at least three further modules from a range of nine options.

Programme Content

Health psychology core courses.

Research methods for health psychology.

Options

Complementary medicine.

Health promotion.

Ageing and health.

Health policy.

Evolution and problem of modern medicine.

Health and the organisation of work.

Health, morality and medicine.

Introduction to counselling and therapy.

M.A./PG Dip. Social Work (Dip. SW)

The M.A./PG Dip. Social Work Programmes offer students the opportunity to combine academic study with professional training. They lead to a university and a Central Council for Education and Training in Social Work. They attract graduates already in social work posts who are seeking training as well as those making change of career. They promote the importance of good social work practice and the development of appropriate and applicable knowledge values and skills.

Programme Content

Social work.

Social problems and social policy.

Anti-discriminatory practice.

Social work law.

Applied psychology.

Community group and family work.

Social work research.

15

New Division of Human Ecology at ICAR

What God wants. The leaf of your body in service to humanity, the flower of your purified heart, and the fruit of your good actions and tears of your devotion.

Working towards capacity building and human resource development in the area of environmental and resource management, poverty alleviation, and socio-economic and gender development.

Asian centre for human ecology in New Delhi at Delhi University for local action in :

- Setting priorities in research to help community in areas of agribusiness, biodiversity and environment, non-conventional energy systems and Human resource development.
- Promote post doctoral research and granting awards for strengthening its focus on rural life.

The main thrust will be directed towards youth employment, income generation and generation of mass awareness about development issues. The activities which are socially beneficial and economically viable like on-farm, off-farm and non-farm will be taken up for the benefit of the community by doorstep and on-station technology transfer through short-term training programme to ensure continuous benefits to the rural poor so that the resource and environment may be preserved for future generations.

Training. Pre Service, Degrees : Ph.D, M.Sc. (2 years), M.A., B.Sc./B.A. (4 years), Diplomas : Postgraduate, Diploma (1 year), In-Service (3 months), Short Term (2 weeks), Doorstep and on-station.

Target Group. Students, Managers, Extension Workers, Government Organisations and Ministries.

Target Area. Bangladesh, Bhutan, Burma, China, India, Japan, Korea, Maldives, Nepal, Pakistan, Philippines, Sri Lanka, Thailand.

To conduct research towards improving the sustainable productivity and to support rural development sector, the project on women agriculture and rural extension will adhere to the NGOs through the collaborative research and training. The projects will contribute to the institutional strengthening of voluntary private sector through the development and delivery of packages for playing significant part both as catalyst and prime mover in rural development.

Thrust Areas of the Centre

Human Ecology for Globalisation.

Partnership and networking.

Restructuring the curriculum for linking higher education with community service to respond to the local needs of advancement/evolution of Home Economics to Human Ecology.

To gain insight from contacts between knowledge resources and socio-cultural realities in the entire curricular system and for higher education, international cooperation/partnership for action, sharing their successful experience, technologies materials, financial resources and learning for pilot studies on :

- Research and training for human resource development in on-farm, off-farm and non-farm sectors.
- Institutionalisation on-farm, off-farm and non-farm sectors for :
  - Case Studies on Conservation of Ecosystems.
  - Studies on Women, Agriculture and Rural Extension with special reference to Biodiversity.

To cope up with greater diversity of agro-ecological settings and producers, a decentralised approach is needed. Such a decentralised approach should focus on individual focus systems and integrate contributions of frontier sciences as well as conventional disciplines and indigenous knowledge in augmenting productivity, stability and sustainability. In contrast to the blanket Green Revolution recommendations appropriate to the needs of the past, the new technologies will have to be tailored to specific locations. Producers themselves will need to participate in setting the technical agenda, contributing their own ideas.

Outcome. Good supply of Extension Worker, Food Security — appropriate technology for agro based industries, sustainability in agriculture, dairy, horticulture, tiny and cottage industries and other agrowaste based income generating activities.

PRIORITISATION OF RESEARCH AGENDA IN AGRIBUSINESS

For undertaking the new research initiative and collaborative research and conducting training programmes for world-wide wisdom socially responsible and gender inclusive science and technology. Establishment of strong and influential networks of individuals and organisations that are engaged in research and grass-roots activities that promotes gender equity in science and technology.

Objective of the Study

- To encourage research into all aspects of gender differentiation in science and technology education and employment.
- To foster gender equity in science and technology education.
- To facilitate the entry of women into employment in the field of science and technology and their progress within such employment.
- To foster socially responsible and gender inclusion in science and technology.
- To provide a forum for dissemination and discussion of research findings and experiences of those in the field.
- To provide a support network for those working towards objectives outlined above.
- Issues of interactions between gender sciences and technology.

Issues of Interaction

- Which scientific and technological advances would be like to see in future?

"A JOURNEY TO SUSTAINABLE LIVELIHOODS"

Ancient Indian sages have said that human beings are composed of both matter and spirit. Our physical body, mind and intellect are the matter components while our soul is the spirit — the real self — that radiates and derives the matter components.

We are equipped to take decision using our intellect and by applying our acquired wisdom, we have vast potential but because of our ignorance of self these potentials remain largely untapped.

Growing activities of human and his increasing demands on the biotic and abiotic component has brought forth a change in his ecological philosophy. Human ecology means to improve people's life.

The most effective path is the attention to the poorest person, where one individual's economy is not at the cost of another's opportunity. We have more than 250 universities and over 11,000 colleges where about 70 lakhs students are pursuing higher studies, still the future citizens and we here are concerned with the professional need as a touchstone to test effectiveness of higher educational programmes in specialised area of national and global relevance to find out the essence of "Karma Yoga" in *Gita*. To achieve total human welfare : the first is the energy of Yoga, the energy of vision, of calm, spirituality represented by Lord Krishna who in Mahabharata War did not take part in the actual fighting but only gave sagely guidance to Arjuna, the hero of action.

Let us then be up and doing/with a heart for any fate/still achieving/still pursuing/learn to labour and to wait to create a positive understanding response to planned philanthropy — particularly corporate philanthropy cause to be recognised as viable instruments for undertaking development programmes using our intellect and by applying our acquired wisdom to attain supreme knowledge of gender and social equity and for fostering harmony within human kind and between it and nature to achieve more active learning to reduce world poverty.

India was first among the global community to have a national population policy with the accompanying programmes. It will be worth-while to know how universities were started in the developed world.

Research is to see what everybody else has seen and to think what nobody else has thought. Today we strive for perfection in every field with the evolution of mind and intellect worldly knowledge has become easily accessible so, we have achieved certain measures of excellence in the physical sciences but physical experiences fails to connect with our true self to shoulder our education as responsible citizens rooting for quality education.

Most of the universities and research organisations in India have collaborated with many Indian and foreign universities for helping them and designing the curriculum on environment at graduate and postgraduate levels. The idea behind it is to reach the grass-root level with the view to implement programmes at the global level for making the worldly of catch them young, for regeneration of eco-fragile areas on an average of irreversible decline eco-tone, restoration of river systems, wetlands and bio-diversity and making the citizens aware of the need to protect our mother earth.

LANDSCAPES OF HUMAN ACTIVITIES

Correcting the errors of other models the endless statistical debates on poverty accords with commonsense.

Modelling tools for environmental and resource management for special skills for resource management. Advanced principles and processes; extensive education and communication techniques, community organisation and research methodologies for the basic concepts of sciences to experiment with real world situation to bring change in curriculum taking higher education with community service towards building and sustaining a productive quality of life. The scientific expertise infrastructure facilities and research need to be strengthened by bonding the relationship between research educational institutions, industry and community in a symbolic mode of conversion of research findings into products, processes and technologies for human resource development.

Interdisciplinary knowledge and skills to deal with problems through vigorous research, active extension education programmes will outreach the community. This will help them to meet the challenges imposed by the new economic and social order and improve their quality of life. The concept and viewpoints developed here will be helpful in framing educational strategies in higher education and research needs in the field of human ecology.

POLICY AND PLANNING CELL

For establishment of new division Human Ecology for Agricultural Extension for new programmes and priorities to changing needs of agroecological and natural resource base with a view to proper planning and coordinated development of Technical Education (TE) system throughout the country, promotion of qualitative improvement of Technical Education in relation to planned quantitative growth, regulation and proper maintenance to norms and standards in the Technical Education system and for matters connected therewith. Technical Education includes the fields of Engineering, Technology, Architecture, Town Planning, Management, Pharmacy, Hotel Management and Catering Technology and Applied Arts and Crafts.

Indian Agricultural Research Institute, New Delhi Vision 2020 addresses the issues, particularly of basic and strategic research, strengthening of system research and integrated management of biotic and abiotic stresses, integrated management of soil water nutrients, post harvest technology and value addition, socio-economic studies and policy research and informatics. Opening of new course programmes, such as agricultural business management and plant genetic resources for participatory technology assessment and transfer for meeting the goal of national progress for sustainable and equitable growth of agriculture.

The earth, nature and human beings have existed for a long time. They must have survived many crises and cataclysmic events. What is so special about the current environmental crises? It is true that the earth, nature and man have survived for long. Earth have existed for 5 billion years, man for 3 to 5 million years and civilisation for 10000 years. Looking back over centuries, nature seems to have absorbed disturbances and stayed always in balance. The Rio Declaration on Environment and development listing 27 principles of sustainable development, Agenda 21, action plan for sustainable development in the 21st century the conservation of biological diversity that we have imbibed from our culture and education. The world works today will work tomorrow for happiness in consumption if economic growth is good to a critical mass of people. We may get begin managing our resources in a wise and sustainable way. Colleges in the purview of VGC network through the help and support of state governments.

Objective. To develop strong centres of education, mission oriented, fundamental and applied research around outstanding scientists of proven leadership in leading Agricultural Universities and Research institutes engaged in discipline of Agriculture, Horticulture, Agricultural Engineering, Animal Science, Fisheries, Natural Resources Management, Home Science and agricultural extension.

There are two main requirements for putting programmes into effect :

(1) Information. There is more information more readily available today than even before. However some essential information for living a sustainable lifestyle in either missing or distorted.

(2) Motivation. Information does not necessarily lead to action. The global economy, immensely powerful and difficult to change over night, the most fundamental and permanent change occurs when an individual adopts a new perspective through deep identification. There are powerful vested interests which oppose changing the *status quo* and change itself can be easy for many people, individuals, societies ultimately change through a combination of factors including circumstances, coercion, consciences, peer pressure, and idealism.

UGC chairman Nigavakar says good example and education are the only weapons against narrow-mindedness, be it communalism, casteism, or partyism.

The UGC faces tough challenges ahead as it goes about laying good rules for the functioning of varsities and colleges in India. UGC has dual role, one is plan for future and to do this in totality by looking at the nation's demands for educated human power. For an emerging country like India, higher education is a social as well as an economic infrastructure. Hence while planning this, theme has to be the focus of development. The other role is to ensure that quality education is being delivered to the students. To ensure this UGC has to set the standards and evolve a mechanism to maintain standards. One of the prime task of UGC is to provide funds for development of education and to use the latest tools of modern technology for virtually enhancement of academic infrastructure, strengthening of research and for improving the credibility and efficiency of administration. UGC is connecting each and every university in the country through the UGC network. This will create internet and internet connectivity for students, researches, teachers and managers of education. It will improve quality of teaching and learning as well as that of research in the universities.

HIGHER EDUCATION — EXPANSION AND OUTREACH

The nation is at the crossroads and any complacency and antiquated short-term thinking may not be without negative consequences. The nation has to overcome its weaknesses, take due caution on emerging threats, and capitalise on its strengths and opportunities. Masses are generally unaware of the real implications of new international developments. Nobody has ever come and will come forward to provide support on a platter without taking first into consideration in its own interests. In all its endeavours, the country has to give signal to the world at large that here lies an emerging economic power centre of the 21st century.

In the third world countries, the rural areas are the places where majority of the people live, pursuing the age-old traditional occupation like agriculture/cultivation. As the laboratory technology has not yet sufficiently percolated to the grass-root level of rural countryside, the people are not able to make good out of their profession. As the land is inelastic and the demand is ever growing on land with unfavourable land man ratio, to feed the hungry millions, the only way left out is to increase or multiply the productivity. With majority of the population settled in rural countryside, the development programmes should aim at generating income and employment to one and all. Access to education is a matter of utmost significance not only for the upliftment of women but also for the general betterment of society. Incidentally some of the programmes, with accent on women's participation, have indirectly helped women to earn while staying indoors without disturbing their normal household chores.

Concept of Development

The term 'development' is used to mean 'organising things' so as to change existing conditions in favour of a better state. There may be many variants of development drawing their nomenclature from the sphere of activity where the change is managed or the type of change or the 'method' how the desired change is attained. For several decades the term was used, solely, for economic change, inclusive of the conditions which affect economic betterment. The concept was later extended to its wider meaning to embrace 'changes' of political, social, cultural, technological, economic and also the psychological frame of society. In its current meaning 'development' is used to express animated change for reaping utmost human potential. Technically, development is the name of a 'policy' and its 'consequent programmes', designed to bring about a 'desired change' in social, economic, political, or technological spheres of life. It is concerned with the promotion of human capacities : physical or mental, to attain the cherished social goals.

Consolidate and institutionalise successes as sustainable and equitable alternatives. Slow pace of laudable success has hurried the field-based studies in torrential scale to attempt an answer for the failures in alleviation of poverty from the rural scene in spite of the rapid growth of output. Sociologists and political scientists have also tried their test-tablets to comprehend the strange situations of oxymoronic rural growth. Planners, as well as development enthusiasts have been frustrated by the collapse strategies of 'automatic trickle down effects' and consequent, 'spread effect'.

The present endeavour is intended to analyse the issues and highlight the prominent trends in Indian context, as a whole. The developmental trends have been picked up from the macro level perspective. The filtration frames the wider Indian experience in rural development and examines it in the frame of wide range of theoretical inter-relations already settled in Growth Theory. It draws considerably from historical evidences to reach the policy-making part of analysis.

DIVERSITY FOR LOCAL ACTION AND ULTIMATE ANSWER

Despite the occasional Hindu flavour, the core philosophy of Bastar's tribals remains charmingly untouched.

Life is friendship; to live to have friendship why should we quarrel? We should show mercy to everyone, starting with trees, the tribal might have added. For wasn't trees it sheltered Ram during his *Vanvas*? And which metaphorically, still shelter us today from the spiritual wastelands that threatens to engulf us.

Science attempts to define the nature of reality. Reality however, presents itself in variety of names and forms : Physical, mental and psychological realities; linguistic and mathematical reality. But science is yet to define physical reality conclusive... hence the quest continues....

If there are so many realities, what then is absolute reality? Spiritual Science or adhyatma is concerned with the understanding of this absolute reality which the Vedas call Brahman and which we refer as to God or paramatma.

The central focus in all the six Indian language systems namely Sankya, Yoga, Nyaya Visheshika, Purva Mimansa or Vedanta is to answer this question and present the experimental knowledge of absolute reality by perceiving pure joy everywhere through speech and action by expanding our "I"ness spanning the entire universe. By seeing oneself in all names and forms of objective reality and by believing in and discovering one's own and everyone else's infinite nature and infinite capabilities; being pure in body, mind and intellect. So to find God and have to find our own self. Ultimately reality presents itself as our pure and infinite self.

ESTABLISHMENT OF ASIAN CENTRE FOR HUMAN ECOLOGY

India was first among global community to have a national policy population. Today we strive for perfection in every field with the evolution of mind and intellect worldly knowledge has become easily accessible. So, we have achieved certain measures of excellence in the physical sciences but physical experience fails to connect with our true self to shoulder our education in India have collaborated with many Indian foreign Universities for helping them and designing the curriculum on environment at graduate and postgraduate levels. The idea behind is to search the grass-root level with the view to implement programmes at global level for making them worldly. Catch young for generation of eco-fragile biodiversity and making them aware of the need to protect our mother earth.

Sustainability is fundamentally an ethic that of reverence for all life forms and respect for their rights to exist to express themselves and evolve. An ethic is far more than a set of practices applicable to only one sphere of activity. Therefore, the sustainability ethic should inform not only our relationship to the environment but to all aspects of life and society. Nature works therefore it is necessary to understand and apply ecological principles in all spheres. Justice and equitable access to essential resources (clean air, water, food, shelter, education, health service etc.) is an inalienable right for all regardless of sex, social and economic status to act locally and think globally. Quality is more important than quantity, conservation than consumerism as within so without it is important to cultivate a life-enhancing inner perspective.

The act of wise living involves four steps : plant purposefully, prepare prayerfully, proceed positively and pursue persistently.

Mental setbacks are hinder to cope with than the physical because it makes people ineffective. They operate from the I "cant" rather than I "can" they operate from scarcity rather than abundance. They are rooted in poverty consciousness rather than in prosperity we have to learn the art of coming from abundance rather than from scarcity. Creativity happens in this space. In the international field, new concepts are emerging in the wake of the end of the cold war and advances in technology. Satellite systems that operate from low earth orbits are being planned with the prospects of providing mobile and communication links world-wide through hand-held and other portable terminals. Other development include the testing of single stage-to-rockets, the use of imagining radar to penetrate clouds and satellite monitoring of the delicate greenhouse equilibrium of the earth's atmosphere. On board space vehicle experiment continue to evaluate the capacity of the human system in space the scope of making new materials.

Ancient Indian astronomy has assumed that the sky extends to as much as-is illumined by the rays of the sun. The concept of Brahmand meaning the extraordinary big, was quite popular in work on cosmic phenomena. Though the space age offers unique opportunities to probe the sky from above the Earth's atmosphere, ground based telescopes continue to play a useful role. In India a big optical telescope the largest facility in Asia — scan the sky over the equator with the most modern equipment. It is designated and fabricated in India. A few civilisations who may be actually monitoring some of our television and broadcast programme may conclude that there is no intelligence on earth worthy of their attention! Even we try to contact other civilisations. Several scientists have called for urgent slips to preserve the diversity and beauty of our one and only home, the earth. The blue Jewel in black space needs to be protected from wanton destruction and pollution.

For a warrior, nothing is higher than a war against evil. There can be no security where there is fear. One has to abandon altogether the search for security, and reach out to the risk of living with arms. One has to court doubt and darkness as the cost of knowing. One needs a will stubborn in conflict, but always to total acceptance of every consequences of living and dying.

The art of getting what I like and liking what I get this, one should cultivate through spiritual practice. Most of us are searching for happiness. We search for happiness in the world of objects and things. However, we fail to appreciate that the world of objects can give us pleasure but not happiness. People do not see this distinction; hence they suffer in life happiness really exist within. The art of going within is one of the arts we have to learn. Once we discover the art of being happy within, then we will participate in the miracle called life. Once learn the art of dissociating ourselves from the ideas of misery we will see so much of joy around us. To come to the relief of the distressed and help the oppressed, act as amends and explanation of many sins. There can be no security where there is fear there is no such thing security. There never has been. But you do not participate in this battle against evil, you will be violating your Dharma and your honour.

Towards the Crises of Development

From the fact that 20% of population remains desperately poor even after several decades of international development aid. The indigenous people, children and women among the poor are under great stress in many countries of the earth.

To begin with, each of us should see the environmental crisis as a real one needing urgent action from us. We have to move from linear thinking systemic or circular thinking that recognises complex interactions and natural cycles in the world.

The first step in the ecological journey is to fall in love with the beauty of the planet. It shall be duty of every citizen of India to protect and improve the natural environment including forests, lakes, rivers, and wild-life and to have comparison for living creatures. The initial steps of care and protection can alone eventually change the appearance of community lands in a very positive way. The actual method for reclaiming "wasted" lands comprises five essential steps :

- Fencing.
- Soil water conservation.
- Introduction of pioneer species.
- Planting secondary species.
- Enhancement of soil life.

Water and energy are going to be the two most crucial determinants for the society world over — water for survival and energy for development. We one ancient nation and have acute stratification socially.

HUMAN ECOLOGY FOR GLOBALISATION

Humanity stands today at the head of new age of a large synthesis of knowledge to collaborate in bringing out concerted action for knowledge. In this new age, great cultural achievements of the past have to be recovered and enriched in the context of the contemporary advancement so that humanity can successfully meet the evolutionary and revolutionary challenges, and bring about a new type of humanity and society marked by integrated power of physical, emotional, dynamic, intellectual, ethical, aesthetic and spiritual potentialities for universal upliftment.

Frontiers of knowledge, age, therefore, bond to expand unimaginably and new researches will oblige humanities sciences, technologies and fire arts to arrive at new equations and new combinations. Development in communication information and technology will open up new and cost effective approaches for providing the reach of higher education for meeting the demands of explosion of information, fast changing nature of occupations and life long education.

India has been in the forefront of all global initiatives that have communicated in the philosophy of human ecology. The scientific expertise to increase the relevance of higher education by making courses more oriented. To enhance empowerment in human resource with special emphasis on education the disciplines of agri-business, biodiversity and environment, biotechnology, non-conventional energy system have been merged to make a unified field of Human ecology for systematic vision of the strategic issues like :

- Perspectives of higher education for community empowerment in human ecology.
- Education extension and outreach updating the clinics with special reference to Home Science.
- Prioritisation of research agenda in Agribusiness, Biodiversity and Environment, Biotechnology, Non-conventional Energy systems.
- Institutionalisation for action for Human Resource Development.

Preservation of the environment and conservation of researches such as fossil fuel and water is a matter of international concern. Action that threatened survival of various aspects of plants and animals, created renewed interest in ecology, the science concerned with interrelationships between organisms and environment both organic and inorganic.

The Meaning of Research

Human beings one unique products of their emotion and evolution. In contrast to other forms of animal life, their more highly developed nervous system has enabled them to develop sounds and symbols (letters and numbers) that make possible the communication and recording of their questions, observations, experiences and ideas. Over many countries, people began to develop what seemed to be plausible explanations. Attributing to the forces of nature to the working of supernatural powers, they believed that the gods, at their whims, manipulate the sun, stars, wind, rain, and lightning. The appearance of the medicine man or priest, who claimed special channels of communication with the gods, led to the establishment of a system of religious authority passed on from one generation to another.

It was only when people began to think systematically about thinking itself that the era of logic began. The first systematic approach to reasoning attributed to the Aristotle and Greeks, was the deductive method. This deductive method, moving from the general assumption to the specific application made an important contribution to the development of modern problem solving. But it was not fruitful in arriving at new truths.

Centuries later Francis Bacon advocated dissect observation of the phenomena, arriving at the conclusions or generalisation through the evidence of many individual observations. The method of inductive reasoning proposed by Bacon, a method new to the field of logic but widely used by scientists of his time.

The deductive method of Aristotle and the inductive method of Bacon were fully integrated in the work of Charles Darwin in the nineteenth century failed to lead to satisfactory theory of man's development. The concept of the struggle for existence in Thomas Malthus suggested that natural selection explains the origin of different species of animals. This hypothesis provided a needed focus on his investigations. The major promise of the older deductive method was gradually replaced by an assumption or hypothesis that was subsequently tested by the collection and logical analysis of data. This deductive-inductive method was now recognised as an example of scientific approach. Many students of research rightly feel that problem identification is one of the most difficult and most crucial steps of the research process.

RESEARCH AND DEVELOPMENT COOPERATION

Science and technology has made great strides and has brought much material wealth within the reach of mankind. This has led to improvement in quality of life, enhanced physical standard of life, lasting happiness and the resultant progress. This quality of life is dependent upon the values followed in a home. Home is responsible for the proper development of individual personality. It inspires one to adopt necessary skills and attitudes for harmonious family and community living.

Home Science is the field of knowledge and service primarily concerned with strengthening family life through :

- Education the individual for family living.
- Improving the services and goods used by families.
- Conducting research to discover the changing needs of individuals, family and finding ways and means to satisfying them.
- Improving community, national, world conditions favourable for family living.

Home Science is the education which makes life meaningful for all. It is unique subject wherein one gets an opportunity to apply knowledge in day-to-day life experience. The study involves the development of individuals efficient management of resources and contributing gainfully to the community of home science included in the curriculum are Food and Nutrition, Child Care and Development, Home Management, Textile and Clothing.

Food and Nutrition for Self and Family

Food is one of the important basic needs of the very existence of mankind. The human beings made from food. Food can be defined as "any nutritive material of plant or animal origin which when taken into human body meets the needs for growth, maintenance, tissue repair and work". Food cán be defined as anything solid or liquid when consumed digested assimilated in the body. Food is made up of small chemical units called nutrients. The molecular clock at which mutation charges accumulate in a certain type and is not involved in adaptation to environment.

Using fossil molecular and other types of evidence, biologists have determined the evolutionary relationships known in general the history of life's diversity. Many organisms have evolved various solutions to the same fundamental problems. All materials must acquire energy, protect themselves and reproduce. The amount of biomass was enormous, trees underwater do not decompose well, and their partially decayed remains because covered by sediment. Sedimentary rocks applied pleasure and the organic material became coal, a fossil fuel. Geological upheavals raised the deposits to the level we are today, without these ancient forests our life today would be far different than it is because they helped and bring about our industrialised society. Individual trade and economic relation debt issues and so forth, the central question first, in what ways does. The Netherlands contribute to strengthening research capacity in developing countries? And, second, how does Netherlands perform with regards to development issues? To consider, how development related research can perform for local action in India?

Development related research has many forms. Feasibility studies or evaluation research differ certainly in approach and content from anthropological field work or agricultural experiments. Research not only involves scientific research at research institutions and universities, but also research in planning office, statistical bureaus and other institutes, pure science, strategic science and applied science and often distinguished. Most development related research has both pure and applied elements — good quality development related research in terms of quality, cooperation, continuity, and management of research programmes, preparation of research programmes takes a great deal of time. Funds should be available to adequate preparation in which researches and policy makers from developed countries should participate in the developing countries to the reinforcement of the local research infrastructure for interdisciplinary research approach for long-term cooperation on an institutional basis with sufficient organisational flexibility for upgradation of personnel and on dissecting biotechnology research to local issues and problems.

The role of universities as dynamic centre coming at promoting active interplay between dynamic, scientific productive and political communities. The economic and political crisis in this large geographical region severely limits this interplay. Foreign support may play an important role in alleviating this situation. Cooperation agreement should be carried out on the basis of respectful dialogue between priority areas, including both long-term capacity building and medium term, result oriented plans, should include different fields of science. The task ahead are immense and there are no simple answer to these problems may be of utmost importance in cooperative research programmes on a permanent basis in donor countries.

GLOBALIZATION AND QUANTITY TRANSNATIONAL EDUCATION

The boundaries have shifted to take on a order scale social context. What is needed in more socially sensitive epistemology that includes the 'soft' visions of science (including the explicit involvement of people, and social and cultural aspects) and its 'hand' body of knowledge. Non-scientists, accounts of scientific events and experiences are proliferating and while this is unpopular among scientists. Scientists have lost their authority to define for society the nature of reality in respect of the natural world. At the same time, their ability to intervene and manipulate that world is increasing. The balance of scientific authority in relation to different interests and values in an issue to be constantly addressed and re-evaluated. Discovery, and actions arising from it are now almost instantaneous.

In creating novelty, scientists create uncertainty. This creates fear, which has to be managed. Scientists should embrace this rather than seeing it as a threat to their existence. A new concept is needed to describe the public space within which science and society, the market and politics interact. The coming into being and the expansion of a new world force. These include the aiming of the loam global economy. The expansion of transitional links among economic units in ways that have created new ways of collective decision making, the development of supernational institutions and in the intensification of transactional communications and creation new regional orders that globalisation is the intensification of world's social relations linking distant localities so that what occurs in one locality is determined by the events occurring miles away. However, owing to multidimensional characteristics of globalisation process, globalisation also effect science, technology, finance, communication, education, culture, and politics. It is important to mention the influence of globalisation on education sector especially on the universities linked to the quality and reorientation of their educational systems and to the formation of human resources. Competitiveness means to incorporate the technical process of productive activities. Thus the education system is general especially the universities must play a very role that at present by outstanding researchers and intellectuals the instruments that would allow for new challenges without changing the current educational system to analyse the nature of impacts of globalisation on the educational system to understand some of the multiple and complex effects of globalisation of educational policy and institutions.

Globalisation influences employment, a fundamental aim at every level of education. The new global economy requires workers capable of learning quickly and who periodically, during their active lines, will re-enter in the education system. The workers should be able to confront severe competition from other groups of international workers. Political aspects in defining national policies, considering the external demands of transitional institutions. The situation is very similar to that faced by the international economic sector in which important supernational institutions have been created to coordinate and regulate such activities. However, although international conflicts have increased the political field (crime, terrorism, perturbation, environmental problems etc.) no solid institutions exists for facing these problems efficiently through a real global vision.

Cultural Aspects

Global change in culture are having considerable effect on educational policies, practices, and institutions. Particularly in the advanced industrial societies multiculturalism has a special meaning in global context. How, indeed, can the capacity to live together with different social groups in the same society, be extended towards a global context in which the level of difference is even higher, the interdependence and sense of interest and the concept of affiliation, more abstract or indirect? How can education teach students to correctly envisage the meaning of local, regional and national while understanding the cause of transitional conflicts? How does one introduce and secure the vision of a global culture while preparing and consolidating one's own national culture?

The Neo-liberal Agenda

In terms of education Burbules and Terreo (2000) evoke the idea particularly implemented by bilateral, multilateral and international organisation is being translated into educational agenda that privileges or imposes policies regarding evaluation, financing standards, teachers training curriculum instructions and evaluations. Owing to these pressures additional studies on possible local and national responses are required so as to strengthen public education in order for it to achieve a balance between the strong international requirements that it must meet and the needs and conditions of the respective natural education system.

Virtualisation of Universalities and Globalisation

While globalization represents a powerful world force, one that is external to the different social and educational sectors on which it exerts a certain influence, virtualisation refers to an internal transformation process affecting institutions and educational processes by which to better achieve the objectives of the latter. Virtualisation is both a process and a result of treatment and communication by computers and data information and knowledge. Virtualisation particularly contributes to the making of important transformations and innovations in the educational sector, particularly in telematic technologies. It has become a fundamental support to stimulate the extension of globalization but also to facilitate and support its function in different areas of knowledge and different human activities.

Network of Networks *i.e.*, the Internet. It is worth mentioning that these new educational developments require a close relationship between technology and pedagogy. Internet is the society, it expresses the social processes, social internets, social values and social institutions. A global dimension is its global character, which makes it global, with an almost instantaneous communication, and a possible interaction.

As a result of these new ways of learning and the recent demands of globalisation, open and distance modalities learning and virtual universalities, globalisation universalities and corporate universalities are giving extraordinary importance throughout the world.

Globalisation of Agriculture

The impact of globalisation and liberalisation on the agricultural sector likely to be equally unfavourable. Globalisation would lead to corporatisation of agriculture and would cause dispeasantisation and reduction of labour absorption. The changing face of this country in 21st century shall be determined by way we handle the side effects of globalisation process. We should take pro-active approach on these issues and develop our own package of non-tariff barriers based on considerations of environment and food security.

Food security today is a function of purchasing power. It is best measured in terms of million person years of jobs, rather than million tonnes of grains. Therefore to ensure that jobs for Indians in the over-riding concern in designing our agricultural research and production strategies and trade policies to safeguard the livelihood security of the rural and urban poor and the ecological security for : restructuring and improve agricultural and rural infrastructure in education, sanitary and phytosanitary measures, this will call for substantial new investment in post harvest technology. We must take care of horticulture and aquaculture — both provide opportunities for improving restriction security at home and export earning abroad. The key constraint relates to poor quality control and inadequate investment in post harvest storage processing, packaging and transportation.

The eco-development technology revolution which permits the blending of the best in traditional knowledge and technology with the frontiers for uncommon opportunity. India's strong institutional and human resource base in science and technological transformation of agriculture paving the way for an evergreen revolution. The hallmark of its well structured scientific programme covering all relevant aspects relating to the theme, such as (i) improving productivity and alleviating poverty, (ii) post harvest processing and value addition, (iii) managing resources for increased term sustainability, (iv) complementing new technologies with traditional knowledge, (v) nutritional needs for human health, (vi) livestock for nutrition and financial well-being, (vii) environmental and agricultural development and (viii) public policies for food nutrition and environmental security. In addition to (i) science and technology, (ii) GMOs and Genomics, (iii) now food secure in India, (iv) WTO and Indian agriculture to the outstanding contribution made by the scientists in various basic and applied fields especially agriculture regarding magnitude of the problem and the possible approaches and strategies to address comprehensively expected that globalisation of agriculture will made required public awareness for their participatory role to make India a food nutrition and environmentally secured nation.

Social Development in a Global Context

It raises many questions and offers mere hypothesis than provides answers. Its objective is to take advantage of some of the best minds in and on India as well as solicit reactions from other Indian experts, to some basic indicators of performance and their possible explanation. To set the stage of developing a better understanding of the 'levers' for accelerating India's socio-economic performance and help India to truly join India's socio-economic performance and the possible explanation. For drawing on a number of comparative data sources and research studies on various aspects of development.

China has faired much better across the broad spectrum of performance indicators, including overall and per capita GDP growth, population growth as well, India has lagged behind; in progress on poverty reduction, adult and particularly female literacy, infant mortality, health and nutrition agricultural production and productivity and reveal non-farm employment. China has clearly been more agile and skilful in adjusting its old command and control approach to the use of market forces and incentives to 'get things done' be they in the economic, social and environmental sectors, despite a long history of markets and private entrepreneurship in modern times, India has been slower in dismantling controls.

Apart from a strong natural ambition about its position in the world, the desolation has occurred despite the lack of a 'western style' democracy *i.e.*, in the form of free and frequent multiparty national and state level decentralised responsibilities and accountabilities are well worth investigating further learn lesson, despite the social barriers in India to fill the wide gap that exists in its social economic performance *vis-à-vis* its comparators.

Reemergence of Ecological Perspective

Concern increased over the effects of human actions on the environment, including widespread pollution, which endangered human health. Actions that threatened survival of various species of plans and animals created renewed interest in ecology the science concerned with interrelationships between organisms and the environment, both organic and inorganic. Conceptualising the phenomena from a holistic system perspective emphasising interdependence and connections between seemingly disparate parts of a whole because widespread. The term ecosystem cause into use and the ecological roots of home economics were rediscovered. 'Ockology' the German word that was in the use in 1892 Richards had announced to the world "let Ockology be henceforth the science of (our) normal lives...the worthiest of all the applied sciences which teaches the principles on which to found... healthy and happy life. Richard saw home ecology as means to improve people's lives and environment. This should be done in the home and family where basic needs are met and human character is formed. Women were the major focus of home ecology. Like ecology an ecological perspectives Michigan State University (MSU) rediscovered the ecological basis of home economics. The family as an ecosystem.

Frequently researchers are interested in complex problems, the full investigation of which requires a series of studies. This approach is known as programmatic research and usually combines the inductive and deductive methods in a continuously alternating pattern. The researcher may begin with number of observations from which a hypothesis is derived (inductive reasoning). Then the researcher proceeds deductively to determine the consequences that one to be expected if the hypothesis is true. Data are then collected through the inductive method to verify, reject, or modify the hypothesis. Thus the researcher is continually moving back and forth between the inductive methods of observation and data collection and the deductive method of hypothesising the anticipated consequences of events.

Science. The term science may be thought of an approach to the gathering of knowledge rather than field of subject matter. Science, put simply consists of two primary functions : (1) the development of theory and (2) the testing of substantive hypotheses that are deduced from theory. The scientist, therefore, is engaged in the use, modification and/or creation of theory. The scientists begins with a set of ideas that direct the effort and with the goal that entails the development of testing theory.

By attempting to apply the rigorous, systematic observation and analysis used in physical and biological sciences to area of social behaviour, the social science have grown and have advanced humanity's knowledge of itself. The field of anthropology, economics, education, political science, psychology and social anthropology have become recognised as science by any authorities. To the extent that these fields are founded on scientific methodology, they are sciences. Some reject the concept still defining science in terms of subject matter rather than methodology. Historically their position can be readily explained. Since scientific methods were first used in investigation of physical phenomena, tradition has identified science with physical world. Only within the last century has the methodology of science in terms of subject matter rather than methodology.

Because human value is so complex it is much more difficult to develop sound theories of human behaviour than to predict occurrences in the physical world, research on human subjects has numerous problems.

Today we live in a world that has benefited greatly by the

progress made by the biological and physical sciences, infant mortality is decreasing, and life expectancy continues to increase. Automation and computerisation touch every aspect of our lives reducing our physical labour and increasing our leisure time. The splitting of the atom, space travel and developments in the field of electronics such as the laser, superconductivity and silicon chip, promise improvements and adventures that are beyond the scope of most people imagination science for meeting the challenges of a college science course. In expensive supplement offers students practical guidelines for recycline and conserving energy.

Science Popularisation

Man is an important element of the environmental complex. His activities growing population, industrial and human settlements, social rèligious and economic set ups are posing newer ecological problems. Understanding his ecological role the anthropologists, sociologists, psychologists, economists, demographers supply data to persons working on human ecology. To be acquainted with various disciplines of physical and biological sciences in order to get integrated picture of the environmental complex in relation to organic world. In order to quantify his data an ecologist has to collect information which could be subjected to mathematical formulation for precise communication to other working in the field.

Indian culture is deeply rooted in two different but intricate traditions. In India rethinking has begun. More and more of the scientists, artists, scholars have started looking into their rich traditions. A large number of NGO's and voluntary agencies have now entered the value education in India. Some of them have evolved innovative programmes.

Home science, in reality is deeply and closely related to life. A model home science curriculum world, therefore, care to cover all such factors, fields, and interests which affects a person's development, his life, in the family and in the community. A change to meet the challenges and opportunities of today's higher education enter. Today higher education enterprise an immensely broad based discipline full of rich academic vocational and professional elements which need to be exploited to the fullest extent in future educational needs.

Professional courses would provide under spectrum of experience of graduating students hence sufficient weightage have to be given to make students professions and befitted in development departments for the effective enterprise development. We have to be risk taking and innovative in view of the dynamic changes of global liberalisation and making strategies and knowledge that improves daily lives of current and future generation.

To develop proficiency in students for planning, organising and evaluating rural development programmes especially programmes for youth and women to be supported by field work and field projects examining the family as a significant ecosystem.

Management programmes explores design and function in conjugation with technology, user satisfaction and perception.

Relation with neighbouring countries and high on operand. However "India needs to focus on economic development now".

ORGANISE NATURALLY FOR BEST RESULTS IN STUDIES IN HIGHER EDUCATION

Science Attempts to Define the Nature of Reality

We make large promises to avoid making small presents. Those who are quick to promise are generally slow to perform globalisation for local action.

Biological systems are adaptable, resilient, and capable of generating perpetualness. Natural systems not only change, they change how they change. The challenge today for our organisations is to appreciate the "Strengths of natural systems, and design and operate to embrace their logics for globalisation of agriculture".

On course work, than the final thesis Ph.D thesis is an area in need of further research and development.

Man is an important element of the environmental complex. His activities, growing population, industrial and urban settlement, social religious and economic setups are posing newer ecological problems. Understanding his ecological role the anthropologists, sociologists, psychologists, economists, demographers supply data to persons working on human ecology. To be acquainted with various disciplines of physical and biological sciences in order to get integrated picture of the environmental complex in relation to the organic world. In order to quantify his data an ecologist has to collect information, which could be subjected to mathematical formulation for precise communication to others working in the field. Indian culture is deeply rooted in two different but intricate traditions. In India awakening has begun. More and more of the scientists, artists, scholars have started looking into their rich traditions, for large synthesis of knowledge. It has to collaborate in bringing out concerted action for knowledge, universal upliftment and lasting peace and unity. For humanity to successfully meet the evolutionary and revolutionary challenges of contemporary advancement — great cultural achievements of the past must be revised and enriched to bring about a new type of humanity. A society marked by integrated power of physical, emotional, dynamic, intellectual, clinical, aesthetic and spiritual potentialities.

Frontiers of knowledge are henceforth bound to expand unimaginably and new researchers will oblige humanities, societies, technologies and fine arts to arrive at new equations and new combinations. Development in communication, information and technology will open new and cost effective approaches for enhancing the reach of higher education to meet the demands of fast changing nature of employment.

India has been in the forefront of all global initiative that have communicated the philosophy of *Human Ecology*. The scientific expertise to increase the relevance of higher education by making courses in use career oriented. To enhance empowerment in human resources with special emphasis on education the disciplines of agribusiness, bio-diversity and environment, biotechnology, non-conventional energy system like a perspective of higher education for community empowerment. To meet the challenges imposed by new economic and social order, and improve the quality of life to make a positive impact on the immediate society to which they belong. Adequate field experience in academic programmes coupled with practical work experience combined with outstanding teaching and strong foundation in applied and social sciences which will provide graduate students with the vision on the study of behavioural aspects implied with the interrelationship of the biotic components with the practical application.

Community resource management concerns for the management of resources for the development of needs of the family and community for social equity and people's participation in a tree interactive process. Large number of NGO's and Voluntary agencies have now centred the value of education in India. Some of them have evolved innovative programmes.

Home Science in reality is deeply and closely related to life. A model home science curriculum would, therefore, are to cover all such factor fields, and interests which affects a person's development, his life, in the family and in the community. A change to meet the challenges and opportunities of today's higher education centre. Today higher education enterprise, an immensely broad based discipline full of rich academic, vocational and professional elements, which need to be exploited to the fullest extent in future educational needs.

Professional courses would provide wide spectrum of experience to graduating students hence sufficient weightage have to be given to make students professions and befitted in development departments for the effective enterprise development. We have to be at risk taking and innovative in view of dynamic changes of global liberalisation and marketing strategies and knowledge that improves daily lives of current and future generations.

To develop proficiency in students for planning, organizing, and evaluating rural development programmes especially programmes for youth and women to be supported by field work and field projects examining the family as a significant ecosystem.

Management programmes explores design and function in conjuction with technology user satisfaction and perception.

The university community should make special effort to increase the relevance of higher education by making the courses career oriented by developing interdisciplinary knowledge and skills for research, extension programmes to outreach the communities. It must empower human resource with special emphasis on educating the disciplines of Agribusiness, Biodiversity and Environment, Biotechnology, Non Conventional Energy System, to raise unified field of *Human Ecology* for community empowerment.

A living organism and environment surrounding it cannot be separated from each other. The system arising from the interaction of a biological community with its non-living surroundings is called ecosystem as an ecological unit that has both structure and function. The structure includes an analysis of biotic communities living in a habitat and the physical features of the environment, including edaphic factors, nutrition, and climatic conditions.

Man's relationship with his environment now occupies a major place among the problems. Therefore, it is necessary to demonstrate the scientific programmes in a way towards meeting the safe and sustainable future to mankind.

To respond to human needs the main thrust will be directed towards the activities which are socially beneficial and economically viable; like farm, off-farm and non-farm sectors.

The national agricultural technology project has made stride under three major components :

1. Agro-ecosystem research,
2. Innovation in technology dissemination, and
3. Organisation and management system.

Let us be set up for balancing higher education for community service :

- For the hope of a better and safe future needed for the management of human and environment to improve people's life and environment in the view of rapid technological advancement and community belonging to the poorest of the poor families.
- Earth eco-system research: To mobilise community support in understanding, promoting and enabling better child care through education.
- To provide supportive services through education, women's development programmes such as safe drinking water, environmental sanitation, and preschool education below 6 years.

- Nutrition and health education by the community, the referral services in expectant and nursing mothers, and women in age group of 15 to 45 years.
- For institution strengthening and linkages for research capacity building in collaborative programmes in research and training.
- To promote participation in education to bring into sharp focus the central role of human development, into poverty education.
- To promote behaviour studies with practical application of knowledge across the domains of research, outreach and international programmes.

Institutionalisation of Extension Curriculum

The colleges have to become a catalyst in the future learning society, a centre of education and development for the students and the community through both formal and non-formal means. The students would use the community as social laboratory for their practical, moral and attitudinal education and learn by working in and serving the community.

The extension activities be incorporated in the undergraduate courses in foundation courses, applied courses, community service, project work, and in basic or core courses.

Institutionalisation of extension needs academic acceptance which is automatically ensured when the activities enter at a stage of studies and research which enlarges our understanding and contributes to knowledge. Extension activities can enter into research through :

- Project work or field-based dissertation at undergraduate and postgraduate levels.
- Postgraduate courses with research component related to extension activities in the form of case studies.
- M.Phil and Ph.D as well as post-doctoral programmes.

It is essential to transform some selected colleges into Community Colleges. They should be given complete academic autonomy for innovations and experimentation.

Radio, T.V., Video-Audio tapes, VCR, VBCP, etc. are the modern electronic communication media that are reaching slowly every village and house. Colleges can play a great role in organising and maintaining the community education centres and make them very effective centres of extensions.

Universities and the Adult Education Programme

It is within the ability and structural conduciveness of the colleges and universities to assume effectively the role of resource centres for adult education for research, orientation, material development, and evaluation, etc. The colleges are best suited to be developed as local resource centres for adult education as they are the knowledge centres with community of scholars and students pursuing knowledge in different disciplines. For post-literacy and continuing education programmes, the colleges and universities are the most agencies to be involved. Colleges and universities can also be effectively used for the monitoring and evaluation support to be given to the adult education programmes.

Rural Development

Except a few institutions which have taken keen interest in rural development, the universities in general have ignored the aspect. The Agricultural Universities have had a limited focus and perspective of covering only few aspect of rural development and seldom treated its rural development activities with an integrated approach.

The Universities have to seriously plan low cost alternatives in upgrading knowledge levels, employable skills, and attitudes conducive to people's participation in development. While the Universities visualise a co-ordinating/initiating role in this regard, colleges as grass-root units of higher education can undertake meaningful field work within the context of a scheme/programme.

The Department of Adult, Continuing Education and Extension could become a nodal agency to act as a bridge between the departments of studies and the rural communities by promoting programmes of continuing and community education in every branch of learning with emphasis on the following functions :

- Creation and dissemination of knowledge.
- The development of human resources.

- The management and implementation of projects.
- Creating usable literature for integrated rural development.

Environmental Education

The role of education in the ambit of environmental problems and opportunities is a crucial one. Environmental Education should be integrated as part of the system of formal education at all levels to provide necessary knowledge understandings, values and skills.

Establishment of Asian Centre for Human Ecology ăt Delhi University

To generate awareness and to enable handling the problems of environment, the education system needs to be revamped. The curricula could be horizontal embracing all the related subjects or vertical dialing with one package covering the ecological social cultural and other aspects of particular problem, it is inherently interdisciplinary in character. It should be relevant to the problems at home and must help learners to acquire knowledge values and skills necessary to help solve the problems. Environmental education involves learning from the environment as well as about the environment and require changes in the established methods of teaching especially in formal education. With the adoption of this problem oriented and action oriented approach environment becomes a continual and forward looking affair.

Objectives. To create a comprehensive data base.

To strengthen the use of gender analysis in research and technology development to ensure that women's as well as men's agriculture enterprises are fully considered for defining research programmes and setting priorities. To develop training modules and imparting training and publication of manuals for sensitising gender related issues in research programmes and policy development :

- To develop and test women specific models of technology transfer that are to be promoted through regular extension agencies by collaborating with SAUs/ ICAR institutes.

- To promote women specific technology for reducing drudgery on women in forming operations including post harvest and home management.
- To provide leadership and sponsor training programmes in order to strengthen the knowledge and skill related to gender implications, informing system approach for researchers and extension personnel and to provide consultancy service within and outside the country on women specific programmes for research/projects and development.
- To prepare video films and other publicity material on improved equipments/technologies and allied activities for extension work. To establish the Asian Centre for Human Ecology at Delhi University, has multidisciplinary faculty and experienced and trained manpower in the area of rural development, human resource development, conservation of ecosystem. The faculties of Arts and Social Sciences and Mathematical Sciences offer Bachelor of Art, B.A. Vocational studies, Bachelor of Commerce, Bachelor of Library and information science. And faculty of science in Home science, Nursing, and science and pharmacy, the faculty of Music and fine arts offer Bachelor of Arts, (Hons.) in Music, Fine Arts, painting, sculpture, applied art, print making, photography, History of art. The other faculty of education and faculty of technology all offer Bachelor degree examinations and degrees recognised by the Delhi University. However, the certificate diplomas in the faculty of science/Arts/social sciences and Mathematical sciences and postgraduate diploma course in Tourism and postgraduate diploma in Book Publishing and international marketing. One year postgraduate certificate and post control and analytical methods in chemistry and biochemistry, health education, immunology and allergy, medical radio-diagnosis etc.

The diploma course in health education under the faculty of Medical Sciences shall be under the Dean of Faculty of medical sciences. Every candidate seeking admission to diploma course in health education shall have the Master's degree in selected social sciences (*i.e.*, psychology/sociology/anthropology/social work/economics/political science or education or nursing from recognised universities with at least one year's experience in community health welfare programme or teaching in social/biological sciences/physical education/home science. Preference will be given to those candidates who are in service.

Women, Environment and Development

An attempt is made to outline women's role in the management of their environment and the impact of policies, or the lack of integrated and ecologically sound policies, on their work roles and status. In this context, government and NGO responses to ecological needs and therefore related women's needs briefly reviewed.

Gender Justice for Progress

A study of the process and factors that have shaped the progress of the status of woman, reveals a deliberate and organic relationship between emancipation of women and the true facets of development. A brief survey of the areas of women's health, education, economic status and social and political empowerment indicates that nation's prosperity is directly proportional to the progress of women.

Women's Health

The health of Indian women is intricably related to the socio-economic status of the household and their age and kinship/marital status within the households. Given the predominantly patriarchal set-up, women and girls get a lesser share in the intra-household distribution of health goods and services, compared to men and boys. However, in the intra-households distribution of labour, women get the major share of economic, procreative and family responsibility. Due to the competing demands on their time and energy as well as their socialisation, women tend to neglect their health. Statistics indicate that education and employment of women have resulted in reduction of fertility rates. Female literacy postpones child birth, and helps in fewer and healthier children.

Education for Women

In India, the gap between boys and girls participation in education is the quintessential symbol of the girl-child.

To generate awareness and to enable handling the problems of environment, the educational system needs to be revamped. The curricula could be horizontal embracing all the related subjects, or vertical dealing with one package. The relevance of the two approaches will depend on the particular situation ensuring side by side that there is no mismatch between developmental priorities.

Continuing education in the area of environmental sciences and technology to cater the group of teachers, scientists, technologists and others who had no opportunity to learn about environment during their school and college days is becoming popular.

The educational process in this regard underlines certain stages :

- Awareness supported by information (both descriptive and scientific),
- Appreciation.of activities by others in terms of environmental advocacy and action,
- Formulation of the stage of the local environmental problem,
- Initiating preventive action immediately, and
- Participation in the process of area-development and people-development planning.

Towards this end, the following base is required :

- Base data relating to each environmental concern;
- Basic data about specific development plans;
- Development models/perspectives guiding such plans; and
- Information pertaining to the implementational agencies/ personnel.

Legal Literacy

The cause of legal literacy for the people as a meaningful extension activity by the university system has been championed through a process of internal collaboration between departments of adults, continuing education and extension and the law colleges and external collaboration with various governmental agencies and social action groups.

The success of the traditional legal service programme depends upon at least on two factors :

- The person affected should be able to realise that the problem he faces is a legal problem and that a lawyer can help him.
- He must know where he can get such legal help.

The above two preconditions are markedly absent in our country and their absence would render any traditional legal service programme ineffective and deprive it of meaning and utility.

Need of the Hour

- Short-term continuing education programmes dealing with specific aspects of law relevant to social, economic and political aspects of individual lives.
- Utilising existing curricular provisions to initiate profiles of injustice/victimisation.
- Setting up curriculum/learning materials, writers' groups to modify existing biases against the poor and oppressed.
- Study groups of experts examining existing development programmes as also persistent and recurrent problems (structural injustice) like floods, droughts, etc. and identifying legal aspects of implementation of social and economic development provision.
- Taking up socio-legal surveys and initiating socio-economic and legal action.

Out of six hundred and eighty-four million men and women in this country, only a very small number of persons are already aware of the laws. Even if the persons who can easily afford to purchase legal know-how are also discounted, it will still mean conscientisation of about five hundred million persons.

RACISM

The natural seminar on Racism in New Delhi on 11 August 2001 made some suggestions and views that emerged increasing

OVERVIEW OF WOMEN'S INTERFACE WITH THE ENVIRONMENT AND RELATED CONCERNS

Resource/Environment Problem	Women's Interface with resource	Impact of resource degradation/ environment problem and policy	Other issues
(1)	(2)	(3)	(4)
Rural Context			
Croplands	Most rural women involved in agricultural activities either as wage labour, unpaid labour or supervisors of agricultural activity. Predominant role in terms of both number of activities and time spent. Women usually perform unskilled activities entailing greater drudgery.	Increase in women labours and decrease in women cultivators. Reduced availability of crop waste and animal waste as fuel and fodder with the green revolution technology. Increased demand for wage labour with irrigated agriculture. Increased work burden for marginal/small cultivators, households with irrigated agriculture.	Gender differentials in wage earning. Marginalised from extension services. Negligible access to land and credit.
Common Lands	High dependence for fodder, fuel and food.	Erosion of rights and benefits with change in ownership and management. Decrease availability of fodder, fuel and food and increased work pressure. Adverse impact on livestock maintenance.	

(1)	(2)	(3)	(4)
Forests	Gathering fuelwood & forest produce. Sale of firewood. Production. Management in Plantations. Predominant role in shifting cultivation.	Decreased availability of products for domestic consumption and income generation. Increased investment in time and effort for collection of products. Fall in tribal women's economic role and status.	Exploitation in terms of returns from MFP collection. Absence of processing technology and marketing infrastructure to maximize returns on MFP.
Water	Principal collectors of drinking water. Limited visible role in water management for irrigation.	Increased workload and drudgery on account of dried up and polluted water sources.	Complete neglect of Women's knowledge relating to water quality and needs.
Urban Context			
Deteriorating urban development		Higher exposure to slum environment and therefore greater susceptibility.	To related problems.
Urban/Rural Context Pollution		Women affected differently or disproportionately on account of the activities they perform which increases their exposure to pollutants or due to their biological functions.	

the level of literacy and awareness led to a better understanding of rights thereby reducing if not totally eliminating any form of discrimination. It was also opined that there was a need to increase the capacities of the people so that they know that their rights and duties are. Though untouchability has been abolished in the country it is still widespread in villages. Caste based exploitation becomes an instrument for the cause of legal literacy for people as a meaningful extension activity through a process of internal collaboration between departments of adults, continuing education and extension and the law colleges.

Trafficking in women is one of the worst form of violation of human rights — a form of modern day slavery where the victim is subjected to violence. Violation of personal integrity and total humiliation without any hope. The victim of such devastating violence may also end up with life threatening HIV/AIDS on a lifetime of human and personality disintegration. Trafficking is thus a violation of several human rights — among them, the very right to life, the right to liberty and security of person, the right to freedom from torture or cruelty, inhuman and degrading treatment, the right to home and family, the right to education and proper employment, the right to health care — everything that makes for a life with dignity.

Today, trafficking in women and children is one of the fastest growing areas of national and international criminal activity. It has created a complex criminal network at times, with the patronage of those in power. Lack of suitable laws and law enforcement machinery add to the problem. The term "trafficking" is most often used interchangeable with "prostitution". It is not widely known that prostitution, though at the case of trafficking is not the only form of trafficking, and even made children in addition to female children can be and are being trafficked by various nefarious purposes.

The problem of trafficking in women and children has received significant media coverage over the years. But the debate on its social, legal and political aspects is still at the initial stage. The folder attempts academics, NGOs, National/ State Human Rights Institutions, civil servants, lawyers, media and UN agencies to bring forth various aspects of trafficking —

its forms the estimates, the causes, the consequences the *modus operandi* and role of national human rights commission (NHRC). The contents should in no way regarded as exploratory to indicate areas where much work needs to be done; proper data needs to be gathered and solutions need to be debated; worked out and made operational to eliminate caste-based discrimination by civilised society by increasing the level of literacy for better understanding the rights; addressing the issues of poverty, empowering the women in eliminating the caste based exploitation. So that caste being local problem could use vehicle of education to climb up the ladder of respectability and take up the issues and raising in international fame. When people form all castes should be encouraged in forming their view against racism.

The relevance to the issues of children living in a world with HIV/AIDS. It has changed the world in which all children live. Research has pointed out that women and children are increasingly becoming infected, with the majority of new infections in many parts of the world taking place in young people between the ages of 15 and 24. Younger children are predominantly infected and died world-wide, since the beginning of the epidemic infected by HIV positive mothers. Who are not aware of their infection and transmit the virus to the children before or during birth or through breast-feeding.

Adolescents are also highly vulnerable to HIV/AIDS and more so because their early sexual experiences often take place without access to proper information. The epidemic has also increased victimisation of children living in particularly different circumstances who are at a greater risk to infection, which in time leads to stigmatisation and greater discrimination. HIV/AIDS is often seen primarily as a medical problem, while the holistic rights entered approach is more appropriate to tackle the much broader range of issues involved. Promotion and adaptation at national level of approaches inspired by the international guidelines of HIV/AIDS and human rights jointly issued by the office of United Nations high commissioner for Human Rights and the joint United Nation programmes on HIV/AIDS. States, programmes and agencies of the United Nation system as well as NGOs should contribute to the dissemination and implementation of guidelines. National human right commission in partnership with the national aid control organisation, societies, etc. to take up a right-based response to the HIV/AIDS epidemic within the country in close collaboration with civil society.

Human dignity is the quintessence of human rights. Trafficking of women and children both male and female is, for several nefarious activities. Prostitution, drug trafficking, organised crime and begging are some of them. Adoption of child and has become a mode of trafficking. Right of child universally acknowledged and also assumed in the constitution of India, recognise the 'right of development' as a basic right of every child. This requires rigid implementation of convention rights, on enabling environment which protects children from all kinds of discrimination and exploitation and the ending of social evils, such as child marriage, child labour. Coordinated action between parent and community and state is necessary. The information set to inform the society the magnitude of evil and mode of combating in societies involvement in the most effective means of combating social evil.

Trafficking encompasses all of the core and dust contentions part of trafficking women and children in is trafficking...only prostitution? Sexual slavery? Mail order brides? Organ trade? And bonded labour? Is trafficking always forced. Nature of the problem — why does trafficking takes place? For what? For who? For what are the women and children from India are regularly sent to Middle East. Girls in prostitution and bonded domestic service abroad and often tortured, held in imprisonment, sexual abused and raped. Targets — poor women and children from socially and economically backward groups from rural areas and urban slums; adolescent, young girls and women sigmatised in society; unmarried/divorced/separated/widowed women; runaways/lost/abandoned/kidnapped/abducted children; and ethnic minorities/SCs/STs/OBCs/refugees/illegal migrants.

The Asia Pacific forum established in 1996 in Darwin Australia to promote dialogue committed to the growth of National Human rights in situations in the region supports through technical cooperation information dissemination and support. It also provides information on country based projects and on regional projects. Technical cooperation is provided to the forum members through common training and activities the objective being capacity building and upgradation of skills. National human right commission in India is an autonomous body set up under the protection of Human Rights Act, 1993 of the Indian Parliament to perform and undertake and promote research in the field of human rights through publications, the media seminars and other available means for the promotion of human rights, concerning population policies and trafficking within and across the national boundaries for the purpose of sexual exploitation, marriage, domestic work, or labour trade to combat trafficking coordinating and cooperation at national, local levels to review develop and strengthen comprehensive, essential and integrated strategies and measures so as to facilitate national/local level agenda to set up a time frame and network with civil society. To coordinate with international organisations, working in the field, including UNICEF, NIFEM, UN centre for Human Right, BLO, UNESCO, UNDP, WHO, UNAID, UN Crime Prevention and Crime Justice Division, UNFPA, World tourism organisations, UN high commission for human rights to suggest strategies for implementation and to set up a time frame and network with the civil society to facilitate local national level agenda.

Trafficking in women and children as of not to pull and push. Industrialisation; urbanisation; poverty; deprivation of low status of women and girls; lack of earning income opportunity; lack of alternate employment, disintegration of rural communities break down of joint family system; and erosion of social values; social conventions like dowry, polygamy, child marriage, etc., and a single status of women (unmarried, divorced, separated, widowed) create a platform for women's vulnerability. Desirability of easy life performed by consumerism, globalisation and liberalisation, which has served the traditional, social-economic fabric and have made the Indian women and children vulnerable, making their commodities in the market; lack of awareness about legal protection, and rights, lack of political will and corruption, lack of effective policing and law enforcement, lack of research and documentation for trafficking with and across the national boundaries.

Brief Overview

With the objective of ascertaining the views of all sections of society including academics, jurists, human rights activists, NGOs and other on the issue of Racism. Racial discrimination, Xenophobia and Related Intolerance, as well as on issues relating to caste and race in India to combating all forms of discrimination irrespective of the label or nomenclature under which it occurs. The Commission's effort is to eradicate discrimination, wherever it is found. Thus, it did not really matter whether the discrimination fell under the label of caste, race, descent or any other category. None are acceptable.

The Chairperson reiterated the statement made by him at the Bangalore Seminar to the effect that the Commission had not formed its opinion on the issue of whether discrimination based on caste and race were co-terminous or similar, and that is would formulate its position only after the Public Consultations had taken place and the Commission had learnt the views of all concerned persons. He assured the gathering that the commission "had not mortgaged its mind to any preconceived notion or thought on the issue of racism," an issue which was being hotly debated. Justice Verma clarified that he had politely declined the invitation to participate in a Committee constituted by the Prime Minister to prepare for the World Conference for the obvious reason that would have been inconsistent with the autonomous character of the Commission. Additionally, he stressed that the NHRC formed its opinion only after taking into account the views of all concerned groups, howsoever diverse they might be.

He then invited opinions on two of the main concerns that had arisen prior to the World Conference : whether 'race' included 'caste'; and views and suggestions for combating discrimination based on caste, which was expressly prohibited by the Constitution of India and was contrary to various International Instruments to which India was a State Party.

FOR WHAT ARE THESE PERSONS TRAFFICKED?

Trafficking is a fast growing industry and its network far and wide. It may be planned involving family acquaintances/

It may be a		
'small'....	'medium'.... or....	'large scale'
	NETWORK	
Trafficks one woman/child at a time.	Specialises in trafficking women/children from one specific country.	Recruits and/or sells women/children to the clientele.
	Keeps women/children under its control in clubs and brothels.	Very sophisticated network usually difficult to combat.
	Does not sell women/children but recruits them for clients.	Have easy access to fraudulent documents.
	Has political/economic/ national and international contacts.	Infrastructure in transit and distribution countries.
		Strong political/economic national/international contacts.

pumps/procures/organised criminals or unplanned — the lost, runaways, pickup by opportunists.

While loud proclamations are made of the sanctity of human rights and the dignity of human beings, flesh-trade remains rampant, which is a negation of all the pious declarations of development and equality.

Human beings in general and women and children in particular are bought and sold to cater to a variety of needs.

It is facilitated by the **'porous borders'** marked by an absence of effective regulations.

It may be in the form of **'wired trafficking'**. Today, the internet is the latest trend in promoting trafficking in women and children. It is actively used to buy/sell them.

Catalogues of **'mail order brides'**, **'commercial sex tours,'** **'live strip shows'** have become common. The scant regulation of the NET has today made **'virtual trafficking'**, a raging success.

TRAFFICKING WITHIN AND ACROSS THE NATIONAL BOUNDARIES

CONSEQUENCES OF THE PROBLEM

Trafficking is detrimental to the individual as well for the country involved, be it a sending, receiving and/or transit one.

TRAFFICKING IS A FAST GROWING INDUSTRY — ITS NETWORK FAR AND WIDE

It may be		
'Planned'	or	'Unplanned'
Involving... Family/acquaintances; pimps/procures; organised criminals.		When the first move is made by the individual itself, for instance...the lost...the abandoned...the runaways, who are then picked up by the opportunists.

The magnitude of consequences to the individual cannot be exaggerated. These women and children are constantly under mental, physical and psycho-social trauma :

- They face continuous sexual abuse and severe health risks;
- They may not possess the necessary documents and thus be subjected to forced dependence;
- They are deprived of basic human rights;
- They are under perpetual debt at the hands of the madams/'gharwalies' and/or the fraudulent bank agents;
- They have serious health problems and are exposed to life threatening risks such as HIV/AIDS;
- They suffer from infectious diseases, STDs, injuries from violence at the hands of madams/pimps/clients, drug and/or alcohol addictions.

The mental and emotional trauma never fails to leave an indelible scar that lasts longer than the physical injuries.

Being part of the global trafficking nexus questions India's dedication to 'Justice'...'Equality'...words that have come to hold very little meaning for the most vulnerable citizens.

Furthermore, linked to the trade is the growth in corruption, forgery of documents and expansion of other criminal activities such as drugs and arms traffic that undermines the safety and security of the nation.

Learning to gather Conservation and Development

Technologically enhanced teaching and learning in this view, is not new? They imply that the internet need, therefore not be seen as any great hurdle. And yet, at the same time, they introduce a set of case studies as the struggle of tertiary teachers as they attempt to harness technology and to realise positive potential. Peer tutoring is a form of active and interactive learning found in all sectors of education. However to explore more than traditional methods of "using" graduate students as surrogate teachers. It focuses instead of learning interaction between true "peers" (*e.g.* fellow undergraduates) organised in such a way that the learning of both tutor and tutee is enhanced. The form of peer-mediated learning should be well organised for maximal effectiveness involving staff development for professionals involved and training for the students involved. Particularly during the phase of initial innovation, saving in time and researches cannot be expected, and these methods should not be ceased upon as a quick fix for organisational stresses. However properly developed peer mediated learning can add significant value and quality to the educational process in terms of learning and the development of transferable skills. The expected readership for the courses is teachers and staff developers in higher education as well as teachers trainers, and education researchers focal theme of this course is on :

- Conservation strategies.
- Methods of conservation of living resources.
- Politics education and environmental ethics.
- Restoring ecology in relation to developmental activities for the topics relating to the conservation of plants, animals and microbes.

Genetics and ecology of extinction, cultural significance of natural protection; code of conduct; seeds and sovereignty, ethics and environment, international regulation of trade in endangered living resources, international and national institutions/organisations associated with conservation; restoration ecology, in relation to development; raising agricultural productivity; renewable sources of energy, farm and community forestry, stabilisation of chemical cycles, designing sustainable economics for projects based on field investigative study for field-cum-laboratory oriented exercise giving arguments in favour or against the globalisation of agriculture desirable to keep the agriculture sector away from the limelight of globalisation. However, the side effects to be pointed out for the policy framework for agricultural resources management in an integrated manner. So as to diversify it and make it realistic to safeguard the sustainable advances in agricultural productivity to face the challenges, with the provisions of the world trade agreements relating to the relaxation of the quantitative restrictions in imports, non tariff barriers in areas such as ply to sanitary conditions, and trade related intellectual property rights. We should take proactive approach based on considerations of ecological and food security agreement in reference to technology development natural resource management. Concern must be integrated with the security cause of restricting imports of food grains and dairy products, open revolution for molecular understanding of the genetic basis of living organism to develop new processes and products for agriculture the environment and for human and animal health. Dissemination of relevant timely information to access the universe of knowledge and communication through low cost electronic network. The ecotechnology for evolution *vs.* revolution of gene. Information explosion and managing agricultural resources with detailed geographic information useful for land and natural resource management in times of ecological and social stability and sustainability of eco-technology. Thus there is need to conserve traditional wisdom and practices which are often tending to become extinct. The traditional knowledge innovation and culture is an important step in widening the concept of intellectual property principles. FAO has been a pioneer in the recognition of the contribution should also undertake the task of preparing an integrated concept for interdisciplinary research on expertise in a range of subject areas such as agronomy, plant science genetics, soil science entomology, physiology, plant pathology, ecology and economics, using information technology to play an important part in crop production and national research management in soil health care, water harvesting, crop and pest management, energy management, post harvest operation etc., to define the nature of reality. But science is yet to define physical reality conclusively...hence the quest continues for physical, mental, and psychological realities; linguistic and mathematical realities with the advent of computers and internet. With the central focus in all the six Indian knowledge systems, namely, Sankhya, Yoga, Nyaya, Vaisheshika, Purva mimansa and Uttar Mimamsa and Vadanta for ultimate answer to present the nature of man for all names and forms of objects — for seeing oneself in all names and forms of objective reality; and by believing in and discovering ones own and every one else infinite nature and infinite capability being pure in body, mind, and intellect. So find God we have to only find our own self to the ocean of Viveka or discrimination, the sun for (causing the bloom) the roots of the bees of all Dharmas who is the full moon giving delight to the ocean of viveka for any particular religion, community or individuals. Yet unknown to sciences quality transnational education for the coming into being and the expansion of new world force, the intensification of transnational communications.

Studies in Higher Education

Students attributes to examinations on the present undergraduate course were borne out by their attributes to examinations on previous courses. Yet, support for an end of course examination must reflect the conservative nature. Undergraduate attitudes to the gravity of examinations are reflected on observations contributed a focus and scaffolding for their revision. It is not only academically able students at the end of the course, the postgraduates on the second course value their final assessment to tailor their own synopsis. They are confident in their ability to construct an understanding of the subject area in response to individual needs and circumstances. The final assessment may be more appropriate at certain stages of academic development and for varying level of self-direction in learning than others. The students in the early undergraduate year value the extra 'push' of all impending examination to assist them in achieving some overall understanding of the course, contents with closed book examination can do well, may be an alternative for the campus based students when considering benefit to students in the early stages of undergraduate education and may also act as scaffolding to assist them in studying appropriately at the end of each course. An intrinsic motivation to engage with course contents, and are ready to take responsibility and manage their own learning. They may also have been more familiar with the discourse of the subject because they were already working in the area, or planning to do so. It is likely, therefore, that they were more proficient at reaching an overall conceptual understanding of the subject area, without assistance or encouragement from the assessment strategy.

Variation in Vivas : Quality and Equality in Ph.D Assessments. In the new market culture of consumer rights with students constructed as paying customers rather than recipient of a welfare service, the problems of doctoral assessment are like to increase, as investigators in the educational products want more certainly and reliability of outcome.

Networks and collegiality. A community of assessors one of the key justification for inserting quality assurance procedures and an audit culture into higher education has been the call for transparency and accumulativity of a previously self-referential professional group. Currently, standards in the Ph.D are ensured through the assumption that what can be achieved in around three years, full time students by a reasonably diligent student is comparable in physics, sociology and history that peer examiners know what the thresholds are for the awards they examining there is a system of external moderation. The code of practice for postgraduate research programmes does not dial with the problematic issues of : (1) who is selected to be the examiners; and (2) the conduct of the viva itself.

In practice of examination of doctoral degrees in Britain is left to informal networks and a belief in a motion of collegiality. The collegiality is one of those words that often marks the complex power relations and the manipulative practices to which these can give rise. The supervisors, examiners and members of appeals committees which disturb as professionals. The research supervision needs to be recognised as a form of teaching to give good code of conduct within professional associations, but which are not regulated by universities' quality assurance procedures as a whole. Examiners sometimes complain that the viva is increasingly used as a formative assessment with 'uncooked' thesis submitted within the research council's time limit the many viva stories that permeate the academy give accounts of students negatively affected by power struggles between the supervisor and external examiner.

New managerialism in the UK has transformed the priorities, culture and practices of the academy, including many aspects of postgraduate education and doctoral studies. It has not had a very significant influence on the regulation and quality assurance of assessments of doctoral degrees and especially not on the oral component.

The research supervision to the guidelines to students about doctoral assessment need to be recognised as a form of teaching, not as a private activity between two consenting adults. Same could be said for viva. It has a major gate-keeping function in terms of entry to and exclusion from the international academic community. As such the central site of power and therefore open to a range of situated interpretations should be open to scrutiny and independent evaluation for doctoral studies and assessment as it has been in other areas of academy and polity. The synoptic and motivational effects of closed book examinations may be of particular benefit to the students in the early stages of undergraduate education and may also act as scaffolding to assist them in studying appropriately at the end of each course the programme content for the purpose of interaction is included to enhance students' ability to determine the exercise in decision making on certificate programmes aims to (a) sensitise the students on gender related questions to function as specialist as women issues and (b) help in generating a social environment through the interventions of distance education free from inequalities disfavouring women for taking initiatives and hope that open universities and others will contribute to an approach that aimed at raising and promoting awareness of rights of women and human rights towards women empowerment.

MISSION AND VISION WITH VALUES AND NEW UNIVERSITY PLATFORM

Humanity stands today at the head of a new age of large synthesis of knowledge, and it has to collaborate in bringing about concerted action for universal upliftment, and lasting peace and unity. In this new age, great cultural achievements of the past have to be recovered and enriched in the context of the contemporary advancement so that humanity can successfully meet the evolutionary and revolutionary challenges and bring about a new type of humanity and society marked by integrated power of physical, emotional, dynamic, intellectual, ethical, aesthetic and spiritual potentialities.

Frontiers of knowledge age, therefore, bound to expand unimaginably, and new researches will oblige humanities, sciences, technologies, and fine arts to arrive at new equations and new combinations. Developments in communication, information and technology will open up new and cost-effective approaches for providing the reach of higher education to the youth as well as to those who need continuing education for meeting the demands of explosion of information, fast-changing nature of occupations, and lifelong education.

Student-centred education and employment of dynamic methods of education will require from teachers new attitudes and new skills. Methods of teaching through lectures will have to subordinate to the methods that will lay stress on self-study, personal consultation between teachers and pupils, and dynamic sessions of seminars and workshops. Methods of distance education will have to be employed on a caste scale. As we move towards a learning society, every human activity will require contributions from experts and this will place the entire sector of higher education in sharp focus.

Aims. To bring about a new type of humanity and society marked by the integrated powers of physical, emotional, dynamic, intellectual, ethical, aesthetic and spiritual potentialities.

- Diversity pluralism and equal opportunity.
- Strengthening relations with the equal environment work cooperatively with public and private institutions, legislative bodies industry, state and community organisations and other units in the university.
- Close linkages of faculty and students with the real world.
- Interrelations between the various components of human eco-system with the planning and principles.

Strategic Planning

- Improve access to quality education and expert knowledge.
- Achieve more active learning.

- Generate new knowledge and scholarship across mission.
- Promote problem solving to address for society needs.
- Advance diversity within community.
- Make people matter.

Future Planning for Action Points

- Expansion of research outreach with people, resources, and facilities.
- Postgraduate degree/diploma programmes for pre-service, in-service graduates.
- Other training programmes short term and doorstep (tailored programmes as per need).
- Research and training programme for wiring the curriculum of school and university.

OVERVIEW

Home Science — Delhi University

The Department of Home Science, Delhi University, comprises of Lady Irwin College and Institute of Home Economics.

Over the years Home Science courses have developed from basic arts and science courses to degrees in masters and doctorate in special fields. The curriculum include basic sciences, social sciences, alongwith subjects like English and Economics. The major field of training is in Home Science subjects like Foods and Nutrition, Child Development, Textile and Clothing and Resource Management. The scope and use of Home Science studies has thus expanded to meet the changing needs of our society, linking education with the needs and aptitudes of those who seek it.

The process is initiated of deriving a new conceptual framework for the discipline of Home Science, based on discussions and seminars conducted over the years, and to operationalise the required changes in order to keep in step with the education needs, notes and identity of Asian women. Reconceptualising the Home Science may take use to reframing the concept to that of 'Women's Development', 'Human Ecology' or 'Human Development'.

Reconceptualising the B.Sc. Home Science pass and honours curriculum is clearly a major activity for the 90s. Several factors will have to be kept in mind to achieve this.

There is now an enormous vocabulary for concepts and experiences available in literature and academics both nationally and internationally, on women centred questions of identity and place. It is now possible to reformulate the three-year Home Science curriculum with reference to a large body of concepts. The 'fragmented' curriculum, which was intended to be as multifaceted as the role of a woman, can now be contextualised with the adhesive of the naturally holistic female self, which has thus far been insufficiently recognised. The curricula, theory and practice of the B.Sc. degree courses can now be reconceptualised to include necessary internship and apprenticeship programmes in relationship with, and under the guidance of, professionals in the field, so as to lead more students, with hands on experience, to choose to specialise at Master's and Doctoral levels.

As important as the need to reconceptualise the B.Sc. curriculum is the even more urgent need to work on school curricula so as to socialise boys at an early age, to develop their home making and nurturing abilities and create thereby a real equality of the sexes in later life.

University Grants Commission

The University Grants Commission (UGC) is a statutory organisation listed by an Act of Parliament in 1956. This is a national body for the coordination, determination and maintenance of standards of university education. The UGC serves as a vital link between the Union and State Governments and the institutions of higher learning. In addition to its role of giving grants to universities and colleges, the University Grants Commission also advises Central and State Governments on the message necessary for the improvement of university education.

IX Five Year Plan — Development of Higher Education

Higher education provides people with an opportunity to reflect on the critical social, economic, cultural, moral and spiritual issues facing humanity. It contributes to national development through dissemination of specialised knowledge and skills.

The Ninth Five Year Plan (1997-2000) launched in 50th year of India's Independence is based on a careful stocktaking of the strengths of the country's past development strategy as well as its weaknesses and seeks to provide appropriate direction and balance to socio-economic development of the country. The developmental efforts especially in the social and economic sphere, so that the country will realise its full economic potential and the poorest and the weakest will be able to shape their destiny in an unfettered manner. This will require not only higher rates of growth of output and employment but also a special emphasis on all-round human development, with a stress on social sectors and a thrust on eradication of poverty.

The principal task of the Ninth Plan, therefore, will be to usher in a new era of growth with social justice and active participation of people at the grass-root level. The Ninth Five Year Plan has accorded priority to agriculture and rural development with a view to generate adequate productive employment and eradication of poverty, accelerating the growth rate of economy with stable prices, ensuring food and nutritional security for all, particularly the vulnerable sections of the society and providing the basic minimum services of safe drinking water, primary health care facilities, universal primary education, shelter and connectivity to all in a time bound manner.

As India, is in the throes of major economic and technological changes, the process will affect not only the market economy of the nation, but also, the whole system of higher education which has to prepare its graduates for participation in the social and economic development of the country, and the type of cultural environment and ethos it will need to foster. Moreover, education is, itself, being internationalised and universities are losing their territorial boundaries. Information technologies is further contributing to this change and will have a major impact on the structure, management and mode of delivery of the educational system. We are living through a period of a social and economic revolution which cannot leave our educational system untouched.

These major challenges are coming at a time when the

system has been facing an enormous economic crunch. It does not have a level playing field to respond to the crisis of change which is global, yet, within their scarce resource, universities are striving to meet the requirements of change. Much depends in the IXth Plan on the priority the nation gives to promoting higher education which provides the leadership for the nation's requirements of human resource in all walks of life. On the other hand, the universities must not be found wanting at such a time of crisis and change. Their response will depend on the quality of leadership, the flexibility of their management structures and the response of the academic community.

EMPOWERMENT FOR WOMEN

Introduction

Women's poverty is directly related to the absence of economic opportunities and autonomy, lack of access to economic resources including credit, land ownership and inheritance, lack access to education and their minimal participation in the decision-making process. Actions to be taken by governments to help women to cross the 'poverty line.'

- Enable women to obtain affordable housing and access to land by, among other things, removing all obstacles to access, with special emphasis on meeting the needs of women, especially those living in poverty and female heads of household.
- Formulate and implement policies and programmes that enhance the access of women agriculture and fisheries producers (including subsistence farmers and producers, especially in rural areas) to financial, technical, extension and marketing services, provide access and control of land, appropriate infrastructure and technology in order to increase women's income and promote household food security, especially in rural areas and where appropriate encourage the development of producer-owned, market-based cooperatives.

With the increasing pressure of population and the growing demands of modernisation as well as economic liberalisation on natural resources, livelihood security of the marginalised groups in rural areas is becoming a critical issue. With the threat of displacement and loss of control over basic resources, both land and water, by the building of big dams and taking over of forest lands for industrial enterprises, the development of new, export-oriented agricultural industries by private companies on agricultural land, the situation of the poor, and amongst them women, is becoming even more precarious. Within the traditional gender division of labour, household maintenance functions fall to the lot of women.

The issue of equity, across classes, castes and genders, in the control over resources, is emerging as a major concern. This is because in the process of "economic development" and more specifically the pressure of industrialisation and liberalisation, the livelihoods of the marginalised groups are increasingly threatened. Unable to survive in their traditional mores, there are increasing trends of migration, displacement, deaths due to lack of access to basic needs and so on. Given the gender divisions of labour and distinct gender roles within households, women are more severely affected by these processes. It is time that the development paradigm took note of the survival and livelihood needs of women and marginalised groups, in order to ensure a minimum quality of life to all citizens of the country.

While empowerment has been defined in several ways, its core elements relate to the control over decisions regarding all aspects.

EFFECTIVENESS OF HUMAN RESOURCE MANAGEMENT IN HIGHER EDUCATIONAL INSTITUTIONS

Introduction

There is no doubt that higher education has experienced tremendous quantitative growth. India is the world's largest reservoir of technical and scientific manpower. However, quantitative expansion has smudged the quality of higher education. Teaching and Learning in colleges and universities are no more than a part-time occupation aimed essentially at the award of degrees which have generally lost much of their creditability and value. Most of the courses offered by our colleges and universities have become irrelevant.

Some efforts have been made to improve the quality of higher education like the institution of the National Assessment and Accreditation Council (NAAC) created by the U.G.C. The role of NAAC in assessing the accrediting private and public institutions in higher learning is crucial.

Accreditation fosters excellence in education, encourages institutional improvement through continual self-study and evaluation, provides advice and assistance to established and developing institutions and protects institutions from encroachment that might endanger their educational effectiveness and academic freedom.

The Need and Importance of HRM in Higher Education

Education is one of the most important factors in achieving development goals of the country. Higher education is of great significance for all-round development in a developing country like India. The number of quality of students coming out of its educational institutions shape a nation. The human resources at the collegiate level serve as the backbone of national development. The products of the colleges are the potential nation builder. The future scenario of political, social, cultural and economic sectors will depend on the contributions of the students of educational institutions today. Hence to attain national relevance and socio-economic viability in education the human resource factor has to be managed properly.

The assessment of HRM activity will provide clarity and focus on purpose, organisational credibility, pride and improved moral, as the staff knows what is expected of them and a goal to aim through specific targets. Hence it is important to evaluate the HRM in higher educational institutions.

In modern times personal management is one of the most complex and challenging fields of endeavour. Educational institutions are no exception to this general turned. On the other hand the management of human resources in educational institutions is more complex, because the quality of their teaching work is in no way going to affect the salary. Hence to generate maximum quality from the staff is more challenging in the field of education. Since the human resource is highly qualified, they expect a great extent of freedom in their field of work. The only possible way of increasing the efficiency of human resources is educational institutions are effective management by frequent evaluation and proper motivation mechanisms. The need of the hour is therefore a shift of focus to the people and to treat them with respect and dignity.

Process of HRM

Going through the opinions of a number of authors and the different criteria adopted by them in the process of evaluation of effectiveness of HRM, six variables which apparently seem to be important and most influential in the case of educational institutional are selected *viz.*,

(a) Employ motivation facilities.
(b) Opportunity for employee training and development.
(c) Employee evaluation.
(d) Employee relationship with employer as well as fellow staff.
(e) Upward and downward communication.
(f) Quality of outgoing students and their demand in job market.

Employee motivation in educational institutions is concerned with optimal use of the potential skills and talents of the staff, increasing their work efficiency, removing the frustration and feelings of alienation. If the management enriched the job of the staff in building a good morale and high work ethics, the members are likely to develop greater loyalty towards the management and a strong motive to work to fulfil the institutional goals. Job satisfaction among the staff removes their tensions and draws out a feeling of personal responsibility and sense of mission.

Refresher Courses and orientation studies for continuous improvement of the staff are encouraged as an art of Employee Training and Development in the colleges, enhance the competencies and thereby effectiveness. Special training programmes for handling sophisticated technology like slide projector, computers, overhead projector and other facilities for updating the knowledge and skills will in turn help efficient classroom communication and is useful to make the classes interesting.

Staff evaluation is one of the important concepts of measuring effectiveness of HRM in educational institutions. The Principal plays an important and continuous role in the effort of evaluating the teachers and students in order to improve the teaching-learning process. Staff appraisal by the students is another tool for the assessment of the teacher's knowledge and performance. The discussion of the report with the staff-reward for positive achievements and encouragement for improvement — is part of evaluation. Frequent and continuous evaluation and feedback to the staff is considered as a constant source of support for increasing teacher effectiveness.

Mutual relationship of the staff with principal and among themselves is yet another deciding factor of effectiveness. People oriented management style rather than a task-oriented leadership develops a cordial relationship in the college. Through an effective grievance redressal system even conflicting cases can be solved by discussion. Only in an atmosphere of cordial relationship, human capacities can be utilised to the best level possible.

Proper and timely communication from top to bottom is found to be very important in the colleges. Periodical staff meetings and group discussion with regard to curricular activities of the college is a cordial way of communication. Government order and other official matters of communication are circulated or exhibited in order to reach the notice of the whole staff. Availability of the Principal to listen to the staff personally is yet another chance to nurture trust and build effectiveness.

Last but not least, the criterion considered for evaluating the effectiveness of HRM in colleges in the quality of outgoing students. The teachers can inculcate the desire, to be self-employed, among the students. They can also advise the students to be job creators and not job seekers. Quality can be evaluated by collecting data about the employment market demands and the jobs taken up by the alumnae of the colleges.

To sum up, in this competitive market economy, only quality products can survive. Hence, it is the need of the hour in higher education target for quality output. But educational management, unlike industrial management, is concerned with non-profit making objectives where the inputs are human beings and are processed by human beings with the objective to produce better human beings. To reach this high goal of higher educational human resources have to be managed properly. Thus, effective HRM has great impact on the quality of output and the effectiveness of institutions.

PRIORITISATION OF RESEARCH NEEDS AND ACTION POINTS FOR THE CONGRESS

As we move towards a learning society, every human activity will require contributions from experts and this will place the entire sector of higher education in sharp focus. Although the priorities, which are being assigned today to the task of Education for All, will continue to be preponderant, the country will have to prepare itself to invest more and more on higher education. Simultaneously, measures will have to be taken to refine, diversify and upgrade higher education and research programmes.

Agribusiness

(Linking farmers, technology transfer agents and agriculture researcher. Promotion of human resource development and entrepreneur development and management.)

(a) Agrisystem

- Planning interventions and implementing farming system development.
- Farming system development, concept and approach.
- Farming system zoning.
- Exploratory diagnosis and analysis.
- Identification of constraints and potentials.
- Evaluation of potential improvements.
- On-farm testing.

Action Plan

- To plan, undertake, aid, promote and co-ordinate education, and to act as a clearing house of research and its application in agriculture, agro-forestry, animal husbandry, fisheries, home science, allied sciences and instituting and promoting transfer of technology programmes.
- To provide, undertake and promote consultancy services

in the fields of education, research, training and dissemination of information in agriculture, agro-forestry, animal husbandry, fisheries, home science and allied sciences.

- To look into the problems relating to broader areas of rural development concerning agriculture, including post harvest technology, by developing co-operative programmes with others such as the Indian Council of Social Sciences Research, Council of Scientific and Industrial Research, and the Universities.

(b) Entrepreneurial opportunity in agriculture

Horticulture, Vegetable, Floriculture, Mushroom cultivation, Seed Production, Medicinal and Aromatic Plant production foods, biscuits, confectionary (including cocoa processing and chocolate making), malt extract, protein isolate high protein food, weaning food and extruded food products (including other ready-to-eat foods).

Beer, including non-alcoholic beer.

Alcoholic drinks from non-molasses base.

Aerated waters/soft drinks and other processed foods.

Specialised packaging for food processing industries.

Establishment and servicing of the development councils for food processing industries.

(c) Post harvest technology for value addition and nutrition

- Fruits and vegetable processing industry including freezing and dehydration :
  - Food grain milling industry.
  - Consumer food industry.
  - Bakery, cocoa products, soft drinks, beer and alcoholic drinks, fruit and vegetable.
- Traditional methods of processing cereals, pulses and grains and modern appropriate techniques and reforms.
- Fortification of cereals/cereal products for enhancing the nutritional level of our population, especially women and children.

- Setting up of mobile fruit and vegetable processing unit.
- Person-power development for entrepreneurship and transfer of technology for processing of food products, production-cum-training centres.

(d) Agro-based enterprises

- Introduction of innovative protein rich items with special reference to dairy, poultry, meat, mushroom and yeast.
- Community food programmes, supplementary feeding programmes, school lunch programme.
- Testing and development of new food product for space exploration, novel food products.

Indian Council of Agricultural Research

The ICAR has been the facilitator of Green, White and Blue Revolutions. The technologies generated by the scientists had been the cornerstones of our past successes. To achieve the twin national objectives of poverty alleviation and welfare of the disadvantaged and weaker sections of the society, it has now become imperative to increase agricultural productivity, profitability, and sustainability through judicious and more integrated use of our natural resources. However, our production of agri-horticultural crops has secured a prestigious position within the century.

The agricultural sector with its significant share in GDP plays a significant role in the employment generation especially in the rural sector. It has significant potential as a net foreign exchange earner.

The main approach of the government policy has been to control trade in a manner to ensure adequate availability of essential food items to consumers at reasonable process and to protect farmers from foreign competition.

Agricultural Extension is aimed at promoting agricultural development by providing farmers with information and training on continuous basis regarding improved production technologies and their adoption.

The extension programmes and activities of the directorate are specifically planned and implemented in the following four specific sectors :

- Extension Management.
- Extension Training.
- Farm Information.
- Farm Women Development Programme.

The Ministry of Food Processing

The Ministry of Food Processing Industries was set up to give an impetus to the development of food processing industries in the country. A strong and effective food processing sector plays a significant role in diversification and commercialisation of agriculture, improves value addition of the agricultural produce, generates employment, enhances income of farmers. The Ministry is concerned with the formulation and implementation of the policies and plans for the food processing industries within the overall national priorities and objectives like :

1. Policy Support

(a) Formulation and implementation of policies for food processing industries within overall national priorities and objectives.

(b) Facilitating the creation of a conducive policy environment for healthy growth of the food processing sector.

(c) Promoting rationalisation of tariff and duties in relation to food processing sector.

2. Development

(a) Assistance under various plan schemes.

(b) Widening the R&D base in food processing by involvement of various R&D institutes and support to various R&D activities relating to development of product, process and packaging with special emphasis on traditional technologies.

(c) Human Resource Development both for entrepreneurs as well as the workers engaged in the food processing industry by upgradation of their skills.

(d) Assistance for setting up analytical and testing laboratories, active participation in the laying down of food standards as well as their harmonisation with international standards.

3. Promotional

(a) Assistance for organisation of workshops, seminars, exhibitions and fairs etc.

(b) Assistance for studies/surveys etc.

(c) Publications and films.

4. Regulatory

Implementation of Fruit Products Order (FPO).

Biodiversity and Environment

(a) Conservation of natural resource including forestry, social agro-forest and grassland

- Forestry education, training and extension.
- Wild-life education and training.
- Non-formal environment education, awareness and training.
- Centres of excellence of the country.
- Legislation and institutional support.

(b) Biodiversity, conservation and its ecological sustainability

- Arid and semi arid system.
- Coastal marine and fresh water ecosystem.
- Forest ecosystem.
- Mountain ecosystem.

(c) Environmental technology, education and training requirement

Biogas plants, Energy conservation, Microbes for effluent treatment, Control of metal pollution by microbes, Solid and liquid waste management, and demonstration on the use of internet in research.

Ministry of Environment and Forests

The mandates of the Ministry are conservation and survey of flora, fauna, forests and wild-life, prevention and control of pollution, afforestation and regeneration of degraded areas and protection of environment. These tasks are being fulfilled through environmental impact assessment, eco-regeneration, assistance to organisations implementing environmental and forestry programmes; promotion of environmental and forestry programmes; promotion of environmental and forestry research, extension, education and training to augment the requisite manpower; dissemination of environmental information, international cooperation and creation of environmental awareness among all sectors of the country's population.

Biotechnology

(a) Agrobiotechnology

- Biological control of plant pests and weeks.
- Medicinal and Aromatic plants.
- Biotechnology based programme for women and rural development food biotechnology, microbial biotechnology.
- Biotech process — uses of yeast as food. Development of low cost nutritious food supplements.

(b) Industrial biotechnology

- Industrial biotechnology possibilities.
- Microbial products — enzymes, antibiotics, alcohol.
- Demonstration on the fermentation technology.
- Tissue culture possibilities for future.
- Demonstration on the production of algal food.
- Biotechnology and health care.
- Development of novel vaccines (Infectious diseases — bacterial and viral).

Department of Biotechnology

India is well poised today for a bio-industrial development. The scientific expertise, infrastructural facilities and research leads obtained during the last 10 years are indicative of the rapid progress in the field of biotechnology. What is important is to further strengthen the relationship between research institutions, academia and industry in a symbiosis mode for conversion of research findings into products, processes and technologies.

Some innovations to industry for commercialisation. As evident world over, biological resources would be the most important feed stock of bio-industrial revolution. Rules and regulation for the new patent regime especially in biotechnological innovations and the need for protecting our national biodiversity and intensification of research and development in all areas of modern biology would be the priorities. While supporting basic research, the department has kept in view the Biotechnology based programmes for rural development, weaker sections and women in particular. A number of new initiatives have been launched in this direction in the country.

The Department of Biotechnology through its multifaceted approach in furthering advanced research in modern biology has given a definite thrust to the sectors of agriculture, human health, livestock, environment and industrial development. A number of useful research leads have been generated. Validation and commercialisation of vaccines, diagnostic kits and bio-products have been the thrust areas for support. Genome research, molecular taxonomy, new vaccines and diagnostic, human resource development, expansion of bio-informatics network, repositories, biodiversity conversation and characterisation have progressed well.

Non Conventional Energy Systems

Climate change for removal of barriers for energy conservation and energy efficiency. Promotion the adoption of renewable energy and gas emitting energy technology.

(a) Rural Energy

Biogas production, Improved chullah, Biomass gasification, Toilet linked plants, Biomass briquetting, national projects on biogas development.

(b) Solar Energy

Water heating, solar cooking, solar air heating (drying), solar building, lighting systems through solar photovoltaic devices and power from renewable sources.

(c) Power from renewables

Wind power programmes, Biomass powers, Centres for wind energy technology, Small hydel power projects for power generation, Small Hydro power programmes, Development of commercial projects, Development in upgradation of water mills, Training and manpower development.

(d) Energy from waste

Types of waste and technologies.

(e) New Technologies

Chemical source of energy, Hydrogen energy, Geothermal energy, Alternate fuels for surface transport, urban and industrial waste and their conversion routes and industrial research and development.

Ministry of Non Conventional Energy Sources

India is fortunate to be endowed with an abundance of renewable energy sources These include biomass, sun, wind, ocean waters, urban and industrial wastes, hilly hydro and canal heads suitable for small and mini hydel sets, etc. The biomass includes large quantities of cattle dung and human excreta, agricultural residues, bagasse and other by-products of agro-based industries like paper mills etc. The potential of some of these is indeed enormous as indicated in the following table.

Table : Estimated Potential for Renewable Energy Technologies in India

Sources/Systems	Approx. Potential
Biogas plants (No.)	12 million
Improved woodstoves (No.)	120 million
Biomass	17,000 MW
Solar energy	20 MW/sq.km
Wind energy	20,000 MW
Small hydro power	10,000 MW
Ocean energy	50,000 MW

There is an estimated 232 million cattle in the country and if one-third of the dung produced annually from these is available for production of biogas and for recycling as farm manure, 12 million biogas plants can be installed. Against this potential, cumulative total of 27.65 lakh family type and toilet-linked plants under the National Project on Biogas Development and 2360 plants under the Community, Institutional and Nightsoil based Biogas Plants Programme have been installed up to December 1998.

Another major programme relates to promotion of solar thermal technologies. Among these, solar water heating systems occupy an important place. Hot water is needed for a number of applications at homes, in offices, institutions, hotels, hospitals, industrial units etc. The Ministry's promotional efforts have resulting in the installation of 4,50,000 sq.m. of solar water heating collectors which can heat more than 22 million litres of water to a temperature of 60-70° C everyday. This is no small achievement and the technology of solar water heating is now fairly mature even though there may be scope for some improvements. The advantages of using solar water heating systems are quite obvious. Use of 1000 domestic solar water heaters of 100 litre capacity each will contribute to a peak load having of 1 MW. Use of huge systems, can result in substantial saving of electricity or other commercial fuels like coal, wood, furnace oil etc. Besides this, carbon dioxide emissions into the atmosphere can be prevented. According to a conservative estimate, the potential in our country for deployment of such systems is around 30 million sq.m. of collector area, against which 4.5 lakh sq.m. of collectors have been installed. This brings out the enormous scope that still exists in this area of renewable energy. In recent years, the manufacturing base of solar water heating systems has improved substantially and there are 37 approved manufacturers with production capacity of 100000 sq.m. of collector area per year. Large-scale promotion of solar water heating systems, through a number of financial and fiscal incentives, has been taken up. Besides the Indian Renewable Energy Development Agency (IREDA), five banks have come forward to provide soft loan for those interested.

A notable feature of the wind power programme has been the interest evinced by private entrepreneurs in setting up commercial wind power projects. In fact, of the 1000 MW capacity created so far, 950 MW has been established in commercial projects while the remaining 50 MW has been contributed by demonstration projects. IREDA has set up a revolving fund to finance commercial projects and has received assistance by way of sizable credit from multilateral and bilateral aid agencies like World Bank, GEF, DANIKA, KFW and OECF (Japan).

Biomass as a source of electricity holds considerable promise. It is estimated that 405 million tonnes of crop residues are produced every year, a large portion of which goes waste or is used inefficiently. By using only the surplus biomass materials available more than 16,000 MW of power can be generated. In this context, bagasse-based cogeneration has assumed significance. An estimated 3500 MW of additional power can be produced if all the 430 sugar mills in the country switched over to modern techniques of cogeneration.

Renewable Energy Policy

The Ministry is in the process of formulating a comprehensive policy on renewable energy and the necessary supporting legislation. The policy aims at augmenting the grid electricity supply with power from renewable sources, ensuring for the rural areas electricity and energy based on renewable sources for decentralised power generation and reduction in environmental pollution caused by excessive use of fossil fuels. The policy seeks to address issues relating to institutional arrangements, mobilisation of financial resources, promotion of renewable energy industry, and development of human resources necessary for largescale adoption of. new and renewable source of energy.

HUMAN ECOLOGY FOR HUMAN RESOURCE DEVELOPMENT

Globalisation of Education

- To study meticulously the working system of the University and then justify separately the requirement of each non-teaching staff in all the units.
- Expansion and development of base of higher education, as foreign students for its economical, cultural and political development.
- To attract international students to their educational institutes for retaining ,and expanding its share of international students.
- Operation of educational institutes on the foreign land by granting franchise or agreement. Arrangement with educational institutes in host countries.
- Establishment in foreign countries in publicise the programmes, fee etc. for their principal institutes through

various media, enroll the students, offer courses and programmes to them.

- Providing learning material and sometimes conduct classes and hold examinations and finally grant them the Certificates, Diplomas, Degrees issued by their principals for the degree of the foreign educational institutes.
- To make agreement with the establishments or educational institutes in other nations like Australia, Holland, Canada, New Zealand, France and England to provide guidance to the tutors as well as students. Evaluations through inter centric, question paper loaded to solve them on computer itself.
- Local tutors and institutions engages by the principals are empowered to evaluate the student and submit thesis assessment to the foreign universities for granting the Certificate/Diploma/Degree to the students.

Establishment of the Campus/Centres of the Foreign Universities in the Host Countries

Some American universities have established their campus/ centres outside the United States to the countries in Middle East and East European region for developing their interest especially in East Asian Regions for expanding their activities and mobilisation of resources with multiple objectives to enroll more and more international students.

Operation of virtual campuses by using satellite and information super highway for access to India largely through the modes growing chances of the operation of foreign educational institutes in India through Cyber Spaces.

Globalisation to regulate the operation of foreign educational institutes in India and safeguard our national interest for reforms.

To meet the challenges offered by globalisation of education, our country requires the introduction of certain reforms to bring some changes in educational policy.

To co-ordinate and maintenance of higher technical and professional education and regulation of foreign exchange for the international students.

Department of education may establish as an apex body to act as Consortium to attract foreign students and suggest the plans to the member Institutes for their consideration and execution.

The School of Human Ecology for Environment Resources and Development for the excellence in graduate education as well as research activities. Through its academic programmes and outreach units working towards capability building and human resource management, poverty alleviation and socio-economic gender development to place its emphasis on food security and poverty alleviation through the development of technology, promotion of sustainable farming system, human resource development, appropriate to varying stages of development in rural Asia.

The programme is composed of three fields of study :

Agricultural Engineering, Agricultural Systems and Aqua culture, and Aquatic resource management, in two interdisciplinary areas namely integrated development and management and integrated tropical coastal zone management :

- Agricultural Engineering — Technology required to increase the efficiency of food production.
- Agricultural Systems and Aqua culture and aquatic resource management for promotion of sustainable agriculture of study from an institution of recognised standing : have undergraduate framed significantly above average.

To qualify with the degree of Master of Engineering, Master of Science, a student must satisfactorily complete either :

- A programme of course works of 55 credits, including an independent research study of 12 credits.
- A programme of course works of a minimum 30 credits and a research thesis.
- The minimum period of full time attendance required for a degree of Master in four terms; the majority of the students take five terms.
- Diploma of Agriculture Information Technology : a student must satisfactorily complete a minimum of 24

credits, including not fewer than two and more than six credits of special studies, leading to the presentation of a project report.

Processing Technology Programmes

- Food, bio-process and paper industries in relation to the material, process, equipment, for conversion of modification from raw state to more useful forms. Quality enhancement through improved process, better control and regulation practices, cleaner production, waste reduction and energy efficient operations through application of such technologies.
- Gender and Development Studies : highlights both the need of specialised academic degree awarding studies in gender and development, and the incorporation of women centred analysis and a gender perspective within an overall gender specific framework.
- Natural Resource Management : emphasises on natural resources planning, development and management, including land, forest, wild life and environmental conservation.

Regional and Rural Development Planning : focuses on rural poverty, improvement of the quality of life, and social and economic development of rural areas. Community resource management concerns for the management of resources for the development of needs of the family and community for social equity and people's participation in a true interactive process.

The university community should make special effort to increase the relevance of higher education by making the courses career oriented by developing interdisciplinary knowledge and skill for research, extension programmes to outreach the communities. It must empower human resource with special emphasis on educating the disciplines of Agribusiness, Bio-diversity and Environment, Biotechnology, Non Conventional Energy System, to raise unified field of *Human Ecology* for Community empowerment.

A living organism and environment surrounding it cannot be separated from each other. The system arising from the interaction of a biological community with its non-living surroundings is called ecosystem as an ecological unit that has both structure and function. The structure includes an analysis of biotic communities living in the habitat and the physical features of the environment, including edaphic factors, nutrition, and climatic conditions.

Man's relationship with his environment now occupies a major place among the problems. Therefore, it is necessary to demonstrate the scientific programmes in a way meeting the safe and sustainable future to mankind.

To respond to human needs the main thrust will be directed towards the activities which are socially beneficial and economically viable : like farm, and non-farm sectors.

The national agricultural technology project has made stride under three major components :

1. Agro-ecosystem Research,
2. Innovation in technology dissemination, and
3. Organisation and management system.

The Directorate of Extension Department of Agricultural Cooperation has established 'Innovations in Technology Dissemination Unit (TDU)'. The Department is involved primarily in setting of Agricultural Technology Management Agencies (ATMAs) with programme implementation in Andhra Pradesh, Bihar, Himachal Pradesh, Maharashtra, Orissa and Punjab. Four Management and Extension Training Institutes each are being strengthened to train farmers and extension workers under ICAR. Twenty Zonal Research Stations (ZRSs) are being strengthened to perform additional role were KVKs do not exist. They are to provide single window delivering system towards support of the Agricultural Technology Information Centre (ATIC), the project titled 'Shale Development Mechanism' has been launched.

However the Centre of Excellence in Human Ecology at University of Delhi shall work to organise and develop strategic action for ICAR using professional consultants for the establishment of the faculty for Human Ecology under ICAR Centre for Human Ecology linked to School of Human Ecology to be established to commensurate with new challenges and opportunities both at National and Global level for the generation of new knowledge to promote problem solving and to conduct studies on women agriculture and several extension through education and having programmes with special reference to service graduated and its linkages for Human Ecology for Local Action.

Lady Irwin College of Delhi, a pioneer in Home Science with the community outreach programmes in education is held in high esteem throughout the world — attracting some of the nation's brightest students with its community reach programmes and a concern for the management of shared resources, the postgraduate department of CRME of the College looks a head into development of needs of the family and community for social equity and people's participation in a truly interactive process.

Academic Programmes coupled with practical work experience. This is combined with the outstanding teaching and strong foundation in applied social sciences.

A large number of NGO's and Voluntary agencies have now centred the value education in India. Some of them have evolved innovative programmes.

Home Science in reality is deeply and closely related to life. A model home science curriculum would, therefore, care to cover all such factors, fields, and interests, which affects a person's development, his life, in the family and in the community. A change to meet the challenges and opportunities of today's higher education centre. Today higher education enterprise, an immensely broad based discipline full of rich academic, vocational and professional elements, which need to be exploited to the fullest extent in future educational needs.

Professional courses would provide wider spectrum of experience to graduating students hence sufficient weightage have to be given to make students professions and befitted in development departments for the effective enterprise development. We have to be at risk taking and innovative in view of dynamic changes of global liberalisation and marketing and knowledge that improves daily lives of current and future generations.

To develop proficiency in students for planning, organising, and evaluating rural development programmes especially programmes for youth and women to be supported by fieldwork and field projects examining the family as a significant ecosystem.

Management programmes explores design and function in conjugation with technology user satisfaction and perception.

"In the Confrontation Between The Stream and The Rock, The Stream Always Wins.... Not Through Strength but through Persistence"

ESTABLISHMENT OF FACULTY FOR AGRICULTURE AND TECHNOLOGY

(Ref. University of Delhi, Calendar Volume II)
(Appendices and Regulations, 1989)

India is third largest in terms of having scientific and technical manpower. Human Ecology for Globalisation is for adventure of ideas not in economic terms but also in terms of intellectual and scientific manpower to enhance India's contribution to intellectual developments.

UGC Guidelines

- Freedom to determine and prescribe its own courses for study and syllabi.
- Introduce new courses, rename obstacle courses of study and syllabi.
- Changing their content, updating courses and Admission policy.
- The qualifications of teaching staff were proposed to be adequate to discharge their academic responsibility.
- Autonomous colleges to frame courses of study.
- To prescribe rule of admissions and to conduct examinations.

ICAR CENTRE FOR HUMAN ECOLOGY AT UNIVERSITY OF DELHI

Global Education Enterprise for Globalisation of Agriculture and Rural Development for the faculty of :

Botany, Chemistry, Commerce, Computer Science, Electronics, Mathematics, Physics, Sericuture, Zoology, and Bio-Medical Sciences with well-developed library system.

To help the students realise their potential in courses

1. B.Sc. (G) Agriculture.
2. B.Sc. (G) Horticulture.
3. B.Sc. (G) Human Ecology.
4. B.Sc. Nursing (With Bio-medical Science support).
5. PG Diploma in Women Agriculture and Rural Extension
6. M.Sc. Biotechnology.
7. M.Sc. Food, Science and Technology.
8. M.Sc. Agriculture Marketing, Banking and Cooperation.

Establishment of the field of Human Ecology

1. To understand the principles and mechanism that gives creative bent to the scientific and logical thinking.
2. Co-curricular activities with subsidiary courses.
3. Local Area Network for intellectually hungry minds.
4. Promotion of Ph.D. programme for rural development with a special reference to Agro-Ecosystem research.
5. Linking Higher Education with community service.
6. Networking at all levels.

HUMAN ECOLOGY FOR GLOBALISATION AT ASIAN CENTRE FOR POVERTY ALLEVIATION, ENVIRONMENTAL PROTECTION, RESOURCE MANAGEMENT, SUSTAINABLE DEVELOPMENT

The world is looking for magical solutions to its problems. But all intellectual exercises to bring about pace and happiness in the world have failed because they are not based on humanism, universalism and love.

Everything in the universe is changeable and mutable because everything is in motion...once causes are destroyed... the original state of 'casuallessness' is achieved.... Spiritual masers experience this motionless, actionless, causeless, spaceless, timeless state of existence.

IN COLLABORATION WITH TEXAS A&M UNIVERSITY, USA MICHIGAN STATE UNIVERSITY, USA

ASIAN INSTITUTE OF TECHNOLOGY, THAILAND

WAGENINGEN UNIVERSITY, NETHERLANDS

HUMAN ECOLOGY FOR GLOBALIZATION

"Society and science provide knowledge to create human ecology. Its interactions between human and their environment is in making the technical concepts more realistic and meaningful."

"To make human social ecology conducive, human ecology through education and outreach to make up science and technology for ecological needs for any multi focal integrated ecosystems of the community for the values of holistic perspectives in addressing the human environmental issues."

ESTABLISHMENT OF ASIAN CENTRE FOR HUMAN ECOLOGY FOR EQUALITY FOR WOMEN AND CHILD IN NEW DELHI

- Adoption of national policy for the empowerment of women with measurable goals to be achieved by 2010.
- To bring about powers of physical, emotional, dynamic, intellectual, ethical, aesthetic and spiritual potentialities.
- Diversity, pluralism and equal opportunity.
- Strengthening relations with the equal environment work cooperatively with public, private institutions, legislative bodies industry, state and community organisations and other units in the university system.

Outcome of Consultative Group Meeting on Human Ecology held on 13th March 2002 at New Delhi

For creation of vibrant new partnership — to reach the most disadvantaged and underserved and the most vulnerable — the young child, the emerging strategy focuses on innovation, fostering decentralised flexible responses for the care of young children and women and reaching through the integrated family and community based interventions for survival, growth and development of socially backward villages and urban slums. With special reference of the society *i.e.* Scheduled Castes, Scheduled Tribes and low income families found in economically backward areas, drought and flood prone areas and areas in which development of social services requires strengthening. It also believes that these goals are an integral part of all efforts to achieve sustained and sustainable social and economic development that meet needs, ensures well-being and protects the natural resources on which all life depends.

The philosophy of human ecology provides the context for developing and serving the individual and their families from a human environment perspective towards building and sustaining a productive quality of life. The scientific expertise, infrastructure facilities and research needs to be strengthened by bonding the relationship between research and educational institutions and industry in a symbiotic mode of conversion of research findings into products, processes and technologies for human resource development.

Recognising the empowerment of woman and development of children for human resource development to enhance the principles of both of gender equality and gender equity.

TOWARDS SUSTAINABLE COMMUNITY HABITATS

We are faced with an information overload concerning waves, droughts, floods, hurricanes, water scarcity, poverty, protests and so on. Many people have the perception that the world is facing meta-crisis, which include the crisis of security. A fourth generation has begun in 2001 and uncertainty continues. There is also the real danger of future was being fought over scarce resources like, oil and water. The disparity between the rich and the poor has only being widening. Each of the five elements : land, water, fire, air and space have been adversely affected through human intervention. Earth has existed for 5 billion years, man for 3 to 5 million years and civilisation for 10000 years. We have to move from linear thinking to systematic and circular thinking that recognises complex interactions and natural cycle of the world. We may yet begin arranging our resources in wise and sustainable way. Local solutions are often the best. Long view is more important than the short-term holistic, co-operative solution. Quality is more important than quantity, conservation than consumerism. As within, so without; it is important to cultivate a life-enhancing inner

HUMAN DEVELOPMENT AND FAMILY STUDIES

1st Year	2nd Year	3rd Year	4th Year (Options)
Sustainable development or agriculture and environment (focus human geography)	Extension education and management (community resource management)	Farm food production and post harvest technology	Local environment for consumerism and public relations, trafficking within and across the national boundaries.
Food and Nutrition	Sociology	Textile and Clothing (Construction and Designing)	Agribusiness, bio-technology technology, bio-diversity and environment, non-conventional energy system.
Gender Issues	Media and Communication	Family financial management and managerial economics	Farm, non-farm and off-farm sections (F.N. & micro-biology).
Computer Basics (graphic designing, interior decoration)	Public health nutrition (Hygiene & Nutritious diet)	Management of formal and non-formal enterprise (entrepreneurial development)	Apparel and Accessories designing.
		Psychology	Child development and welfare. Art of living. Industrial psychology, labour law or criminal psychology. Research methodology and statistics.

perspective. The first in the ecological journey is to fall in love with the beauty of the planet.

Agriculture, if that world still to be used has now little to do with the growing of food, with the reaping of nature's bounty. It is a Herculean task, if not entirely impossible. Although we will concentrate on the social and economic issues of the India's total land usage of 329 million hectares, there are so-called marginal lands. According to 1985 report of the National Remote Sensing Agency, Hyderabad, 53.3 million hectares of the marginal lands are to be considered "waste land". Water is the driving force of nature. Pioneer plant is used as tool to tide over difficult times. When the tool is no longer needed, it has to be set aside.

Low maintenance of waste water treatment system, development of technologies and dissemination strategies for know-how of possible solutions in order to adapt the technology locally, to bring in operation and steering in appropriate and realistic approach, the treatment systems, quality, reuse of waste water, reuse of sludge, use of biogas etc., extensive training of local standardisation of plant design for operation may be the solution — for active dissemination for development planners and project managers, to disseminate decentralised waste water treatment system to improve the practical application of knowledge to ensure the field study approach and the results are directly applicable in field for the foundation for sustainable development through optimum involvement of teacher and students. The departments and centres of the university to adapt a multidisciplinary approach to developmental and problems and solutions. For the conflict at community, family, local market level, link and support and advocacy work to grass-root action and networking in social relations and institutional perspective to combine expertise in political science, behaviour science and management studies in the organisational context the factors goals and objectives micro and macro strategic, human resource development structure, operational management, organisational learning, value and culture to enhance the capacity of NGOs in poverty alleviation on which organisation is most relevant to basic needs.

EFFECTIVE ENTERPRISE DEVELOPMENT

Managing high performers can be even more difficult than managing poor. The implication is that the top people should be rewarded. The gap with the others should not be too great. The mistake is to pretend that pay is about formulae and systems. No work is perfect; there is always scope to improvement. In many cases interventions have to rely on second hand information in order to function.

Understanding the peasant household system *i.e.* the goals, knowledge and activities of rural families is important in order to facilitate their participation in project work and design project activities in accordance with people's needs. For successful participation of rural people in project work are : political will and appropriate institutional framework, time, patience and resources, supporting services, open-minded attitude, flexibility to adjust plans and programmes, training, learning and education towards participation. In broad sense monitoring is to be understood as creation of imperial knowledge about specific situation concerning health, nutrition, state of environment education, income needs and value of participation.

Rural household is seen as a central decision making unit in rural development. This refers not only to utilisation of existing development potentials introduction of innovations of various kinds, but also social stability in the society. To help make poverty elimination programmes it will be the combination of a scholarly productivity and modelling to achieve critical mass of knowledge to function ecologically. Human Ecology begins with look at communities for their development ecologically with the basic aim of developing appropriate technologies in harmony with social goals to make poverty innovation programmes more effective. These can act in the view of natural resources of the village and other human and agro climatic conditions aiming towards sustainable development of enterprise.

Democracy does not guarantee equality of conditions; it only guarantees equality of opportunities. In order to function where "they" possess vital knowledge of which we are ignorant and most of us attempt to avoid. And very avoidance results in greater pain and inability to grow both mentally and spiritually.

The road is less travelled for new psychology, traditions, value and culture.

Reality, however presents in a variety of names and form : Physical, Mental and psychological reality; linguistic and mathematical realities and with the advent of computers and internet, digital reality. But science yet to define physical reality exclusively...hence the quest continuous.

If there are so many realities, what then is absolute Reality? Spiritual science or Adhyatma is concerned with the understanding of this absolute reality which the Vedas call Brahman. Brahman is defined in the Vedas as one that presents itself as absolute truth. How do we find God? Simply by understanding this definition and by striving to be one with this definition. Being truthful in thought, speech and action and upholding the truth; by acquiring the highest knowledge by experimental knowledge of the absolute reality; by perceiving pure joy everywhere through steadiness of mind. Theologists are always bothering about the origin of evil, but evil is just natural behaviour, it is the origin of human goodness that is really so extraordinary and inexplicable. The modern theory of everything posits that space time actually has 11 dimensions but most of them can be ended up like a loop in a carpet pile, solving we do not notice them. We live in one of the lucky universe evil is a fact, not to be explained away but to be accepted; and accepted not to be indented, but to be conquered. It is a challenge neither to our reason nor to our patience, but to our coverage. There is no explanation to evil. It must be looked upon as a necessary part of the order of the universe, to ignore it, senseless for the cases of harassment often drag on for years, during which both the perpetrator and the victim are left hanging. Justice delayed in this case is pretty much the same as justice denied.

A person can proceed rapidly on the path of soul growth and self-realisation through devotion. It endows with true wisdom. A subtle, uninterrupted current of divine energy starts flowing through the inner being, cleansing his intellect mind, emotions of the prevented and dark thoughts feeling and desire.

The sadhana is worship of supreme knowledge will never be lacking in spiritual enlightenment and worldly happiness.

Ever since the beginning of vedic era chanting mantra, sadhana, and Yagna have been considered the most potential means of invoking divine energies, latent in the deeper consciousness of human beings.

With the view of accelerating the process of transformation of human consciousness from the astral plane. It contains all which is worth knowing about mantra, sadhana, yagna and it is hoped by logically establishing correlationships of sciences with spirituality in the modern age, it will provide to the aspirant deep inspiration and guidance and firm faith in sadhana and fulfil the true purpose of human life. When life is very complex the value of biodiversity may be judged considering the economic, ecological, anthropological, provided on philosophical basis. In 1970 the college of Human Ecology Michigan State University was the second major institution to challenge its name from Home Economics to Human Ecology.

Application to Education

Teaching for transfer requires emphasising the similarity between the current subject and the situations to which new learning will transfer to which the principles. In general when the student has practised the basic problem to a higher degree of mastery and has experienced with a variety of similar problems to ensure generalisation of the principles with a wide variety of problems without time to learn anyone to a moderate degree of mastery. Skills in high school course to use reference books, interpret charts, and summarise results not only in substantial gains in that specific course but in transfer of these gains to other courses. It is equally true that history can be taught in order to provide an understanding of current political and economic problems and arithmetic in the way to provide positive transfer to the study of algebra. Introductory lessons on study skills if the two subject area are general principles or concepts.

Experimental biological analysis. Provides biological basis of psychology for the developmental process. Biological and developmental processes for the introductory approaches to the study of psychology neurobiology, behaviouristic cognitive, psychoanalytic and humanistic. These approaches provide a thread of cohesiveness and helps the student understand why theories about a given psychology topic often seem to be saying quite different things.

Psychology as a scientific and humanistic endeavour for the family to discover the relationship between bodily processes and behaviour from the neurobiological viewpoint as for physiological psychologists, developmental, personality, clinical and counselling psychologists, industrial and engineering psychologists, educational psychologists. A new term in the area in environmental psychology.

The methodologists with the development of modern methods of experimentation and treatment of data symbolised by the high speed computer, problem of research design, statistics and computation have become so complex that the methodologist has become a specialist in social behaviour in societal ideology and behaviour science and public policy.

Relations with neighbouring countries are high on the agenda of minister of state. However "India needs to focus on economic development now." The military deployment on Indo-Pak water is part of coercive diplomacy. Now that troops are being withdrawn from border, what kind of diplomacy will the government follow? Our position is known to every body. Science attempts to define the nature of reality.

Principles of sustainability : The 1st step in the ecological journey includes :

(a) Wide scale environmental restoration.
(b) Minimising pollution and waste.
(c) Widespread recycling and reuse.
(d) Substitution of renewable energy generation for the use of fossil fuels.
(e) Adoption of environmental accounting practices.
(f) Paying the true price of goods and services which involves environmental and social devastation.
(g) Favouring natural health remedies over chemical and invasive systems.
(h) Substituting organic farming practices through empowering them to manage local resources, and through community supported agriculture schemes, alternative currency system etc.

(i) Promoting universal education involving environmental and social literacy programmes.

(j) Empowering minorities, including indigenous peoples.

(k) Planning and building for people's real need with love and compassion may be celebrations.

In India we have to go in that dissection, even though it will be necessary slow because it involves change of machinery. There is no use of imposing pseudo leftist presumptions for development for the reason we can visualise India in three streams :

1. Renewable energy technology options — solar thermal, wind power, small hydro power, biomass on site micro power systems.
2. Microbial hydrogen from biowaste, full cells, zero emission vehicles.
3. Eco-enterprises — micro power system, eco-communities, low energy architecture, green cars, decorating of appliances for white goods such as vacuum cleaners, refrigerators, washing machines, TV, ovens, etc., to provide loans at lesser interest for green goods.

Conference of economic and ecological stability integrated with psychological perceptions of the users is absolutely essential for any real sustainability. Condensation of spirit of times and needs to be discarded.

The ICAR centre for Human Ecology and University of Delhi to take up programmes for science and environment at University of Delhi for M.Sc. Environment Biology examination under the faculty of interdisciplinary applied sciences for theory papers.

(a) Earth systems.

(b) Cell biology and genetics.

(c) Environmental philosophy and behaviour sciences.

(d) Evolutionary biology and systematics.

(e) Organisational and population ecology.

Courses and their Contents

Earth systems — the major attention to community ecology ecosystem dynamics and modelling.

The aim of this course is to provide an insight on :

- Community structure and organisation.
- Ecological succession and ecosystem development.
- Ecological energetics.

A field-based investigation study for a Conservation and Development on : Conservation strategies, methods of conservation of living resources, politics, education and environmental ethics, patent rights and genetic resources, International conventions and environmental laws, restoration ecology in relation to developmental activities.

The practicals in all courses for laboratory exercise and field-cum-laboratory oriented exercise (in the form of microprojects).

Topics relating to community ecology for Human resource development based on *in situ* and *ex situ* conservation strategies; principles of preservation; design and management, legislation; people's involvement and public concern; cultural significance of natural protection; code of conduct; society, government and environment; seeds of sovereignty; ethics and environment; international regulation of trade in living resources, international and national institutions; organisations associated with conservation; restoration ecology in relation to development; raising agricultural productivity, renewable resources of energy; farm and community forestry; stabilising chemical cycles; designing sustainable cycles; designing sustainable economics.

Biotechnology in Resource enhancement and ecosystem redevelopment oriented to provide information on :

- Conventional technologies applied for agricultural and forestry importance.
- Application for non-conventional technologies for ecosystem redevelopment.

This course is essentially oriented to provide information on : conventional technologies for the improvement of plants, animals, microbes of agricultural and forestry importance.

- Application of non-conventional technologies for evolving genetically improved strains of biota.

- Technologies relevant to : (i) enhance the biological productivity on degraded lands (ii) soil and amelioration and protection (iii) purification of polluted environments (iv) renewable resources of energy and biocycling of industrial, domestic and agricultural water.

Applications of genetic engineering to enhance levels of plants, productivity on degraded lands; soil amelioration and protection; purification of polluted environments and renewable resources of energy and biocycling of industrial domestic and agricultural waste management and sewage disposal and their management, tissue culture technology in relation to reforestation and afforestation; restoration concepts for terrestrial and aquatic ecosystems, technological.

Technological inputs into restoration and cost effectiveness based on :

(A) The urban waste crises in Delhi, unsustainable ground water use :

- Concept of water harvesting the case of Delhi : (1) How to harvest rain water? Case studies on elements of typical water harvesting systems catchments (2) Conduits (3) Runoff (4) Storage facilities (5) recharge facilities.
- Solid waste and sewage disposal and their management in respect to : tissue culture technology for field based investigation studies for health and hygiene and adaptive strategies at the organism level microbes, plants and animals will be taken for organismal and population ecology.

(B) Organisational and population ecology : the major focus on adaptive strategies at the community level — the population structure in relation to spatial distribution; population dynamics, regulatory mechanisms; kinds of interspecific intentions, population models — microbes, plants and human relationship context to community structure and organisation, bionomic strategies and population parameters, models for two interacting populations, human behaviour system.

(C) Evolutionary biology : One single stream of love for the gems of wisdom on pulsating divine life — the philosophy of biology; concepts — single mindedness of purpose is what is required for the attainment of the goal by ego fouls and the spiritual atmosphere to combat minor everyday health problems, home-made remedies (to deal with an emergency before the medical aid in providing some relief to the user) for : courses in evolutionary biology and systematic in evolution of molecules to organic diversity; genetic vanability and evolutionary mechanism, genetic structure of populations; changes in gene frequency; small populations; components of variations resemblances; altruism; selection, and gene flow for long term evolution; adaptive radiation, level of biological diversity.

Practical based on the environmental philology and behaviour science. Major emphasis on community ecology, ecosystem dynamics, growth and development, physiological, biochemical and genetic mechanism with organismal adaptation for environmental stress and behavioural aspects.

The focus would be both basic and applied aspects of physiology, biochemistry and behavioural ecology.

(D) Environmental physiology : Environmental aspects of carbon, nitrogen, sulphur and energy metabolism, the crises of environment is often in the news. All environmental problems arise from the abuse and misuse of natural resources of human beings each of the five elements land, water, fire (energy), air and space have been adversely affected through human intervention.

Land, soil and plants have been affected in the following ways :

- Tropical deforestation.
- Desertification.
- Soil erosion.
- Biodiversity loss.
- Water is becoming the scare resource. The vast ocean is also in trouble.
- Fishery resources are being over exploited and we are now close to maximum sustainable limits of 100 M tonnes.
- Many marine animals like whales are depleting in numbers or becoming endangered.

- The ocean is being polluted with nutrients from sewage and agricultural chemicals, sediments from mining and farming, pathogens from sewage, toxic effluents from industries, urban waste water, oil from land, ships and drilling, plastics from nets, ships and beach litter etc.
- River, lakes and wet lands are being degraded.

India is a country of diversities in the social and economic sphere. Although there are wide variations in rural and urban areas, as well, notable differential exists in the levels of living as measured by indicators of human development such as literacy and schooling, health and longevity, employment wage security, and access to public programmes. Although relative differentials exist, absolute deprivation is high in most part of rural India. About half the population of rural India is illiterate and suffers from "capability poverty" about 40 per cent have extremely low incomes. About 8% of households' income is spent on health and primary education.

Land is the dominant source of income and economic security. Land of village development has a clear influence on income. Public action is therefore needed for synergetic efforts should be made to enhance rural incomes and also generate broad based employment opportunities along with the guaranteed real wages. Advanced research methods to unvailed the intricacies of the social and economic inequalities in India are now in the process of implementation in India.

Human development is a process of enlarging people's choices. The most critical of these wide ranging choices are to live a long and healthy life, to be educated, and to have access to resources needed for the decent standard of living. Additional choices included political freedom, guaranteed human rights and personal self-respect. Human development is the end-economic growth a means, so the purpose of growth should be to launch people's lives. The quality of life in developing countries is lined with institutions and public programmes meant to provide for the basic needs of the poor and vulnerable sections of the society creating structures and institutions which ensure the basic human needs are met and that alternative choices are available should be the priority to generate the data for investigate and analytical studies.

In India, the national constitution recognises the state obligation in clear terms in Article 47 which provides that the raising of the level of nutrition and improvement of public health are among the primary duties of the state. This is a directive principle of state policy contained in part IV of the constitution which lays down the principles fundamental in governance of the country and obligates the state to apply them in making laws. Another directive principle in Article 48A imposes the duty to protect and improve the environment and to safeguard the forests and wild life in the country, which too is related to improvement of public health. The linkages between human rights and human development is recognised and so in the significance of public health. There is felt need for genuine partnership, the primary targets for the year 2015 of the world bank also include public health issues such as improvement in the reproductive health of women, reduction in infant, and material mortality rates etc. However, there is less confidence about the improvement of the non physical aspects of our world.

However, there is less confidence about the improvement of non physical aspects of our world. Scientific methods must be applied with greater vigour and imagination to the behaviour aspects of our culture. The development of the behavioural sciences and their application to education and other human affairs present some of our greatest challenges.

Theories about the relationship between the position of the earth and other moving celestial bodies were essential to the successful launching and return of manned space vehicles.

Traditional knowledge, innovations and practices are of importance for the conservation of biodiversity and sustainable use of components with respect to our biological and intellectual heritage. There is serious threat to our ancient wisdom, a threat to the extent of its total elimination, a threat which may cause the complete loss of this magnificent heritage of our traditions and culture. Yet there is hope that agricultural research institute and university agriculture remains the backbone of India's food livelihood and ecological security as well as natural sovereignty. Since our agriculture is now at the crossroads due to globalisation of economic and liberalisation of trade of our farm families will have to be enabled to achieve the following four revolutions. If they are to survive the present emerging threats to our agricultural trade by productivity revolution, quality revolution, income and employment revolution and small farm management revolution for synergy between science and technology organisation and public policy to bring about sea change in the area of agriculture, food and environment to support rapidly increasing population, per capita income, increase in life expectancy, erasing the memories of the famine and mass starvation.

The globalisation of markets will influence domestic production employment and price stability. It is necessary to establish a clear difference between internationalisation and globalisation. The first refer to nations and exchanges among nations. While the second includes a super nationalism that ignores national frontiers as well as the wishes of nations in regards to higher education.

Despite of cautions recognition of global responsibility for development opportunities in all nations of the world, wealthy countries have yet to demonstrate consistent attention. In the Netherlands, a great deal of development related research is carried out in the field of health care, rural development, demography, the role of women, food issues conservations and environmental problems.

ICAR SCHOOL FOR HUMAN ECOLOGY FOR LOCAL ACTION AT PUSA CAMPUS

Preservation of the environment and conservation of resources such as fossil fuel and water is a matter of international concern. Action that threatened survival of various aspects of plants and animals created renewed interests in ecology; the science concerned with interrelationships between organisms and environment — both organic and inorganic.

Home Science roots from Ecology to teach the principles of healthy and happy life. The term ecosystem provided a philosophical basis for much of subsequent work in human ecology as it is applied to the family and to the home economics.

The glare of modern technology is constantly pushing back our old knowledge and philosophy until we may forget it all together.

The development of computational and models of the physical, chemical, biological processes.

In fact, science and mythology are not different but mutually exclusive disciplines of learning. They are merely two different languages of describing the same reality. After all human brain is common, with common reflexes, stimulus, inspirations and aspirations.

Human Ecology attempts to break the barrier between rational scientific thought and the dogmatic beliefs of our ancient mythology. The wisdom contained in the ancient mythology is to be explained with the view to accelerating the process for the astral plane.

ASIAN CENTRE FOR HUMAN ECOLOGY FOR ESTABLISHMENT OF NEW FACULTY FOR LOCAL ACTION GLOBALISATION OF AGRICULTURE AT IARI, PUSA CAMPUS

Establishment of new faculty for effective enterprise development at undergraduate level to enhance empowerment in human resources with special emphasis on education. Today our country is proud of having one of the world's largest national agricultural research and education network. State Agricultural universities apart from training graduates in diverse fields of agricultural sciences have established strong higher programmes in specialised areas of national and global relevance.

State agricultural universities apart from training graduates in diversified fields of agricultural sciences for active extension education programme, imposed by the new economic social order and improve their quality of life.

The trained human resource development by stage agricultural universities, five deemed to be universities, including Allahabad Agricultural Institute, one Central Agricultural University, Imphal, 3 central Universities (BHU, AMU & Vishwa Bharati) and fifty colleges outside Stage Agricultural University system. India has developed requisite expertise to meet the future challenges. Owing to the non availability of composite data base on institutions, programmes, prerequisite eligibility condition have been instrumental in propelling all these transformations at the national level such as biotechnology and molecular biology, environmental sciences, agro-business management, post harvest technology, information technology, communication development, remote sensing, non-conventional energy sources, disease forecasting, wild life management.

The community resource management and extension with its community outreach programmes coupled with practical experience to work in the community and how to address larger issues concerning the quality of life of people. The postgraduate courses in CRM&E offers a well meaning theoretical base with hands on practical orientation and a month long placement in suitable NGO/GO.

Resource management with advance principles and processes and extension and communication techniques, community organisation, in farm food production.

Objectives

- Reorientation of land grants. University System to integrate information on the issues such as widening gap between advances of science and development of technology in our agriculture, lack of interaction, admission policies.
- To promote ecologically sustainable agriculture performed by individual scientists and interdisciplinary team.
- To provide promising scientists on harnessing and management of resources for enhancing agricultural production.
- To promote contact among research workers in different institutions and organisations within the country and world scientists.
- To provide a forum to agricultural scientists to interact of important issues of agricultural research education and extension.
- Publish documents and specific studies including those intended to policy makers for advancement of agricultural research and development relevant to public interest.

- Integration of education research and extension education in all branches of agricultural sciences.
- Utilisation of graduates, postgraduates and doctorates in state agricultural university.
- Postgraduate education training programmes and information system at SARS.
- Special training courses and refresher courses in specialised areas for the benefit of farmers and extension workers.
- Training to other Asian countries, extension workers to receive training in biotechnology, virology, genetics and horticulture.
- 1 year postgraduate diploma for service graduates for exploring into entrepreneurship development in agriculture by development of training modules for extension functionaries.
- Current development in plant biotechnology, DNA cloning etc.
- Division of floriculture and landscaping, Modern cultivation of ornamental bulbous crops.
- Division of fruits and horticulture, technology for post harvest management of fruits, vegetable and flowers.
- Production of technology for fruit based drinks and fruit nectars etc.
- Institutional arrangements for building a strong base in specialised area of national and global relevance.
- To seek collaboration for solution to what, how, why and when the best alternative for action on global vision and mission for human ecological needs.
- To study significance of education for sustainable development at all levels.
- To promote networking in view of objectives and importance of the grass-root level. NGOs and global forum for wider access to higher education for diversity.
- To use distance education for training skills in virtual classroom with an advance of communication technologies to upgrade education and research programmes.

IN COLLABORATION WITH TEXAS A&M UNIVERSITY, USA MICHIGAN STATE UNIVERSITY, USA ASIAN INSTITUTE OF TECHNOLOGY, THAILAND

FUND SUPPORT FAO

Science Popularisation

Man is an important element of the environmental complex. His activities, growing population, Industrial and urban settlement, social religious and economic set-ups are posing newer ecological problems. Understanding his ecological role the anthropologists, sociologists, psychologists, economists, demographers supply data to persons working on human ecology. To be acquainted with various disciplines of physical and biological sciences in order to get integrated picture of the environmental complex in relation to the organic world. In order to quantify his data an ecologist has to collect information, which could be subjected to mathematical formulation for precise communication to others working in the field. Indian culture is deeply rooted in two different but intricate traditions. In India awakening has begun. More and more of the scientists, artists, and scholars have started looking into their rich traditions, which are lost.

Humanity stands today at the head of new age of a large synthesis of knowledge. It has to collaborate in bringing out concerted action for knowledge, universal upliftment and lasting peace and unity. For humanity to successfully meet the evolutionary and revolutionary challenges of contemporary advancement — great cultural achievements of the past must be revised and enriched — to bring about a new type of humanity. A society marked by integrated power of physical, emotional, dynamic, intellectual, clinical, aesthetic and spiritual potentialities.

Frontiers of knowledge are henceforth bound to expand unimaginably and new researchers will oblige humanities, societies, technologies and fine arts to arrive at new equations and new combinations. Development in communication, information and technology will open new and cost effective approaches for enhancing the reach of higher education to meet the demands of fast changing nature of employment. India has been in the forefront of all global initiatives that have communicated the philosophy of *Human Ecology*. The scientific expertise to increase the relevance of higher education by making courses in use career oriented. To enhance empowerment in human resources with special emphasis on education the disciplines of agribusiness, biodiversity and environment, biotechnology, non-conventional energy system have been merged to make a unified field of Human Ecology for systematic vision of the strategic issues like a perspective of higher education for community empowerment.

To meet the challenges imposed by new economic and social order, and improve the quality of life to make a positive impact on the immediate society to which they belong. Adequate field experience in academic programmes coupled with practical work experience, combined with outstanding teaching and strong foundation in applied and social sciences, will provide students with the vision on the study of behavioural aspects implied with the interrelationship of the biotic components with the practical application of university based research for interdisciplinary programmes.

ASIAN CENTRE FOR HUMAN ECOLOGY FOR LOCAL ACTION FOR BIODIVERSITY AND FOOD QUALITY

The politicians of our time might be characterised by their vain attempts to change the world and by their inability to change themselves.

Veda means supreme knowledge of spiritual being, self-realisation and fulfilment towards peace of mind. It will appear that its consciousness moves within these four spheres, the four directions of knowledge flow :

1. Rig — Spiritual well-being and fulfilment,
2. Yaju — Valour,
3. Atharva — Prosperity (Arth), and
4. Sam — Enjoyment.

For the spontaneous development of these four aspects, four stages of human life and four social divisions (varnas) have been formed : childhood as the stage of playfulness and self-development, youth of advising a family and earning money, vanaprastha or virility and Sanyas of doing well sane activity.

According to this fourfold division, Brahman is Rig; Kshatriya is Yaju; Vishya is Atharva and Shudra is Sam. Just as water manifests in four different forms of ice, vapour (cloud, dew, fog etc.), air (hydrogen, oxygen) and liquid; Fire too manifests in the form of burning heat, light and movement.

'Life is full of unexpected suffering.' Even so, as Eleanor Roosvelt says : 'If you can live through that (a difficult situation) you can live through anything. You gain strength, courage and confidence by every experience in which you really step to look far in the face.'

Agentine poet Almafueret wrote : "To the weak; difficulty is a closed door waiting to be opened." Difficulties impede the progress of those who are weak. For the strong, however, they are opportunities to open wide the doors to a bright future. Everything is determined by our attitude, by our resolve.

In the *Bhagvad Gita* God is portrayed as being eternal and all-powerful. God is the great Creator who began and who will one day end the universe. According to the Hindu calendar, as recorded in the ancient scriptures, the year AD 197 corresponds to 1,972,949,078 years since the present world came into existence.

It was Herschel, the British astronomer who observed that the universe extended, much beyond the solar system which was itself only a small part of a much bigger star system, the galaxy. So the mysteries of the universe continue to unfold. Our search for celestial truths could well be an eternal one. Because it seems even the cosmos is not free from the cycle of birth and death.

Conclusion

Human Ecology for Globalization of Agriculture for Community Based Approaches

Man's relationship with his environment now occupies a major place among the problems agitating mankind. Therefore it is necessary to demonstrate the scientific programmes in a way towards meeting the sustainable and safe future to mankind.

Our life depends on one thing called oneself. Who is the self is an important truth to be arrived at. To know and not to act on what you know is equal to not knowing. If you have not acted then you have not known. Not knowing is ignorance. People fall in love with words and concepts. We have started loving words and not action. We have started believing that a word is knowledge and not action. Treat action as knowledge and not words. We live in jargons; we give power in words. We should learn to give power in action to treat action as wisdom and not words as wisdom. The wisdom will grow with the power. It teaches us, that less we use our power the greater it will be. There will be no end to the troubles of states, or of humanity itself till philosophers become kings in the world. The political power and philosophy thus come into the same hands. It is an illusion that we are one — the person we assume ourselves to be and what we really are. If we observe ourselves can we see that we are the observer and past of us is observed or else the observer pollutes the observations and creates an imaginary self.

It is an imposing status — the aquiline features of great educationist visionary gazing far into the distance — and fitting for one of the greatest universities in the world. To solve in and to make sure that it is for real global terror and communal tension on seven sins of public life — Politics without principles, wealth without work, pleasure without consciousness, knowledge without character, commerce without morality, science without humanity and worship without sacrifice. We have to notice that the way we walk, talk, think, feel criticise, praise, like, dislike. If we notice these movements closely our life will start transforming itself mysteriously. Also it will guide us to demonstrate effectively the sustainable solutions of healthy communities.

Human Ecology is the study of interaction between human beings and their environment. It is a means to improve people's lives and human environment emphasising the study of reciprocal effects that take place physically, socially, economically and aesthetically. The philosophy of human ecology provides the context for developing and serving the individuals and their families from a human environment perspective towards building and sustaining productive quality of life.

The concept of ecology by way of introducing the field of botany to contribute to international research in relation to other sciences for rural development, human resource development and promotion of education and economic interest for all sections of society. It combines the interest, theories and studies of geographer, ecologist, agricultural scientist, economist and biologist for the major themes :

- Linking higher education for community service.
- Changes required in the area of Home Science programmes to make them relevant to all sections of society.
- Setting priorities in research to help community in the area of agribusiness, biodiversity and environment, biotechnology, non-conventional energy systems and human resource development.

Indian Council for Agricultural Research (ICAR) proposed new division of Human Ecology at Delhi University for the establishment of new faculty for Human Ecology for research, education, extension and outreach with the fund support of ICAR, Department of Agriculture Cooperation (DAC) and Food and Agricultural Organisation of United Nation (FAO), New Delhi (In partnership for international linkages) :

- Home Science to Human Ecology for graduate programmes to investigate the interaction of people across life span with their natural, social and designed environments in partnership with College of Human Ecology, Michigan State University and Texas A&M (U.S.).

- Establishment of Department of Human Ecology for international linkages in partnership with school of environment resources and development, Bangkok, Thailand. For interdisciplinary approach for making difference in society with School of Social Sciences, Middlesex University (U.K.) for postgraduate and post experience programmes on criminology, social policy, psychology, geography and environmental management, social science research methods, social work and research degree for social science support including taught master programmes, M. Phil and Ph.D. Underpinned by teaching and research training for lively research culture focused around conferences, seminars, forums and other activities together with the lectures from invited speakers. In partnership with Wageningen University, The Netherlands to interact with environment in environment management, Bio-technology, Food Science & Technology, Forest and natural conservation, geo information science, consumer studies and modelling tools for environment and resource management, water supply, drainage and sewerage engineering.

Mission. Strengthening and empowering individuals and families to interact effectively with their environment.

Vision. To meet the society needs, to develop unique culture by linking several disciplines and professionals for ecology of individuals, families in their diverse socio cultural, physical, biological environment where diversity of ecosystem is a way of life.